KI   JAN - - 2006

		DATE DUE		

On the
BATTLEFIELDS

On the BATTLEFIELDS

Two World Wars
That Shaped a Nation

Canada at War, Volume II

From the archives of **MACLEAN'S**

Edited by
MICHAEL BENEDICT

PENGUIN
CANADA

PENGUIN CANADA
Published by the Penguin Group
Penguin Books, a division of Pearson Canada, 10 Alcorn Avenue, Toronto, Ontario, Canada M4V 3B2
Penguin Books Ltd, 80 Strand, London WC2R ORL, England
Penguin Putnam Inc., 375 Hudson Street, New York, New York 10014, U.S.A.
Penguin Books Australia Ltd, 250 Camberwell Road, Camberwell, Victoria 3124, Australia
Penguin Books India (P) Ltd, 11, Community Centre, Panchsheel Park, New Delhi – 110 017, India
Penguin Books (NZ) Ltd, cnr Rosedale and Airborne Roads, Albany, Auckland 1310, New Zealand
Penguin Books (South Africa) (Pty) Ltd, 24 Sturdee Avenue, Rosebank 2196, South Africa

Penguin Books Ltd, Registered Offices: 80 Strand, London WC2R ORL, England

First published 2002

10 9 8 7 6 5 4 3 2 1

Copyright © Rogers Publishing Ltd., 2002

Printed and bound in Canada on acid free paper ∞

NATIONAL LIBRARY OF CANADA CATALOGUING IN PUBLICATION DATA

Main title under title:

On the battlefields : two world wars that shaped a nation : Canada at war,
volume II / edited by Michael Benedict.

Articles originally published in Maclean's.
ISBN 0-14-301341-6

1. World War, 1914–1918 — Canada. 2. World War, 1939–1945 — Canada. I. Benedict, Michael,
1947–

FC603.05 2002   940.4'0971   C2002-901954-0
F1033.05 2002

Visit Penguin Books' website at **www.penguin.ca**

Contents

Foreword

J. L. GRANATSTEIN

Canada must be one of the very few nations never to have waged an aggressive war. This country has never fought a war for the joy of conquest, for territory, for economic reasons or for racial vengeance. Not that we have been a pacifist state. Far from it. But Canada's wars have been fought for the right reasons—to defend our soil, for our friends and allies, for democratic values and, yes, for freedom.

Our warriors have usually not been professional soldiers, schooled in Clausewitz's dogmas or trained in staff colleges.

Instead, they have been ordinary Canadians thrown into situations of horror and terror, ordinary men and women who performed extraordinary deeds in conditions that frequently defied the imagination.

This sense of the heroic ordinary Canadian at war comes through very clearly in this new collection of reportage from the archives of *Maclean's* covering the two great world wars of the twentieth century, during which Canada played major roles and became a nation in its own and the world's eyes. You can see it especially in the chilling first-person account of a Lieut. C. W. Tilbrook, who takes the reader right under the German trenches in the First World War and describes the tunnelling operation designed to blow up the enemy as he slept. And in W .W. Murray's two pieces on Great War Victoria Cross winners—the deeds are stirring, a tribute to the extraordinary courage that few men show in battle. Or in the epic tale of farm boy William Barker, who became one of the deadliest, and most heroic, fighter pilots of all time. Barker's rise to international fame—he piloted the Prince of Wales through action—is admiringly recounted by Maj. George Drew in a 15,000-word, nearly breathless tribute.

But there is little vainglorious heroism in these patriotic accounts, not even much flag-waving or deliberate attempt to paint the Germans as weak or cowardly. The enemy's strength and military skill made the courage of the V.C. winners all the more astonishing. Yes, George Pearson's story of "The Last Stand of the Princess Pats" features a naïve patriotism, but that was certainly long gone from the soldiers' ranks by 1918. The tastes and attitudes of *Maclean's* readers then were different. The magazine was beginning to become part of the Canadian fabric, even though it was much less of a news magazine than it later became, and the difference in tone with the more mature journalism of the Second World War is striking.

There is one point, however, that unites these two world wars for Canadians. In 1914, Canada had a tiny army, untrained and equipped with little more than enthusiasm. This comes through clearly—astonishingly enough for a nation that practised censorship with some ruthlessness in the Great War, in Pvt. Harold Peat's "You Will Yet Be Glad." Peat, who enlisted in 1914 and served at the front, became one of the most popular writers on the war. In this article, he admits readily that the 1st Division of the Canadian Expeditionary Force that went to France in early 1915 was "raggedly equipped and partially trained." The censors likely let that pass only because Peat drew a sharp contrast with the much improved equipment, training, fighting efficiency and great reputation of the 1918 Canadian Corps.

In September, 1939, Canada was just as unprepared for war as it had been 25 years earlier. The regular forces numbered only 10,000, the reserves perhaps six times that, but neither the professionals nor the reservists—and certainly not the civilians who made up the great bulk of the Canadian forces that eventually numbered 1.1 million men and women—knew anything of war.

Again, the ordinary men stepped forward, learned their increasingly high-tech trade and set out to face their country's enemies. Many of them were air crew, youngsters, like Manitoba's "Mark Brown, Fighter Pilot," who flocked into the Royal Canadian Air Force to learn how to soar like eagles. Most of these men became part of RCAF and Royal Air Force bomber squadrons overseas, carrying the war to Germany's heartland.

Other young Canadian men took part in the raids early in the war when bombers sometimes had to navigate in darkness by dead reckoning. Jack Calder, in "I Flew into Trouble," describes that challenge in telling how his bomber ended up crashing in neutral Ireland—where he spent almost two years in internment. Another crash story in this collection, "Three Against Death," is much more harrowing. It tells how a three-man air crew survived Arctic conditions for 10 days on a rock just off the icy cliffs of Greenland.

By 1943, the Royal Air Force's Bomber Command, in which Canadians served, mounted raids using 1,000 aircraft that blasted the industries of the Ruhr into rubble. One such harrowing mission is vividly told by Flt.-Lieut. Coleman Perkins to the legendary Gordon Sinclair in "I Was the Wireless Operator." This was war at its most savage, and service in Bomber Command cost more than 10,000 Canadians their lives.

Some in this country today scorn this sacrifice, viewing the bomber crews as dupes used to wage a genocidal war against civilians. What the critics forget is that the Nazis started the bombing of cities and reaped the whirlwind. These critics sometimes claim that neither Canadians at home nor aircrew in Britain knew that German civilians were dying during these raids. In his 1943 article "Bombs Away," D. K. Findlay, who wrote for *Maclean's* throughout the Second World War, gives this claim the lie. Findlay makes no pretence that heavy damage was not being done to homes and factories and that thousands were dying.

This collection also includes several articles on the war at sea in the thankless North Atlantic campaign, where Canadian vessels played a leading role, and three pieces by the legendary Lionel Shapiro, who later went on to win a Governor General's Award for his D-Day novel *The Sixth of June*. In one of them, Shapiro tells the stories of the Canadian soldiers who fought the Wehrmacht in Sicily and Normandy. The tone again is quiet and reflective; the soldiers doing the fighting are ordinary Canadian boys. Some had to take their Sherman tanks into unequal combat against Nazi Tigers and Panthers; others had to perform battlefield surgery under the most trying of conditions. But what comes through very clearly in Shapiro's articles is that Canadians understood that they had a vital job to do if their country was to survive.

Defeat was not an option in the Second World War. Mistakes aplenty were made by commanders at sea, in the air and on the ground, and ordinary Canadians paid the price. Was it worth the cost? Forgetful of our past, cynical about the propaganda that washes over us, we might question this today, but *Maclean's* readers in the Second World War did not. They understood that if the Axis powers won, Canada's lot included racial-purity laws, death camps and total economic exploitation. Sometimes wars must be fought; sometimes wars are just. In an era when the democracies face new threats, it is well for us to remember these truths.

Canadians tend to dig their toes in the dirt and mumble when highfalutin words such as "freedom" and "democracy" are used, but most of us realize full well how these ideas shape the way we live. *Maclean's* splendidly written articles on the struggles of Canadians to prevail in the two world wars of the last century are a useful reminder that our forebears also understood what was at stake, and performed their duties with courage.

Preface

When Penguin Books decided in 1997 to publish the first in what has become six volumes of collected articles from the archives of *Maclean's*, we agreed that stories about Canada's fighting men and women should be the first subject. Thus emerged the best-selling *Canada at War*, which featured compelling tales from the First and Second World Wars.

The success of *Canada at War* showed the desire of Canadians to learn more about the exploits of previous generations on the battlefields that shaped our nation. The largely first-person accounts particularly resonated with young people, many of whom knew little if anything about Canada's rich history in defence of friends and freedom.

When researching that volume, I found a treasure trove of yellowing but still vibrant articles and bemoaned the fact that there was a physical limit to how many could appear in *Canada at War*. There was so much material to choose from, and the quality was so high, that the final selections could have been made blindfolded.

Fortunately, we can now enjoy more of these accounts of ordinary Canadians performing extraordinary feats on the battlefields of the two cataclysmic events that shaped the twentieth century. Included in this latest collection are articles by some of the best Second World War correspondents working in the English language—Lionel Shapiro, Gordon Sinclair, Wallace Reyburn and the still-productive Peter Stursberg. From the First World War, there are pieces by the multi-talented Maj. George A. Drew (who later became Ontario premier and national leader of the Progressive Conservative Party), Will Bird and Harold Peat, whose *Private Peat* was a sensational best-seller during the time of the Great War.

One constant in the six volumes has been the wise counsel of Kristine Ryall, now the magazine's photo editor, who knows where every historic Canadian picture is located. Not even two babies, one born on book deadline, have distracted her from finding the best possible pictures to illustrate these stories. There have been others who have helped out on all these archival collections, including the magazine's production and technology director, Sean McCluskey, who oversaw the transfer of the words from the aging issues of *Maclean's* to the fresh pages of this book.

For researcher-reporter Michael MacLean, whose job it is to track down the leading players in the stories as well as the writers who told their stories to the general public, this is his fourth book. Few escape his sleuthing.

Michael Benedict
Executive Editor, *Maclean's*
June, 2002

On the BATTLEFIELDS

First World War

The cathedral in ruins, 1918

A Visit to the Western Front

MAIN JOHNSON
January, 1917

How would a person feel if, in the morning, he left Toronto or Montreal or Winnipeg, and, at noon of the same day, arrived at the Front, under shell fire, without any acclimatizing experience or training? How much of a shock would it be, how much of a disturbing of one's very consciousness and existence! It is not physically possible to make this exact experiment, but it is possible to do something which, although different geographically, does approximate it in feeling and sensation, and which does plunge you from one world and one form of life and civilization headlong into another.

One morning, not long ago, I had breakfast in the peaceful city of Paris, and had luncheon the same day in Reims (Rheims), a town under almost constant bombardment from the Germans, and at the immediate and actual front. An hour or two later, I was still further up, with the French artillery during a bombardment, and still further yet, in observation posts, where the German trenches lay in front of us in full and unobstructed view, surprisingly close at hand, with shrieking shells, both French and German, crossing each other on their devastating paths.

Although we had already been in Great Britain and France for a month, and thought then we were close enough to the war, in reality everything we had seen up to that time, however significant, had been comparatively secondary and remote. The astonishingly violent change even from Paris to the actual front was such as to jolt one's very personality.

One morning there came to the door of our hotel a motor to take us to the front. Immediately I felt myself keyed up to a point where the most casual things stood out with all the vividness of a silhouette. The boulevards of Paris were no longer merely delightful thoroughfares—they were roads leading direct to the focus-point of all our world, the Western front! It was about to become as actual as a house or a street.

As we speeded out of the suburbs into the open country, we were travelling on one of those famous roads of France, straight as a railroad line into the farthest distance, and lined by wonderful trees. This particular road was the one over which a large section of the spectacular taxi-cab army was rushed from Paris to Meaux at the Battle of the Marne, and the one, too, along which the Germans would have marched into Paris, if it had been they who had won the battle. West of Meaux, half an hour by motor from the gates of Paris, we saw the wooded slope where German batteries had been placed—the farthest point of the German advance, perilously close to the heart of France.

Up to this point, life seemed fairly normal, but soon we entered the "zone of the armies," and immediately the whole aspect of things changed. Some indefinable human element, some indefinite but deep ingrained feeling of the essential cheerfulness of life despite all its ordinary woe, some psychological impression of normal, secure existence as it is lived by the mass of humanity in average times and average communities, went out suddenly like an extinguished light and in its place came a sinister air, a feverish atmosphere of abnormality, the first currents of an electrical influence which hung heavily and ominously over the whole area of the front. The joy of life snapped off!

As we gradually drove further and further in, the human element became submerged—the machine of war and fate came in. Not that there were the slightest indications of fear or despair. That is not what I mean. But a cheerless colourlessness, a brooding sense of drabness, of the mechanical rather than the human, bore one down; coupled with an immense feeling of pity for these towns and for the women and children who still had to live in them, where all the pleasures of life had been snuffed out so long ago, that now it seemed as if the world never had been happy, and never would be again.

We came, in time, into the region of dust—dust from the countless motor cars and motor lorries—dust from the transport wagons and ambulance cars—dust from men marching up to the front, and dust from other detachments marching back into rest billets. Soon we swung into a little village, passed through its narrow stone streets, filled with soldiers, and, in this case, with no one else, except a few old women, bent and withered, and a noticeably large number of black cats; turned a corner, and entered the headquarters of a French army, where we had the opportunity of meeting the general in command. Then we drove away, and, after some unspecified time, like people in a dream, for the reality of the thing seemed almost impossible, we entered the town of Reims.

The Germans held this city for a few days in August and September, 1914, were driven back during the engagements marking the Battle of the Marne, and entrenched themselves in sight of the town. During these whole two years and a half, the town has been subject to a persistent bombardment. One never knows when a shell will come crashing through the streets or over the roof tops. A group of civilians, including a woman and children, had been killed a day or two before we were there; another heavy bombardment had occurred just previous to that, and, still another might begin at any moment.

We drove directly to an hotel for luncheon. It is one of two principal hotels—the other lies in ruins; the one in which we had our meal hadn't been hit yet, although several shops in the neighbourhood had been demolished.

What a meal eaten in this hotel at Reims! Every moment of the hour we spent at luncheon in this bombarded town stands out with an inerasable vividness. I remember feeling the pathos of the situation—two lonely-looking women preparing and cooking food for us; such a normal occupation in such abnormal circumstances. We ate *hors d'oeuvres*, I remember, and an appetizing omelette, juicy lamb chops, a huge plateful of green peas, French pastry, coffee, and bread, which for brownness and a touch of sourness and sogginess, was the nearest approach to "war bread" we met in France.

After luncheon, we went for a walk through the town. Grass was growing through the cobbles of the street; many shops were closed; the thoroughfares, although not deserted, were depressingly quiet. And yet there were signs of ordinary life too. Water was running in the fountain in the middle of the square; the flowers at its base were gay and showed signs of care. Butcher shops and bakeries were open, and the post office. In one window was arranged quite a display of corsets, and, in another, some children's hats.

We went into the largest shop in Reims, a department store, which, in its advertising, boasted that it had an elevator, and which had been hit twice. All the windows were shattered by shell shock. There were not many customers that afternoon, but there were women attendants ready to look after us, all dressed in black, and all with sorrow stamped on their faces. Yet they were still prepared to sell a strange hodgepodge of merchandise.

We bought some articles which I believe reveal the pathos and tragedy of war as well as any incident we encountered. For example, I bought a little toy doll's trunk for 10 centimes, and four or five celluloid animals, a frog, a fish, a duck, a dog, for five centimes each. We bought some wooden forks and spoons, and a shaving brush. In the very centre of the war, here were people selling trinkets and toys and the most conventional articles.

After we left the shop, we came into an area where the destruction was much greater than in the other parts of the town. Hardly a stone was left one on top of the other; whole blocks were razed to the ground. Not a place was habitable. Complete destruction lay all about us.

Rising out of the midst of the ruins, but itself a ruin too, stood the Cathedral of Reims, considered by many the finest in all Europe, and the destruction of which by the Germans has aroused such world-wide condemnation. We spent about 20 minutes inside the wrecked building, and could see for ourselves the extent to which the Germans, in their two years' campaign against it, had ruined the sacred pile. Without going into details, the damage is very great, and, for the most part, irretrievable, although the outer walls still remain.

On the floor I picked up fragments of the medieval glass of that peculiar quality and colour that no one has ever been able to duplicate. These glorious windows are now lying shattered on the stone pavement of the cathedral floor. Huge craters gape where the altar used to stand, and the pillars are scarred by the marks of heavy shells. It was a dangerous 20 minutes, that time spent within Reims Cathedral, for, almost daily, the Germans keep hurling their bolts against it.

The most inspiring thing about the cathedral in its present condition is the statue of Joan of Arc standing in the square immediately in front. Unscathed it has remained from all the attacks; banners and wreaths of flowers, emblems of supplication and thanksgiving, from all parts of France, are strewn about the statue, and Joan of Arc, herself, holds aloft in her upraised hand the tricolour of her country. The soul of France, the matchless spirit she has shown, the courage and devotion and love almost surpassing human comprehension, qualities that have raised France and the French people to unique heights in the estimation of the world, and that have given her one of the very noblest places in history—all this miracle is symbolized in the tricolour of France, held aloft defiantly, and yet lovingly and sadly, by Joan of Arc in the courtyard of Reims Cathedral.

That afternoon we drove up and down the front for many miles, stopping at times to visit the artillery trenches and the batteries, and then to go further forward into observation posts.

On one of these visits, as an example, it was a surprisingly short walk from the automobile to the artillery dug-outs. As we went through a wood on our way to the trenches, we saw a number of French privates, some of the world-honoured *poilus*, cooking bacon for themselves on little wood fires, and breaking off, from long French loaves, huge chunks of bread. Through the trenches, we made our way to the artillery positions, and saw a battery of the famous French 75 guns. Everything was so quiet at the moment that we were able to examine the guns closely, pat them affectionately and gaze around at the stores of ammunition. The gunners themselves, as, indeed, all the French soldiers, artillery and infantry, which we had seen that day, were the sort of men we had expected to see—those wonderful French soldiers, reserved, serious, unflinching and determined, who in the last two years and a half have raised France's military reputation, already high, to a point where it has become the marvel and admiration of the world.

But it is one thing to read about the French *poilu*; it is another actually to see him, not on paper, not on parade, not at any base or headquarters, but actually on the firing line, where all theories meet their tests, and all reports meet their true interpretation. To see these French soldiers at their posts of danger, to see the coolness and deliberation of their demeanour, was to realize, once and for all, the essential fact that makes France great today.

While we were with the battery, there was no indication of any immediate firing. Although for several hours we had been within range of German fire, we had not heard a sound of war. But it was now four o'clock in the afternoon, the period of the day when a renewal of activity, after the respite of late morning and early afternoon, might be looked for.

It came even sooner than we expected. We had left the guns,

walked through the trenches, and climbed to the level again. A cross-road, leading in the direction of the German lines, lay in front of us. One of our party, an officer, motioned us to wait a moment; he peeked out from behind a tree, drew back, peeked again, and then signalled us to follow. This incident brought home the realization that this was no picnic excursion, but that we were so close to the Germans that we had to take precautions before crossing a road.

On the other side was a vineyard. We were in the Champagne district of France. We had seen women and old men working among the vines within range of German shells, in constant danger of death, which all too often really came. We saw this visible proof that French agriculturists, men and women, fear death for France no more than do her soldiers.

This particular vineyard, in our personal history, will rank before all others. As I said before, we had just left a battery which, to all appearance, was quiescent. No sooner, however, had we begun to walk across the field than these French guns opened fire, one after the other, in steady succession. One of the officers who was with us was diplomatic, if not entirely reassuring. "I think we'd better hurry a bit," was his quietly expressed advice. "Our battery have opened fire, and although the Germans don't know the exact point from which the shells are coming, they have a pretty good idea, and they often try to return the compliment as accurately as they can. This is a long vineyard, and rather exposed. Shall we move on?"

The invitation was accepted. The French officer was right. That *was* a long vineyard, and exposed to a dangerous degree. All around us, as we walked, the ground was ploughed and churned in obviously recent shell holes, and many of the vines were scorched and burnt by the heat of shells which had coursed through them not long ago, and which might sweep through again at any minute.

Something else beside vines was growing in this ground, something we saw all along the front—blood-red poppies. Before we went to France we had seen a number of poems in London journals about the poppies at the front, but had never realized their true significance. When there, however, we saw that red poppies did blaze everywhere, in the fields, among the vines, along the edge of fences, overhanging the very guns themselves. All the heat, the feverishness and the pain were symbolized in one of the most suggestive influences in the world, that of colour. Afterwards, likewise, we saw the white lily-flowers growing on the battlefield of the Marne, a symbol of the peace that follows even the bloodiest battle—the peace, alas, of death; cool and white, but death nevertheless.

Before we reached the end of that vineyard, making our way by every step closer to the front, the bombardment became heavier, and the long drawn whistling of the shells, going and coming, from French and German batteries alike, became more frequent.

Observation posts are always ingeniously placed to escape the notice of enemy batteries. We were guided to one point of obser- vation near this section of the line, but for obvious reasons it is impossible to give any description either of the post itself or of the circuitous route by which it was reached. It was evident that it had not been left unscathed by the storm of shell that breaks over all parts of the line.

There, stretched before us, was a section of the supreme panorama of the world, French and German trenches facing each other, close at hand! It was a particularly favourable place to see the front, for here was a valley, with one slope (on which we were standing) held by the French, the other by the Germans, with No Man's Land lying between, along the floor of the valley. For observation, this reduced the distance between us. The quality of the soil also added to the clearness of the picture. The ground in this region has large deposits of chalk, which, when thrown up in the digging of the ditches, marks every twist in the trenches with surprising detail. There, in front of us, plainly to be seen by the naked eye, and startlingly close through field glasses, lay the first, second and third lines of German trenches, with the communicating trenches running between them, all marked off to their every zigzag, as if one were looking at the irregular furrows of a field.

We hadn't been looking for more than a minute when a great upburst of earth was hurled from between the first and second German lines. A French shell had landed. And for a long time we watched similar shells landing at various points along the line. If any one thinks it is exciting to sit in a grandstand and watch where a batted ball is likely to fall, imagine the tenseness with which we stood in that observation post looking through an aperture in the wall, watching the landing of French shells on German trenches!

And, as before, the shriek and wail of shells were not all travelling in the one direction. The Germans were firing, too; we were on the route for them. It was not only the noise of German shells in the air which assured us there were Germans opposite us. An observation balloon began to be inflated behind their lines, reached its full size, and rose gracefully above the trees.

What sort of landscape were we looking upon? One of the most beautiful countrysides I have ever seen, extraordinarily beautiful even in a land of rural charm. First there were the vineyards, thick and green and cool looking, in the feverish air, stretching from beneath our feet to the advanced French lines, and beginning again on the German side. In addition, in one direction, were ridiculously small tilled fields at harvest time, glowing under the French sun, with various colours of earth and produce, the whole producing that variegated effect you do not see in the larger, American farms and which, when I used to see it depicted in paintings, I thought was exaggerated and impossibly colourful. Here was a combination of all the charm of French nature, vineyard and field, in the very territory of the opposing trenches.

It was sinister, yes, and electric, so sinister and electric that one felt this represented the very ultimate in existence. All else in the world, pleasant and unpleasant alike, slipped a long way back, and the "front," the trenches and what lay beyond, became so all dominating, all pervading, that the rest of the world, the remainder of existence, seemed an unreality.

The Reims cathedral was painstakingly restored over two decades and reconsecrated on July 10, 1938. In 1945, the city was the site of the Nazi surrender, and in 1991 UNESCO declared the cathedral a World Heritage Site.

Main Johnson worked for the Toronto Star, off and on, from 1910 to 1946, including stints managing its radio station CFCA and as editor of Star Weekly. He died at 72 in 1959.

Canadian and British prisoners of war, 1915

The Black Hole of Germany

JOHN EVANS

April, 1918

"The Black Hole of Germany" will be accorded a place in the history of the war. It is by this name that British prisoners, scattered all over the land of the Kaiser, refer to a prison camp that lies in the middle of the coal fields of Westphalia. The German military authorities designate it as Kommando 47 and probably consider it a model camp. It is here that the severity with which British prisoners of war are treated reaches its height. It is an inferno of rigid discipline, unrestrained brutality and scanty rations. To those unfortunates who have been there, the

Black Hole will always stand as a monument to the worst sides of the German character.

It is my purpose in this article to chronicle unreservedly the life of the prisoner of war. I wish to make it clear, however, that the conditions under which we suffered at the Black Hole are not found in like degree at other camps. All camps have not officers who will stand prisoners at attention before coke ovens until their faces scorch and burn, or put them for weeks at a time in dead of winter into cells three feet by six without any heat. But even the best camps are bad enough.

Life at Kommando 47 began at four o'clock for those who worked in the mines and at five o'clock for the coke makers. I shall tell more presently about coke making which will explain why we considered the early-rising squad the lucky ones. At that early hour the guards would come to the door and rout us out to our day of heavy labour. The work in the mines began at five o'clock and continued without cessation until three-thirty in the afternoon. We were then through for the day. A bowl of turnip soup at seven o'clock and "lights out" at nine were the two remaining official items in the daily routine.

There was little in the life of the prisoner of war but hard work and continued "strafing." Any attempts at sport or entertainment were deliberately checked by the authorities and at best they were undertaken in a half-hearted way. The exercise ground was so small that it was always full to overflowing, and games were strictly impossible. In any case, the detention cells were placed right in the middle of the grounds, so that there was no available space for sports. There was a certain amount of card playing in the evenings in the barracks given over to British and Canadian prisoners, but here again the matter of space was a distinct handicap. There were 250 of us quartered in a space 30 feet by 30. Most of the men found it necessary, if the weather were chill enough to keep them indoors, to spend the evenings in their flea-infested bunks. Competition for places around the two coke-burning stoves that heated the place was keen, and at times acrimonious. It finally developed into a matter of taking your turn.

The camp officers seemed to have one set purpose—to give the "Englanders" the worst of it in everything. They were by no means gentle with the French and Russians, but there was added venom and meanness in all their dealings with us. The French used to hold concerts right along and it served to keep them cheered up. But whenever the officers learned that we were planning something of the kind they would immediately find a pretext to stop it. Anything would serve. One of our number would run foul of some camp rule and by way of punishment the order would be given to stop the entertainment. Characteristically enough, the order of prohibition would be delayed until the last moment. During the 14 months that I spent in this camp, the British were only allowed to hold three concerts.

The strain of the hard work and the monotony of it all told on the prisoners. They became moody and queer. It was not an uncommon occurrence to see a group sitting around and exchanging not a word—just sitting there, silent, brooding. I think most of the prisoners were mentally unhinged. Well, it was enough to upset the equilibrium of the strongest mind.

This condition was most pronounced among the men who had accepted the inevitability of the situation. Most of our fellows were convinced that escape was impossible and they allowed themselves to get into a low condition of mind as a result. They had lost all hope. A few of us were continually on the alert for chances to get away and this kept us stirred up. We had, at least, a shred of hope left.

Perhaps the most inhuman side of the treatment we received at the Black Hole was in the matter of the care of sick and wounded. The medical officer took it for granted that everyone who came to him was shamming. Unless it was possible to show a temperature or a serious wound or sore, the applicant was gruffly ordered back to work. I have seen some of my comrades hustled off to the mine or coke ovens who could hardly walk with rheumatism or who were nearly fainting from sheer exhaustion. Rheumatism was a common complaint, owing to the dampness of the barracks, but the prisoner who applied for exemption from work on that score was taught a painful lesson.

"Rheumatism?" the medical officer would say. "Good! It is soon cured."

The patient would be ushered into a special room where a powerful electric battery was kept. If the part complained of was the arm, the pad would be applied to the arm and a current turned on powerful enough to make the unfortunate man scream with agony. It was kept up until the patient would beg and implore that the current be turned off. "Good!" the officer would say. "That will cure the rheumatism. Back to work with you now, and if the arm still bothers, more electricity will be needed."

A second treatment was never sought. Men crept off to work with stiffened joints that made the use of pick and shovel almost impossible rather than face the torture of that electrical ordeal.

I had very painful experiences with the medical officer myself. Once I developed an abscess under my arm, due, I suppose, to insufficient food and general weakness. I reported it, as it was almost impossible for me to work. The medical officer said gruffly that he would fix me up. He produced some variety of pump with a glass tube attached and placed the tube over the abscess. I protested that it had not yet come to a head, but the officer grunted and roughly applied the pressure.

I could see the flesh rise in the tube. The pain was so terrific that I cried out to him to stop. He went right ahead until the suction drew the blood through the skin. The red drops oozed out like beads of perspiration—but the abscess did not break. Finally he stopped the torture, convinced that he was wrong. I staggered to a window and collapsed, completely overcome with the pain. The officer proceeded to wash the tube without paying any heed to me at all. Then he took a bucket of water and poured it over me as I lay on the floor. When I was sufficiently recovered to get to my feet, the sore was bandaged and I was ordered to report for work.

After my third unsuccessful attempt to escape, I was sentenced to 14 days "black"—solitary confinement on bread and water. I had been brought back from the border in a very weak condition. A high fever was settling on me, the result of exposure and lack of food. I remember very little about the proceedings except that I was forced to stand up before the Kommandant while the room swam around me. I could see nothing and could just barely hear the sharp tones of the Kommandant as he pronounced sentence on me. It must have been apparent to every man in the room that I was sickening for something serious, but it made no difference in the carrying out of the sentence.

I was put into a damp cell, three feet by six, and seven feet high. There was a mouldy, foul-smelling tick [mattress] on the floor on to which I dropped like a log. The guards closed up the window so that not a ray of light came through and then went away. I stayed there alone for two weeks.

I was in a raging fever for the first few days and my memory is very hazy. I can remember that the guards came in at intervals and left hunks of black bread beside me, which, of course, I did not touch. I was frantic for water and eagerly drank all that they would bring. Whether I ever actually lapsed into delirium, I do not know.

At the end of the fourth day, a couple of guards came in and rolled me off the tick with as much ceremony as if I were a bag of potatoes. Then they hauled it out and put another tick in its place. They left me on the floor. I was so weak that it took me a long time to roll back on the tick.

Fourteen days alone in a reeking hole and not a ray of light except when the guards opened the door! The fever worked itself out finally and left me so weak that I could hardly reach the pan of water on the floor beside me. The guards seemed to be at perfect liberty to use us as they liked. There was a young Scotchman named Mennie, a husky lad who literally writhed under the necessity of accepting the treatment. Once he flared out angrily at a guard who had roughly shoved him out of the road. The guard raised his bayonet and thrust deliberately and savagely at Mennie's face. The point caught him in the cheek and ripped the flesh, leaving a gaping wound.

The guard laughed and walked on, flaunting his bayonet with its tip of scarlet. Poor Mennie carried an ugly scar as a result of the guard's little pleasantry. Nothing came of the incident, of course.

The most flagrant case was the deliberate murder of one of our number. It occurred shortly after I arrived at the Black Hole and I can remember still the horror that it implanted in our minds. We lived after that in a state of continual apprehension, never knowing what might happen.

The murder occurred in the mine. Four of our fellows had found a worked-out gallery end and were enjoying a quiet little rest when one of the guards stumbled on them. He was an irascible fellow and he immediately charged at them with his bayonet, roaring imprecations. The four turned and ran with the guard after them. They came to an elevator shaft and found the hoist above with the cable stretching to the bottom of the shaft 60 feet below. Two of them got away by "shinning" down the cable. One of the other two—I won't mention his name—was standing on the edge of the shaft intending to follow suit when the guard came up behind him. By this time the guard was beside himself with rage. He charged at the man standing on the edge of the shaft and deliberately clubbed him until he lost his balance and tumbled headfirst into the pit. His two comrades climbing down the cable saw his body hurtle past them in the dark and then heard a dull thud beneath. The poor fellow was probably killed instantly. The fourth man got away. The guard, who had spent his insane fury, let him go unmolested.

There was an investigation, of course. The prisoners had decided to demand justice and they charged the guard with murder. The fourth man, who had seen it all, gave his evidence to prove that the guard had deliberately knocked his victim down the shaft. The guard was exonerated and the witness was sentenced to four months' solitary imprisonment. I saw him when he came out—weak, wasted, with a look in his eyes that would have startled me if I had not seen a semblance of the same thing in the eyes of so many of the men around me.

I want to describe the detention system in fuller detail. There were 14 cells in all, making up what the authorities called a "rest house." All the cells were the same size as the one in which I spent my terrible two weeks' ordeal. Each cell had a tiny barred window which was sealed up if the prisoner had been sentenced to "black." The place was never heated. If a man were unlucky enough to incur sentence during the winter, he suffered unspeakably in those cold, cramped cells. It was a common trick of the authorities to put three men in a cell, generally an Englishman, a Frenchman and a Russian. Remember, the cells were three feet by six. When three men were herded into one of these holes, it meant that they had to sit huddled together, knee to knee, rubbing shoulders and saturating the air with different national odors.

Each day these were allowed a few minutes in the fresh air. A guard would come and take each man out in turn. This gave an opportunity to get washed. There were no sanitary conveniences in the cells.

Much has been written and told about the scantiness and the badness, nay, the putridity, of the food served to prisoners. No real conception of how bad it was can be gained, however, from a mere description of the fare. It is necessary to tell how it was prepared to get an idea of how it tasted.

We got the same fare always—black bread, turnip soup and coffee. On very rare occasions there was a bit of meat in the soup. It was not very desirable meat, being strong and highly odorous. We often wondered what it was. One day I found out.

I happened to be in the cookhouse. A French prisoner was engaged there around the big pots where the inevitable soup was being prepared. He was a sort of assistant chef. The smell arising from the pots was so nauseating that I thought at first of bolting out.

"That'll be grand to eat," I said to the French prisoner. "What in thunder are you cooking? Dead horse? Dog meat?"

"Exactly," said the Frenchman. "Dog meat."

He lifted the lid and the odour in the room became noticeably worse. Floating around in the thick, pulpy mass of turnips were— yes, parts of dog meat, unquestionably canine. I bolted out. It was more than I could stand even with a stomach inured to eating prison fare. We had meat in our turnip soup that day which I did not enjoy; but I did not say anything to the rest. Where ignorance assists digestion it is folly to be wise.

Before Christmas it was given that, through the benignancy of the Kommandant, we would be given three days' holidays from work. Unfortunately for me I was not to enjoy the rest. I had been charged with laziness in the mine by the staggers (foremen) and so was told off to assist in the cookhouse during the three days. The charge was a just one. I was incorrigibly slow in the mine. It went against the grain to produce coal to run the munition plants of the Kaiser, and I had reduced the matter of non-producing to an exact science. The staggers knew this and were right on my heels all the time. Well, I lost my Christmas holiday.

During the whole of the three days I was kept busy peeling turnips. I was stationed in a corner of the cookhouse and the turnips were piled up in front of me. They were covered with mud and by the time I had been at work five minutes, my hands were thoroughly grimy. I was not allowed to stop and wash, so the turnips left me pretty well mud-caked. They were immediately thrown into a big grinding machine and reduced to a pulp. This pulp, a mixture of turnip and mud, was put right into the pots and made into soup. No wonder we found our mouths full of sand after eating the soup.

Of course, our sufferings in the matter of food were as nothing compared to what the Russians had to endure. We got our Red Cross parcels and managed to eke out an existence, but most of the poor Slavs had to live on the prison fare. It was terrible to see them, big and husky fellows falling away to mere skeletons. They would come over to our side and beg for food. We gave them all we could. Once some bread came through from Switzerland which had become blue and mouldy on the way. We hesitated at first about offering this to them, but the Russians seized it avidly. They soaked it in water and ate it ravenously.

Often, when they were marching off to work, men in the Russian lines would topple over. They were faint from lack of food. We did our best for them and shared our food as liberally as we could. The French, however, exploited the simple-minded Slavs, selling them food at steep prices and trading with them. Sometimes a gaunt Russian would sell his boots for a tin of bully beef. This practice was pretty general among the French and created a certain amount of hard feeling between us.

It was not possible to get very close to the Russians nor to find out anything much about them. They were a dumb, passive lot, knowing no language but their own and quite devoid of intelligence for the most part. They did not cause the German guards any trouble. They worked until they dropped and accepted any form of ill-treatment with the stoical resignation of the Slav race. We knew this, however, that the Russians hated the Germans with a hatred more deep-seated even than our own. It is a racial hatred that has its foundation in the old undying enmity of Slav for Teuton, the heritage of centuries of conflict. I cannot think that Russia will ever be able to live at peace under the dominance of Germany. The old enmity will bring the Slavs back to fight for their independence again.

Most of us worked in the coal mines, but some were selected to look after the coke ovens. Their task was to load the coke, as it came out of the ovens, into cars or trucks to be carried away. Each man had to load 20 tons a day. Close watch was kept. The hours were supposed to be from six in the morning until six at night, but any unfortunates who had not completed their allotted work by closing time had to keep at work right through until the full 20 tons had been loaded. Sometimes there would be a scarcity of cars. It made no difference to the prisoners, however. They had to wait until the cars came and then load the daily amount before they got off duty.

It was terrible work. The heat from the coke ovens was intense and by the end of the day the men would be absolutely played out. They would return to the camp so thoroughly fatigued that not even the activities of the fleas, which infested all of us and which bred in our bunks by the million, could disturb their sleep.

They were allowed every second Sunday off. Sometimes the strain became so unbearable that the coke makers would go on strike and refuse to work. The method followed by the guards in such a case was perhaps the most callously brutal thing in all my experience. The men would be forced to stand at attention immediately in front of the oven doors. The heat pouring out would be so intense that their faces would become scorched and burned. They had to stand in this inferno sharply to attention. If a muscle sagged, the butt end of a rifle or even the sharp point of a bayonet would bring the offender sharply up.

Men would faint after a few minutes of this. The guards would sluice the recumbent figures with buckets of water, drag the men to their feet and make them stand in the most exposed positions of the line. Flesh and blood could not stand it long. Maniacal laughter would break out, sharp cries of pain and frantic appeals to the mercy of the guards.

"Then back to work you go," would be the ultimatum of the guards.

And back they would finally go—with drawn faces that would smart excruciatingly for days after and with a vertigo caused by the intense heat—back to complete their full 20 tons apiece that very day!

Work at the coke ovens soon reduced a man to a mere skeleton. It was the form of punishment that they held over all of us—a term at coke making.

I could go on, piling horror upon horror. Perhaps what I have told will suffice, however, to show why that camp set back in the desolate coal mining country of Westphalia is called the Black Hole of Germany. Perhaps also what I have told will show how necessary it is to wage this war to a victorious conclusion. A nation which will do the unspeakable things that I have witnessed must be beaten to its knees and taught that such crimes against God and man will no longer be tolerated.

Princess Patricia of Connaught, daughter of the governor general, reviewing the Canadian Light Infantry regiment that bore her name at Bramshott, England, 1919

The Last Stand of the Princess Pats

GEORGE PEARSON

May, 1918

The noose of the net we were in was drawing up tighter with each new day. Daily now there came to us of the Princess Pats where we lay at Polygon Wood orders to stand-to and be ready to evacuate. The story ran that we were faced by Prince Ruprecht of Bavaria and half a million men converging on us for a drive to Calais. It took on wild shapes. They said an airman but newly back from a reconnaissance over the German lines had collapsed in a faint at the landing place so that they had to carry him from the machine. They dashed water in his face and brought him to. "Are you all right, old chap?"

He rolled his weak eyes. "Good God, sir! The country's black with Germans—moving men and guns," he wailed.

We had put on everything we owned and stood about, waiting. It was very hard. A pack is never so heavy as when the bearer of it is chained to a tiresome inactivity that places the full weight of the load on one set of aching muscles, as the uneasy twisting of any pack-mule proves. So we waited and blasphemed the Bavarians and our own higher command.

And then the glorious order came: "Take off your packs. The contingent is holding its own. We're going to stick it another day." This thing happened upon several days, and towards the crucial last thrice in one day, so that our nerves were likely to crack with the strain of it all. It was a time of great unease and dread of the unexpected which was for active imaginations harder to bear than all other bad things hereabout.

And with each fresh evacuation order the sullen determination of our men to die, if die they must, here and without giving up one foot of ground, hardened and set into an obsession so that when the order came, officers and non-coms had to go down the trench angrily bidding rebellious privates to stand-to in full marching order and to "Jump to it." And then when the order came once more: "Stand fast," we cheered some more, in growls by this time; flung our packs savagely down, peeled off our great-coats and took one more insuring look at the proper working of our rifles.

At first, the plan had been for the rear-guard of an officer and 15 men to dynamite our trenches, but this was given over, presumably because it would most efficiently notify the enemy of our more important intentions. Instead they were up there in the front line now under the command of Mr. Lane giving rapid fire, from 16 different spots and as quickly changing to an equal number of new ones. They would do this for two hours more, changing rapidly from one spot to another, thereby giving us time to march back to the new position and shake down in it.

We could hear them now up there, shooting smartly. We could imagine it—one man here and another there—from each a shot, perhaps two—a hasty run on the part of each to a new position, a shot, another run, then back again and so on *ad infinitum*, a nerve-racking task. They were brave men. We hoped no ill would befall them.

We selected our loads from the pile at our feet. I chose two one-inch boards, a foot wide, 16 feet long. They were very green and very full of sap and heavy in proportion, so that their floppy ends made much grief for me before I laid them down for good. We stuffed our pouches full of ammunition so that each man had 240 rounds about his middle and in addition to that three extra bandoliers of 25 rounds each across each shoulder so that our load in lead alone was a very great one. We tightened our belts and shifted the bulky packs which contained our all of worldly possessions, from souvenirs to the great-coats which some thoughtful mind had bid us not to wear because there might yet be work in the wood this night not suited to the wearing of great-coats.

We clustered in a small open place amongst the pines. There were these few odd shots from our rear-guard. That was all now, that and the less frequent twitter of some sleepy bird—except for that dull glow of villages which had these many nights become a fixture in our summer sky—just the peaceful twilight of a summer evening that now closed in on us, leaving the world to us and it.

We choked with emotion; we gave our belts one last pull, bent down, picked up our loads and then, with bitter hearts and like the beaten men we knew we were not, turned our backs to a foe we did not fear and trudged out into the night to Bellewaarde and away from him.

The night was heavy with the travail of unspoken woe and with that battle stillness which was the more ominous because of its apparent lack of relation to the evil circumstances of the moment. The dying fires of the blasted villages ringed us in with a dull and sullen furnace glow which in its unconscious art furnished just that bare modicum of light which was necessary to suggest rather than actually to portray the dim mass of marching men and which, because of the strange stillness of the night and all other things, held the greater threat. Queer looking trees and shapeless bundles of men loomed indistinctly for a moment in the poor glare of the villages and then slid slowly by.

The suspended sword of Damocles had fallen at last: Fear had become fact and we, the proud Princess Pats with those precious colours over which a princess had strained her eyes in the making, and which were now up there at the head of the column, were in full retreat! To these other agonies was added that more poignant one of the separation from the bodies of our sacred dead, now left to the unkind mercies of what well might be evil minds. The thought was torture. We stumbled on with our awkward loads of flopping boards and heavy sand-bags, full of a fatigue so keen that it was a physical pain and a heartache that was worse—upwards of a thousand disillusioned children. Dark though it was, it was easy to tell that we were very tired by the way in which our feet slipped on the cobbles, the lack of decision in the dragging sound of them and the utter lack of words.

Now that we had left Polygon Wood the air seemed keener, but although it was not unpleasant, neither was it bracing. But that like all other things seemed merely part of the strange dreams in which we now found ourselves and in which nothing mattered and so that the brain, except in certain rare and automatic moments, took no account of anything that passed: For every shrieking nerve was falsely energized to its own highest pitch to the more pressing need of hounding the tired body on, whipping it harshly whenever its strangely unrelated feet lagged and dipped to the near point of falling. A condition of natural self-anesthesia set in which mercifully dulled the brain to all impressions and the body to all pain—after first driving into the one for the direction of the other that one insistent command—"carry on."

We had fallen in for the retirement of this night march about eight o'clock, but by reason of the heavy loads each man bore it was well on to midnight when we reached the edge of Belle-waarde Wood, three miles as the crow flies from the trenches we had just evacuated in the Wood of Polygon and a slightly greater distance from the still-active lamp of the dying Ypres.

The trench, if it could be called that, lay out from the wood in the middle of a mud-smooth field. We deployed along its course in single file by platoons until the entire regiment had been aligned, after which we were bidden to take off our packs. Our extra loads of lumber and other trench furnishings were already on the ground to which we had let them slide at the first hint of a halt, so that latterly and during this last short trek to our position on the edge of the trench the greater portion of us had been dragging them because we had not the poor strength necessary to lift them up; even as it was our fingers slipped their hold on the loads because there was no longer any firmness in our grasp and our knees gave wickedly at inconvenient moments.

It was raining now. They told us to wait a while. We did so. Our heads nodded so that we slept standing—like horses. In a few minutes an officer wandered along the line giving orders. We reached down for our things, all of a tremble with this sudden new weakness which the unaccustomed rest had brought. We slipped one arm through the sling of the rifle and grasped the straps of the rest of our equipment in that hand, reserving the other for the boards and other foreign loads.

We dragged them so, a separate collection in each hand, still like horses, but between shafts this time. There was no one to see that it was done properly and we did not care, so we did not pile the trench material as we had been ordered to do, but merely let it clatter down, each piece sinking into its own bed of mud and so that the whole was spread out over an acre of ground. We continued to drag our packs as we turned back toward the trench, going further up it this time to make more room, as we had been directed to do. For the first time that night we began to talk. Weak voices lifted up as mate sought mate and, being answered, quietened again.

"Lie down and get what sleep you can. We'll wake you up when the tools come. You can dig yourselves in then—there'll probably be hell to pay in the mornin'." The voice of the officer trailed off in a monotonous repetition as he shambled by, mouthing the order to each group in turn.

We looked at the trench and, weary though we were, longed ardently for tools with which to augment its pretence of shelter. Despite permission, or rather order to lie down without even the necessity of posting sentries, we fell to with our entrenching tools, seeking to deepen our shallow shelter. It was of no use. The pick end was a tooth-pick and as useful, the shovel end good only for the work of a poor pick. We tried loosening it so and then scooping the earth up in double handfuls, but after viewing the united efforts of the three of our group for over a quarter of an hour, we gave it up in despair and lay down, wondering dimly why they had not prepared a place for us, and if they had been too pressed these last few days, why the magnificent ones on the staff had not justified their jobs by doing so before the great battle had started.

The trench was only waist deep and so narrow that when lying on the side one had no room in which to bend the knees as a man likes to do when he lies down, but had instead to lie out straight. Even the bent elbows struck the wall at the back as the hands did in front. The rain had turned into a steady drizzle now, but by preference I turned my face up to it and lay on my back in order that I might make shift to bend my knees. The trench was so narrow that the sides of it pinched both shoulders and when the rain changed into a steady down-pour, I endeavoured to get up for the purpose of exchanging the service of the rubber ground sheet on which I lay, planning to put it over my body. I heard grunts and sighs and oaths on either side of me as others came to the same hard decision only to find themselves stuck, as I was. The narrowness of the trench was such that in my weakened condition it held me in a vise, the wet walls of which slipped from out my grasp and the floor from under my feet each time that I endeavoured to gain a hold with which to draw myself erect, so that for a minute I had to lie back exhausted while I endeavoured to determine how, since there was no room to bend the legs, I might best gain my feet.

I did it somehow and had almost decided to lie out on the top when I saw that the men lay so closely at either end of my six feet of trench as to threaten my ownership of them and so plumped down into my old quarters, which in the brief interval of the thought had already filled with water in the holes my hips had made in the mud. I lay there in the water, listening to the rain strike on the rubber sheet that covered my face until, discovering that each fold of the sheet directed its own individual stream to augment the increasing body of the one I lay in, I cast the thing off with a curse and lay thus for the remainder of the night, as all others were doing, in a pool of water, my face dead to the impact of the pouring rain.

It did not seem possible that people in other places were perhaps going quietly to their sheltered beds, or that such things as sheltered beds could exist when here the deadly cold only crept the further into one's marrow bones and almost ate of courage itself. It was, I remembered, on just such nights as this that somewhere, some time, a long, long time ago, we used to like to gather around the open fire and listen to the lash of the storm. A grand night for a dance—but, of course, no one danced any more—the world was at war—women worked and wept—men fought—there was no dancing. All denied themselves. The last thing I heard before I became utterly stupefied, for certainly it was not sleep that followed, was the threat and counter-threat of a jangling quarrel at my feet.

We were very glad when they routed us out at three o'clock in the morning and bade us go to digging with the tools which had just been received and which they now handed to us. We sought our share of them and found it to consist, for our group of three, of only one short-handled and broken-backed shovel, together with 15 or 20 sand-bags.

We stamped up and down in the pouring rain, flinging our arms about to gain a little warmth, our teeth chattering. Two of us fell to on the bottom of the trench with our entrenching tools, loosening the earth which the third man shovelled into the empty sacks. We had not filled many of these when we discovered that we were cutting to the quick of the water level of that particular section of Flanders and that any further gain in depth meant the same in water. The problem was evidently one of a parapet and that meant more sand-bags; our present equipment of them would never do; we must play the old soldier and get some.

We clambered up on top, and while Shepherd and Stamborough went to an industrious filling of the remainder of the sacks from the field in our rear I cruised along the trench, following my nose and keeping a sharp look-out for sacks or tools. Everywhere men were digging and filling just as we were. I asked each group for picks or shovels or bags, for anything in fact that they might have in the shape of trench plunder. Nothing doing! Everywhere it was the same. Already our minds were shaking off the evil effects of the night march co-incident with the exercise of digging operations, a fact that was reflected in the manner of the reception of my request, for they merrily told me to go to hell. One man did at last give me a pick after taking my name, rank and number, together with most solemn assurances on my part that the tool in question should be returned at the appointed time. I returned with that to my two comrades and found that they had similarly added to our store by commandeering the supply of sacks of the men on our left, who were still lying down and who as the result of their own weariness and domestic and internal quarrels in their group steadfastly refused to do any digging or otherwise improve their and our unsheltered position. There seemed to be no one there to make them do so, so we argued with them, pointing out that the Germans, who were undoubtedly pressing hard on our heels from the Polygon Wood position, would most certainly be down on us as soon as daylight should expose the disposition of our forces.

"———— 'em," they said. "Let 'em come—the quicker the sooner. If we're for it, we're for it! Have an end to this anyhow." Whereat they rolled over and made pretence of sleeping again.

In view of the acquaintance with the ground, which my ear-lier trip had given me, my comrades elected that I should do the skirmishing, get what sacks I could as far away from home as pos-sible. I drifted up the line of digging men until I had passed sev-eral groups and then picked up the first unprotected pile of sacks I saw. I doubt if I even salved my conscience with the weak defence that it was possible that they had no owner. I simply did what Tommy always does in like circumstances, what an honest starv-ing man does when he lacks bread; I stole them from the plutes.

I took a cruise on the other way, but without result. Only Number One and Two companies of ours were here, the others were in support in huts around the chateau and lake behind us; and it was impossible to go far without getting into the lines of other regiments—which meant trouble, so I retraced my steps.

When the last dull cloud of mist had risen and set the seal on the arrival of the new day, which, because of its murkiness, seemed rather to ooze out of the night than to be sharply divided from it, we straightened our backs, wiped muddy hands across our wet foreheads and looked around to see what we could see.

"Well, God love a sailor, Lumme! Look at that will you, mate? Them blokes!" Shepherd pointed a mud-encrusted finger out in the general direction of our front; our eyes followed and this is what they saw.

To the right and left of us there stretched a long and irregular line of knots of our comrades, all digging furiously except for those who were, like us, straightening up and gazing across and at our front where a solid line of other men were also digging furi-ously but without any looking up on their part. Apparently the surprise was all on our own side.

"By the piper that played before Moses." "Well, by ———. What d'yuh know 'bout that?" "They sure know we can't hurt 'em or they wouldn't do that." "Why the Hell don't our ———— artillery mop 'em up?"

Our natural impulse after that first one of numbed astonishment had been to bid us fly to our holes, but by the time our minds had formulated the thought to fling down the tools, grasp rifles, leap down into the trench and go to shooting, we had seen that the Germans continued to dig as phlegmatically as though this was not war. Since that accorded well with our designs on our own poor trench we were glad to observe the unspoken truce they thus initiated and carry on without any such aggressive action. Occasionally a man would stop from his digging long enough to look up, wipe the rain from his face, painting it with mud instead, and swear feebly in a fresh astonishment as he looked over at the industrious Teutons before again resuming his own desperate labour. Except for these small incidents, our surprise had given over on the instant of perception of the major fact to one of a tacit acceptance of a natural and to-be-expected one which was in the final analysis one more in a long succession of surprising facts to which our shock-absorbent systems had long since ceased to react.

So there we were, two long lines of men just so far as the eye could follow which then was until some intervening hill or lot of wood cut off the view in front or perhaps sheltered the other diggers from our curious sight. The Germans were further away from us than on any previous occasion, some hundreds of yards in fact, but still within comfortable rifle range. The rain and the faint mist which now began to flout itself in nebulous and smoke-like wisps gave to their toiling figures a certain indefiniteness which only intensified the strange air of unreality and added to the weird nature of the entire proceeding. A very few shots were fired at first; none of which were aimed, if the fact that no one on either side fell could be taken as any indication. Except for that there was no firing. After that the only sound was that of scraping shovels and falling clods of earth, intermingled with snatches of talk about the manner and the disposition of our work.

Apparently the enemy had not yet got his artillery up or, if he had, was not prepared to use it on us until his own troops had dug themselves in. But in any event his unsurprised acceptance of the present situation undoubtedly proved his acquaintance with the sad fact that he need fear no artillery of ours.

At nine o'clock on the morning of the fourth day of May, a single German gun spoke once, and as though it had been an awaited signal the well-drilled Germans opposite dropped into their warrens in one pretty and simultaneous movement, just as though they had been one man. And without any other warning than that significant action, we just as prettily and I will warrant, because of the handicap under which we suffered, much more swiftly leapt into our own holes, where we scrunched down, a trifle out of breath perhaps with the quickness of our leap and staring at one another in a somewhat startled fashion, but yet saying with a brave attempt at a jest: "This is *der Tag*—Kismet!"

The bombardment was on. That one report was followed by one more, but that one was the vast and accumulated sound of so many lesser ones that the ear lost count of the tale of them; the world turned into a throbbing, pounding terror and we lay there waiting for it to end.

We alternately prayed and blasphemed that our artillery should do something. Were we dogs that they should let us die thus—like rats—and unrevenged? Only once was our prayer answered by our artillery, and by one gun only, quite early in the bombardment. The poor lonely thing barked feebly, twice, after the manner of a plucky terrier facing the annihilating rush of a tiger, and then drew home so fierce a German fire that it was for ever silenced.

The trench then began amid a great rending of flesh and earth and bags to go through all the painful processes of dissolution—began violently to decay and fall apart, to spout oil-wells and otherwise alternately to inter and to vomit its denizens. Men sighed and died and their souls slipped gladly away from the turmoil. The murmur of war changed to the cavernous roar of it and hung there for all the daylight hours of a long, long day. It was a slow, a steady, and a merciless shelling which lasted for hours without respite so that the air throbbed and sobbed and sucked in painful unison with our held breaths and leaping hearts.

The battery which claimed us for its own prey lay in a direct line to the right so that it had an enfilade fire on and swept the trench from one end to the other, almost always, because of the great length of target offering, striking in one place if it missed in another. First there would come the slow and deep-mouthed pair: "Boom! Boom!" and, merging into the heel of that sound, the rapid-fire "Boom! Boom! Boom! Boom!" of the balance of the battery. If one were standing, sitting or kneeling, there was just one thing to do, and that very quickly: fling oneself down at full length on the bottom of the trench before the burst. That came announced by the shell's scream from the moment that that sharper sound emerged faintly from the duller and distant one of the boom until, in a steadily rising crescendo of a million rasping throaty squeaks the thing burst right at our perishing ear-drums in a violent "Bang" and followed by a series of them, each one holding its own vivid flash of addled flame and belching sulphurous odours, as rotten in odour as in colour.

With the body tied down to this merciless inactivity of a rat caught in a trap, and waiting to be killed, it was natural that the mind should roam strangely. I found time to reflect on the strangeness of the fact that I felt no actual fear other than the gasping breathlessness of the shock of very close bursts, while on some other occasions that I could remember, and some of which were not to be compared with this one for pure horror, I had felt fear in its worst form, stark panic, maddening fright. The worst of fear for most men comes later—after it is all over, when there is no longer any need for the mind to brace itself so tensely for the impact of the shock, and so relaxes and invites reaction.

That sharp exhilaration in the air of the night before as we left Polygon Wood was now explained: It was the gas and smoke of high-explosive shell-fire tinged perhaps by errant whiffs of the more potent and distant main body of the asphyxiating gas. The eyes, nostrils and lungs smarted and burned with the contact. It bit sharply and clawed into the chest like the inhalation of an especially rancid cigarette and like that, bringing with it, and in the added proportion of its greater volume, a certain biting, stinging light-headed exhilaration which made even the pain of it not unpleasant to the taste.

Each time as soon as the last clap of the battery which had us in hand had died down, some one of us sprang quickly to his feet and thrust an inquiring head above the parapet, eye sweeping the country about our front and making certain that the enemy infantry were not advancing on us, in which case we should of course man the parapet and, so desperate were we, perhaps go out to meet them fairly in the open field, and charge them man to man, the best, the quickest; and so quickly determine whose was the best claim of being the better man.

Each fresh glance showed some new section of the trench caved in, but beyond the constant recurrence of that painful fact it was impossible to say with any degree of accuracy just what was occurring in a general way. The guns shot with a terrible accuracy so that, in the rare intervals when the fire lifted off our own persons and we could observe its effect on others, our hearts stood still to see the black columns walk up and down the trench 100 yards away just like a living thing—but dealing death. Men were suffering there, being burned alive—dying the slow deaths of wounded worms under tons of suffocating earth.

Once while we lay with our chins in the mud waiting for this spouting turmoil of others' misery to shift on to us as it so regularly did, there came from out in front a cry for help, so desperate, so faint, so cracked with pain and terror that the pity of it tore our hearts. The words were indistinguishable.

"Speak louder," someone cried.

"Is that the K.R.R.?"

"Yes," we shouted, for the sake of brevity, although the King's Royal Rifles were well up on our right.

"Well, then for the love of God, mate, come an' give us a hand—God's sake!"

"Don't do anything of the kind! It's a trap! It's a trap!" warned a voice from the bottom of our trench, for we were not unmindful of the fact that German snipers were by this time crawling up under cover of the shell-fire.

"No! No!" shouted Wostenholm above the din: "It was too good English, an' too broad English! Come on!"

He jumped up and with another man raised himself stiffly over the top and crawled out in front. They reappeared in a couple of minutes with two wounded and very badly shaken K.R.R.'s who slumped weakly down in the bottom of the trench, giving way instantly and completely to the relaxation of the comparative safety our reassuring presence seemed to afford them. They told us brokenly of how they had done rear-guard for their regiment and had then crawled up through the bombardment, not knowing where they were and fearful until they heard our voices lest they had blundered in amongst the enemy. The trench was too narrow to allow of their passage even if they could have walked; so we made them as comfortable as we could and left them in a weak portion of the trench which could be of no use to us in the event of a hand-to-hand struggle. They asked for a fag, sank weakly back, and closed their eyes.

That narrowness of the trench which we had found so irksome when we had sought that impossible rest during the night now proved our one best friend since it offered just that much less of a target to the flying fragments which filled the air. Stamborough had elected to move up on the other side of the traverse, thinking it safer there, and Shepherd, his mate, followed as a matter of course so that I was left alone until Radcliffe, whose mates were dead and buried, came to the vacated place and joined me, both for company and for the greater safety the spot afforded. He sat with his back against the traverse on the other side of which the other two had gone, with his knees up, staring straight ahead at me with eyes that, once naturally protuberant, now almost frightened; they protruded so.

"By ———," he muttered. "This is murder. We'll all be killed!"

Nearly every one said that and certainly all believed it. The utter hopelessness of it all and the feeling and the thought that was the hardest to bear was this: to be killed like rats in a pit, not even swiftly, but agonizingly over a long period of many torturing hours, the sport of these cruel shells. We longed bitterly for the Germans to come on and end it all; for by that time we knew by reason of our depleted numbers and all the other factors of importance in our strength that there could be but one ending to any determined assault, but we did yearn for that, to kill some Germans and go down fighting like men and not like unknown impounded dogs. If only they would come on and finish us quickly! How glorious! Prayers for that and other mercies were not so much prayed as wrung from rebellious hearts, out of agony and sweat and blood.

It was when, in a moment of surcease from the shells, the small-arms fire reached its most furious maximum of intensity that we heard a cry from the far side of the traverse for volunteers to go out and get a wounded man. It seemed a pity, for we had long since ceased to try to do anything for the wounded except to crawl to and bind up those who seemed most likely to live and to tell those who could walk "to beat it" to the communication trench which some said had been dug during the night. As for the other more severely wounded men, we merely adjusted their heads, and if they could smoke, gave them cigarettes. Afterwards we took their papers for their wives.

So, that lives should be thrown away for this wounded man when the rifle of each unwounded man was so badly needed here seemed odd indeed. An unusually painful wound perhaps? No soldier fears death but all dread useless sacrifice. We listened hopefully to the voices on the other side and for my own part I hoped that the volunteers would offer before the call reached us, for the decision either way would be a hard one, since on the one hand it meant certain death without any of the justification of any useful purpose accomplished; and on the other no Pat could deny the plea of a wounded comrade.

The call was answered—the bravest thing in the worst fire we had ever seen. At first the only indication of the fact was the cessation of the call of volunteers. Shortly after that I heard queer voices, rose to my feet, looked around and saw the most inspiring act of pure courage that it has ever been my fortune to witness.

In this terrible fire, so dreadful that the air thrummed and quivered with the countless displacements of turning bullets that struck so thickly that they sent the mud flying in all directions hereabout, two men ran heavily just at my head, carrying a heavy thing on a stretcher. A loaded stretcher is at all times a very heavy burden on the most level of dry ground. Here it was terrible. These men were imbued with super-human strength for, although the ground was full of shell holes and very wet and slippery, they were actually running.

The lead bearer was a boy of less than 20 who was unknown to me although I had from the fine quality of the face noticed it when he had lately joined us in a draft. That face glowed ardently now with the indescribable confusion of the sheer terror and sublime exaltation of his sacrificial moment. The man who ran with him was one who in Polygon Wood had eaten his heart out for his daily punishment because he had once failed the regiment. This was his expiation and his unstudied answer to the worst of his detractors. He was speaking, imploring, commanding, and by the chanting, praying monotone of the words, almost to himself: "Faster! Faster! Faster!"

It seemed incredible that they had lived so long, with the fire so bad and the snipers so close. Those warning roars of the battery boomed out again. I flung myself down. There was a crash: The air was full of falling things. I sprang up to see that all was gone: And have rarely known such sorrow.

"Make way there ———. Gangway!" It was the gruff voice of a sergeant leading the boy out to the communication trench and the dressing station in the wood. The boy was the only living survivor of the trio but seemed not to know that or anything else, for he was quite dazed and gave no indication of pain from the bloody mess of a completely pulverized arm which he carried like a wet dish-rag in the hollow of the other; any more than he felt pain from the bad head wound which had laid bare his scalp and which had already matted his silky hair with blood which now ran down and covered his face, filling his eyes. There was no room for one man to pass another so we crawled up on top to let him by.

As the sergeant took the boy out some rude things were hurled at the former from several quarters. He feigned not to hear. That place out back to which he now was going represented Heaven and safety to us and him—the last place anyone in authority should seek to go to on any but the direct order. Only the courageous nature of this boy's sacrifice could condone even the sending of a man from the ranks out with him, for it seemed certain that the Germans might rush us at any moment, for which reason no man who could bear a rifle was to be lightly spared, even for suffering. And certainly it was disgraceful for a sergeant to go. He knew all that as well as we did and knew that we knew too, so that he was very glad to slip on by with a great show of bluster about his wounded man that sat but poorly on him who had never before shown kindness to any one of us sick, wounded or well. He knew that we saw through his ruse and that he made this brave man whom he dishonoured with his touch the pretext for the carrying of his own carcass to safety. We damned him to his face and just then a flying splinter took him in the head, wounding him slightly so that like as not he won a decoration for bringing a wounded man out from under fire.

Startled men began to crowd down on us from around the shoulder of the traverse. "Orders to evacuate," they said tersely. We did not know whether to be glad or sorry. Some swore wrathfully; others were frankly glad and made no bones about it either. "Anything," they said, "to get out o' this." For the most part we were relieved to get away from so awful a place and terribly cha-grined that we must again retire. But both these conflicting emo-tions were confused by the more powerful one of our soldier anger at an enemy who pounded us with man-made things of iron and steel, for ever keeping us at arm's length and from the fierce assuaging of our insensate lust for his blood in the man test of a close-up *melee*.

"What about the wounded?" we asked when we saw that only whole men were passing us.

"Leavin' 'em," a lack-lustred-eyed man said wearily.

That saddened us: Things must be bad indeed, worse than we had thought possible for the old regiment. We turned slowly and went with them.

The occasion offered the first opportunity we had for ex-changing news of casualties with our comrades from the upper reaches of the trench. There were scores of them, and although it was not long past noon, and although all who could after any fashion walk, crawl or hobble had gone down the communication trench, the main trench was already well littered with the dead and the dying. Owing to the narrowness of the trench we had been forced to lay some of our dead upon the parapet where they now received further wounds. It was either that or walk on them. Only those were buried who had been done so by a shell when the wall of the trench had slid in on them, kicking, strangling, their mouths and nostrils full of mud.

That portion of the trench next to and between us and the communication trench was blown in so that we had to bend our backs well in going over it. As we did so the man ahead of me gave a rasping scream and pointed, staring down at the loose earth: "Look at Joe! Look at Joe!" he cried. Joe had been his mate, and now portions of the battered head of him projected from the earth. It was too much. The man passed on ahead of me, scream-ing his hysterical way down the trench.

Everywhere the trench had been blown in and everywhere we had to mind our step to avoid the unmentionable. We came to the communication trench, and found it choked with the men who had preceded us, and who struggled now amongst the bodies of the narrow passageway, to get back amongst us. An angry officer emerged from the commodious dug-out at the cross-roads of the trenches and drove angrily at the struggling mass with expostulating hands.

"Get back! Go back to your places!" The officer seized a man by the shoulder: "Who gave that order to evacuate? Who gave it?" he cried angrily, looking at all of us in turn, "I'll have him up before the C.O.—getting us all cut up." We made our way back more cheerfully than we had come. We wondered from whence had come the mistaken order and sagely decided, as always in simi-lar circumstance, on the theatrical explanation that never failed to warm our melodramatic hearts: An English-speaking German had crawled up to the trench and breathed the order into our unsuspecting ears.

Wostenholm was sitting on the bottom of the trench, clean-ing his rifle once more as he had already done a dozen times that morning after each nearby burst that had flung its own charge of mud and grit into the mechanism of the breech. He hurried so as to be ready for the next attack which would certainly be only a matter of time and in the turmoil of the moment not dreaming that one was even then under way. It was in this sitting position and with both hands engaged that a German bayonet found a home in him.

It came from the rear and without any warning other than the shock of the impact of the standard of the bayonet against his shoulder blade and which in itself had so much of weight behind it that in the shock of the moment he was quite sure that he was killed. "They're here!" he screamed. He looked down and his distended eyes saw the haft of the bayonet sticking out of his breast so that even in the flood of unreasoning terror that swept over him he found time to wonder why there was no pain. By this time the air was full of the murmur of attack—cries, shouts and blows; the crack of rifles close-fired and the clank of steel meeting steel.

Terror left him because it could find no welcome in any of his breed. He flung his whole weight to one side and wriggled desperately with all the strength of his small body to be free from the

*Exhausted members of the Princess Pats after capturing
a machine gun emplacement on Vimy Ridge*

impalement. He fell off. He was not impaled at all, for the bayonet had merely slipped in between and under the straps of the back portion of his equipment, through the cloth of the tunic, through the lanyard and the straps in front and out the breast pocket, pushing out of the latter as it did so the papers of a dead man which this indefatigable soldier had lately added to his collection for the thoughtful easing of the uncertainty of the mothers and wives of lost comrades. It was thus that the standard had struck home so that the shock had made him quite mad with fear for that one brief moment.

Just then his German, who stood on the parados, toppled over, let go all holds and fell: kicking spasmodically. It was so sudden that his pointed rifle which had been raised to shoot Wostenholm almost speared him as it fell from the dead hand and the bayonet did in fact strike him in the jaw. The lurch that had freed him from the bayonet had caused him to let go his own rifle with so much force that it had fallen under the feet of the struggling men who now filled every corner of this portion of the trench.

He had desperate need of a rifle and was by this time very angry at so rude an interruption of the cleaning of his own. The German weapon was only half useful, for bayonet work alone. He required one that would fit his British ammunition and so began to crawl up on to the edge of the parados, seeking the rifle of one of the several Patricia casualties who lay there and was already reaching out for such a one when there was a crack and a burst of flame; the world briefly and temporarily came to a sudden violent end at his very ear; a heavy blow on the foot turned him completely over and it was only a quick inspection that showed him that it was gone although the loss mercifully enough caused him no pain.

Other shells followed. There was desperate hand-to-hand

fighting all along the line as he could plainly see from his higher position. Many German shells fell amongst these men, killing Canadians and Prussians alike. Great bodies of the latter poured in from all sides and from the front and rear. They had not yet gained the support trench, although in the attempt to do so some were dying all along the length of its parapet from which our lads with their heads well up now poured in a terribly destructive fire on these of the enemy who had not yet found the doubtful shelter of our fire-trench, or the ardour of whose charge had carried them over the latter and on to the support-trench itself, in which event they died in good order in their tracks.

Wostenholm was brought back to the earth by a violent movement at his foot that jerked him violently, sans ceremony, back into the trench, where he sprawled ungracefully at the feet of a German who seemed many times larger than even a very large man could possibly have been and hoped that the end would be a swift one, for he had no arms, was hopelessly maimed and was still dazed from the shock of the bursting shell.

The German growled a guttural something that he could make nothing of, grasped him by the slack of his tunic under the armpits, dragged him further back and laid him against the parapet, more out of harm's way. He growled again in a shame-faced sort of manner and angrily thrust a cigarette between Wostenholm's lips, lit it, picked up his own smoking rifle and strode heavily away to assist a *Kamerad* in the task of dispatching a lithe Patricia who was fighting so well as to threaten that section of *Kultur* which faced them. The two of them killed the one Pat; nonetheless, the heart of Wostenholm warmed to this man who could thus succor with one gentle hand the comrade of a man he killed with the other harder one and so that he hoped that he might some day shake the kinder one.

Someone spoke and Wostenholm made out Barrett lying further up the trench and like himself out of action. Although they were only seven yards apart they could scarcely hear one another for the din of clashing weapons, the smack of rifle-fire, the shouts and groans of fighting and dying men that themselves were only superimposed on the denser background of sound made by the still-falling shells.

"What d'ye think we'd better do?" they shouted at one another. Just then a shell struck home and blew Barrett up so that in front of the other man's startled eyes he catapulted like a hurling tomcat and so that the last that Wostenholm saw of him was his well-bent hips flying through space; thereby causing him to remark to himself and to the whirring shells: "Well, there goes Barrett. His troubles are over anyhow," a conclusion that seemed amply justified by the fact that the traveller failed, so far as his observer could see, to come down even in pieces, and which amply bore out the obvious theory that it was because he was probably travelling in opposite directions.

But some months afterward, on the occasion of an eagerly looked-for garden party which signified the beginning of Wostenholm's convalescence, he was astonished to observe a face that was so familiar as to cause him to later remark: "An' bless my ribs, if it wasn't Barrett."

There was fighting all about. Kelso was putting up a magnificent one. He had exhausted the contents of his rifle and fought now with the bayonet and all the muscles of his body so that he died in the splendour of other souls crashing a path ahead for this one of his which had thus sped them on to pave his greater way.

The sanguinary struggles that had for a few minutes immortalized this strip of trench died down: The trench was cleared and the main body of the Germans hurled themselves over at the support trench. Our men there lined the parapet and gave them "Rapid-Fire" so warmly that those Germans who escaped it were glad to fling themselves down, panting, in the fire trench.

Wostenholm could see, however, that they had broken through on the right of the support-trench line and were making for the farm in which we had found the cow and the rice on the 4th and the seizing of which would enable them to enfilade the support trench and perhaps to envelop it in a surrounding movement. He decided that it was time to go if he did not want a trip to Germany. Better a quick end from a sniper than that. He crawled forward as rapidly as his smashed foot would allow, keeping his head well down so as to avoid all unfriendly observation.

The communication trench was the same chamber of horrors through which he had clawed his way with the message of succour on the 4th. But if it had been that then, it was infinitely worse now; for it was blocked and choked shoulder-high with the dead, theirs and ours, a head there, a leg there, the cries of the tortured and buried wounded running through and dominating all other sounds and making of it an inferno of blood and mutilated suffering, the materialization of a maniac's dream.

Wostenholm crawled over them. They stirred and squirmed under his affrighted hand like uneasy worms, each move as much a fresh torture to the shocked man who caused it as to those beneath who suffered it until his mind could neither stand nor his limbs make any progress through so cruel a charnel-house. He pulled himself forthwith to the level of the ground and fell to, hopping on one foot along the broken rim of the communication trench. At that he overbalanced and fell down so that he went instead to creeping, a procedure that was in its turn more rudely interrupted by the bullet that creased his scalp and knocked him down again so that he thought that he had surely died this time, and had, too, in so far as shock counts for that. However, it was only a glancing blow which did not harm beyond the dazed condition that it left him in and the channels of blood from it that persisted in getting into his eyes and so obstructing vision.

He crawled on, one foot gone, a hole in his head and a bayonet thrust along his breast, but still going strong. He had passed the support-trench and was in the act of drawing his mutilated body through the wire that fronted the wood and safety when he saw the sergeant-major of his company, or rather the upper end of his six feet four of stringy length, peering mildly over the top of the trench at him: "Get down ———. You silly ass! Get down," Wostenholm shouted. There was the usual crash, flame and crowding pressure of an air that rained missiles and he saw "Big Mac" crumple up and go down in a manner that could mean only one thing and that not a good one.

The tortured wood behind was blown away and all signs pointed to the swift approach of the inevitable end. All knew by this time that the regiment was now unsupported on either side and had been left as picked troops to stem the Teuton tide and if need be ——— go down in it. After the main crash of the assault had subsided, small waves of it ebbed and flowed with the private and terrible tragedies of soldiers who had been left alone between friend and foe, exposed to the raking return fire of each and, if they could muster strength to travel at all, not knowing which way to go and by nature of the circumstances denied all help of friends. Some came swiftly to a longed-for end at the hands of embittered foemen who thought it sporting to shoot down crawling men who were already stamped with death.

There was one Pat who came mercifully to his end at the hand of his own mate. He was a badly wounded survivor of the fire-trench who had managed to get over the top and part way home when what may have been either a chance or a directed German bullet wounded him afresh in the head and in such a manner that although he was not dead it seemed certain that he soon would be, and in any event the most casual glance disclosed the fact that it would prove a great misfortune if he should have the great ill fortune to live. A certain man saw this and in hysteria implored that some one should put out of its misery that bloody crawling bundle of mewing rags that writhed aimlessly and that once had been his own dear mate. The others looked at him with dead eyes, seeming not to hear, so that his own face froze at their silence. He seized his rifle and after sighting it with great care, held it rigidly to his shoulder, shut his eyes, pulled the trigger and turned away without looking with his face of stone since he well knew that he could not have missed.

By the time the worst features of the second attack had subsided it was half-past 10 o'clock. A hasty survey of the situation disclosed the main feature of it, most of the men out of and only four officers in action, and all of them lieutenants. And such was the personnel of the regiment that one of them was that Talbot Papineau who was a grandson of the rebel of '37 and a cousin of the Nationalist, Bourassa, of today, whom many call worse than rebel.

With the elimination of the active participation of the commanding officer in the command, that had fallen some time since to the diminutive Nevin. He had been a "full" private that day at Ottawa on which we had received the colours that now reposed back there in the skeleton of Bellewaarde Wood and he was now temporary commanding officer of this skeleton of a regiment which still held fast to those same colours. He proceeded to reorganize this remnant to the best advantage for the holding of whatever ground was still intact.

The guns rolled on, the vast key-board of the front registering the hammering unison of their simultaneous striking so that the ear-pans could no longer register anything more definite than sound-chaos and so that the brain, the head and the entire structure of the physical body reacted and rocked with the dull boring insistence of a grinding corkscrew pain that hurt to the racking, screaming point.

At half-past one, the reinforcements which had been so long hoped for leaked stealthily out from behind the skeleton trees. It was only a weakened platoon of the reserve battalion, but they seemed a miracle to the hope-dead men here, although the inarticulate souls of them would permit their acknowledgement of that fact only in the grateful manner in which their dead eyes hung on and followed these new men as they slipped into the flattened trench and oozed themselves along and into position on the right. They lay there on their bellies and behind the trunks of blasted trees in that tortured wood, behind the whisp of a hedge, in shell holes, anywhere in the cemetery that offered the least cover to men so that at the last and necessary moment they could to advantage rise up, surprise the foe and in the good company of their comrades of the Patricias — die.

George Pearson worked for Hardware & Metal, *a Maclean Publishing Co. magazine, before he joined the Princess Pats and served five months at the front. Pearson was subsequently hospitalized and discharged, rejoining the publishing company. He continued to write about the war for* Maclean's *and others, including two books, until he died in 1928.*

Still smiling, even with a useless right arm

You Will Yet Be Glad

PVT. HAROLD R. PEAT
August, 1918

Pvt. Peat is a young Canadian who has broken publishing records with his war book and has electrified audiences by his war talks from one end of America to the other. In the accompanying article he addresses a message to the men of the new Canadian army—a message of good cheer.—The Editor, 1918

Gee, but the army is h——, isn't it? Everything has gone wrong—officers crabby, Colonel crazy, and everything in general is no darn good. Well, all that may be as you say—but say, old boy, have you tried to look at the army the other way? Have you given the army a chance to make good? Who has made the officers crabby and driven the O.C. crazy—have you? Come, old man, be honest about it.

And fellows, listen to this. You have a picnic to-day, honest you have, if you only care to make a picnic out of it. Here is something of what all of us old originals went through. I had a pretty cushy job when the war broke—but I quit. Oh, just for the fun of it. Away I went all the way from Edmonton and for five nights the whole darn lot of us sat up or doubled up on the hard wooden seats of accommodation cars, but never a murmur (except the usual army grouse) from any of the crowd.

Our final stop in Canada was Valcartier, Que., and there we tumbled out stiff and travel weary—to rest and billets? No, boys, to pitch our own tents, to collect from the stores our own waterproof sheet each, and not the big, heavy kind issued now, but the narrow, light sheet. We were also given a pair of blankets; but for bed underneath us, all we had was the cold, cold ground. It was nearly always frosty in the early mornings toward the end of the month, and oh boy, when it rained—good night!

But we went through it all right and reached Salisbury Plain. Valcartier was a rosy dream to the nightmare of the Plain. If we had had hardships in Canada they were nothing to this. When we went on route marches, to take one item, we had not the nice light web equipment which was issued later, but we had the heavy leather harness, the Oliver equipment, or as we boys commonly knew it, the Oliver torture. We wore that torture on parades and at reviews. Taking things all in all, nothing that was issued us at that time was up to the standard of present day equipment, excepting our badges, numerals and matters of that sort.

The hardships of Salisbury are too well known to everyone

now and have been too well thrashed out and explained to need repeating. We went from the awfulness of the Plain to the greater awfulness of France.

Take a look at the France of yesterday and to-day; the France of 1914 and 1918; a France just invaded and a France under fighting trim for four years. The Hun had it on us at every turn, though fortunately he did not know it then as we do now in looking back on those days.

Take us as samples of typical troops. We had recruited with vague ideas of why we were at war or why we had enlisted. We had trained at Valcartier for five weeks. We had been instructed by officers who knew the same amount of war as we—and that was nothing. But as "good scouts" those officers were second to none. In later days, after experience, they turned out second to none as officers and instructors.

There was little chance for any one at Salisbury. Rain! I could well believe the oldest inhabitant of the nearest town when he said he'd never seen the like before. Noah was the only man who ever saw anything approaching it. It rained practically every day in England. The resultant mud and awfulness made it impossible to train. We forgot everything we had ever learned at Valcartier, excepting how to erect tents. We had tents for a large part of the time at Salisbury. Not once, but twice in a night it has been my lot to be half smothered under a flapping flattened tent, kicking free from an almost inextricable confusion of legs, arms, blankets, mud and deluging water—and this not on one night alone.

We passed much of our time in building railroads across the Plain and later in putting up buildings for our own housing. Useful work, a something very excellent to know, but not training for a fight with the most inhuman devices that monsters in the shape of men could conceive.

You see the brilliancy of the army—the Canadian Army—as it was on arrival in France. But, you say, "There was your time at the base—your intensive training, your bomb drill, gas drill, hand grenade drill—"

Of the base we saw nothing. Of intensive training, we never heard. Bombs and gas were unknown quantities to us then and for weeks after. We were wanted on the front line, in the front trenches, alongside the English, Scotch, Welsh and Irish who had been shot in just as we were, only some months sooner than we could get across. Our intensive training went on in the foremost positions. We got hints from the English troops who initiated us, just as they shared a ration with us.

And then consider that front line. Long before we got to France—and we were there good and early—Fritz had introduced trench warfare. He had dug himself in and he had chosen the best location. Fritz is very wide awake to the main chance. He is a wily foe, and one we can't afford to underestimate. He had taken up the high, dry positions, he had entrenched on the hillsides and places where he overlooked and commanded. We were left the low, swampy ground.

It was nobody's fault. There was no alternative. We had to dig in or give in. Literally we could not dig in, for it was a mere shovelling of water and blood thickened to a broth with earth. We had no high rubber boots as the boys, I am thankful, have today. A few of us got knee rubbers. I never did myself, but the boys who had them suffered more than we did without. The liquid went over the knee and into the boot. There was no means of changing or drying, and that mud froze inside the rubber till the boys were crippled with rheumatism, frostbite and trench feet. We fought in puttees and boots, dressed in fact as we would have been on parade ground.

Our dugouts were a joke. Officers and men alike depended on

the uncertain stability of a fire trench for rest, but during our four days "in," sleep and rest were joys few and far between.

Take the hand grenades. The Boche used these on us when we had never heard of them. We invented grenades of our own. We collected old jam tins and constructed bombs in the trenches. It was exciting work. The Boche had perfected his gas. We were the main unlucky recipients of that, and we had not even respirators let alone gas masks of rubber with oxygen reservoirs attached—lucky to have mud and water enough to wet a handkerchief or muffler so that we could throw it over nose and mouth.

Take our artillery. For every shell our men put over, and they were doing their best, Fritz could drop 10 on us, and he dropped them with calculated accuracy. In the matter of men, I can only refer you to official statistics. The enemy had 12 men to our one. We British are fighters, but a 12 to one handicap is as much as any single Britisher can carry.

And on top of all these sufferings, there was something worse. Did our civilian population back home realize then, as now, what war is? Boys, they did not. Some were bewildered, some indifferent, some, it almost seemed, hostile. You see we got glimpses of home papers at times.

It was nine months after I had been at the front that I got my first parcel from anyone back home in Canada. It wasn't that my folks forgot me. No, they just didn't think of it. They didn't grasp what I was going through, nor why.

Take the letters from "home." Some of the boys actually feared to open their letters. They lacked the sympathy of realization. The folks wrote of themselves and their troubles and worries and wanted the boys to sympathize and find a solution and remedy for them. We had as much as we could stand ourselves without the added thought for those at home.

Today, the trouble with the soldiers is too much sympathy, too great a petting and fussing. Maybe folks are going now to the other extreme. Gee whiz! I went for four months when I first enlisted without talking to a woman. Today if fellows are not quartered in big cities or near them where folks give frequent entertainments for them, then the entertainments are brought to camp. Singers, players and speakers are always on hand in the huts of the "Y," the Salvation Army, the K of C.

But hardship is easily forgotten. Let's forget it. Let's look at the war from an individual standpoint, from the point of view of the new soldier himself. Once or twice before I reached France I asked myself why I had enlisted. I had no clear, definite reason. I had everything, apparently, to lose and nothing to gain. For "reasons" there was fun, there was adventure, there was the favourite "reason" of most of the men, a trip to England, maybe a sight of France, and a war ended.

We got to France, raggedly equipped and partially trained. We made good. And we made good, not because we were better men than the boys who are drafted or who are enlisting today, but because we realized war as war is. We realized why we must fight and fight to a finish. We learned, as you boys will learn, to say with reverence and deep faith:

"Thank God, that I have the privilege to fight over here and not back home. Thank God, that now when war has come I have the honour to keep my own country free of invasion."

Just come with me to Ypres for a moment—the Ypres of 1915, the Ypres of flame and murder, of falling masonry, of bombs and pitiless outrage; Ypres with streets of gaping shell holes strewn with glass, with broken carvings, with the mutilated bodies of dead babies, little innocent clinging infants. Boys, think of it. I saw the refugees pouring out of Ypres—old men, old women, young women and children, young girls horribly outraged and dragging along in a shame not their own. I tell you, Comrades, I cried—yes, a lump would rise in the throat of the toughest to see that dismal procession.

I thought of my sister, safe with her mother in Canada, and I could see scores no more than her age weeping miserably, not daring to meet our eyes as we marched by. And my sister's safety, the safety of a thousand sisters, a million mothers, sweethearts, wives, depended on the fact that we—no, even that I was there. That made me, as it will make you boys who are joining today, realize why we must fight and fight to a finish. Why we "must be men," where the enemy show themselves beasts. And yet in those old days we shivered at the thought of meeting the enemy. We knew he was our superior in numbers, in every material thing. We could only guess his spirit; but we knew our own.

Today, there is at least a 50-50 chance on material things and we are the superior of the Hun in morale. It is the spirit and the will to do and endure which will carry on through to a triumphant close.

Personally, despite a partly useless arm, a half-gone lung, loss of weight and less strength, I am glad I went to the fight. Personally, I believe every man who goes will be glad of it long before he comes back. A fellow can and does learn more about his fellow man over there in two weeks than he does in a lifetime back home. No university, school or college can teach in four years what a man learns in four weeks of life in the trenches. We see the soul of humanity in the War, the soul of humanity in all its glory and magnificence. We see greatness and valour, honour and glory where we had never thought to see it. We recognize it because we ourselves are in it, facing death, facing eternity, facing God Almighty.

It is only when it is all over, when those who have gone and are going return home, that with us *all* Canada will see the good which comes out of evil. If this War does good personally and individually, it must do good nationally. If you are Canadian born, or of French descent, or of Irish, English or Scotch, or anything else, remember you can make the Army a Hades for yourself, or you can make it a darn good place. It is in your own hands. I know your choice ahead of time. Canadians were always good sports and always will be.

Don't think anyone is against you; everyone is for you. Fellows, realize it, we are all pulling for you. You are really having things easy, why take it hard? You have a great bunch of officers to start with, as great as our officers became.

Keep smiling, boys. Learn to know your officers, co-operate with them. More than you think, they have your interests at heart.

Boys, above all, as a Canadian you can thank God Almighty that this War is not being waged on the banks of the St. Lawrence, the Humber or the Saskatchewan.

I tell you, Comrades, in going to this fight, no matter what comes to you from it, *You will yet be glad.*

This article, in fact, was a speech Harold Peat delivered as part of a war bond and recruitment campaign that he joined after a wound left him with a useless right arm. He and his wife, Louisa Small, a successful writer and editor, campaigned for peace after the war. After their divorce in the 1930s, Peat ran a lecture bureau in New York City for a decade before returning to his native Jamaica, where he died of a heart attack at 65 in 1960.

Canadian sappers at the front, 1918

An Unsolved Mystery

LIEUT. C. W. TILBROOK
December, 1918

We had finished our front line system and, when we looked at our work, we knew that it was good. In all we had located 14 chambers under strategic points of the enemy line—chambers that were loaded and ready to "blow" whenever the word came from headquarters. That the Hun had not located any of these chambers we knew, because we inspected them regularly and found them untouched. It provided us with a strange sense of elation, the knowledge that we were prepared to literally blow his line, opposite our sector, into smithereens whenever the G.H.Q. in its wisdom deemed the time to be ripe.

We of the tunnelling corps were very much satisfied with ourselves those days. We had beaten the Hun at every turn in mineland. The God of Battles had been with us. The enemy had started work before us, digging galleries under our lines like the tentacles of a huge devil fish before we had been aware of the danger. Since we had started to fight him at his own game, however, we had been able to completely checkmate him. By luck or by hard work, I am not sure which, we had been able to find his chambers every time and to draw the fangs before he could strike. On the other hand we had often "blown" his line at important points. Up to the time I write we had never lost any of our works. Our system was still intact and we took a huge pride in the network of narrow passages that we had delved out under No Man's Land.

Matters had reached the stage, in fact, where there was little for us to do. No new work was being undertaken. It began to look as though we might be moved to another sector or drafted into another branch and the probabilities of some such move being made was the main topic of conversation with us. One night I made bold and asked Major Henry at dinner what would likely be done with us. "We'll be kept here, of course," he snapped. "There's plenty more work for us to do."

At the time, I could not imagine what work there was to be done but the O.C.'s tone did not encourage further questioning so I let the matter drop. I was not to be kept in suspense long, however, for the next afternoon Maj. Henry took me with him to Cassel, the second Army Headquarters. Here I was introduced into a conference on a scheme to extend the underground system for the purpose of housing a battalion between the first and second lines. It was an ambitious scheme and I listened with intense interest as I realized that I was not being taken into the confidence of the staff officers for nothing. Gradually the plans were shaped and at the finish I learned to my delight that the work was to be done on our sector.

On the way back Maj. Henry said to me: "I am going to put you in as works officer." I expressed my great delight, and he added: "This will be all plain sailing—no stopping to listen, no fear of the Hun being around. You'll be far enough back to sail right in."

But for once he was wrong—I think it was the only time I had ever known him to be in error. As a matter of fact I was due for the most exciting experiences perhaps of my whole underground career.

The work outlined for us was to put in a system of tunnels behind the front line that would be large enough to accommodate a battalion and to provide a safe means for troops to pass to and from the front lines. It would be unwise to specify the exact part of the line where the operation was to be carried out but when I say it was in the Ypres salient the reader will understand the need for the underground passage to the front lines. The salient was then, as always, under heavy bombardment and the casualties from snipers had been shockingly heavy. It was largely to overcome the losses from sniping that the staff had decided on the underground route. Such, at least, was the information given out. We had all heard a different reason and we used to talk it over as we bent to our task.

"The Big Push is coming at last," some would remark. "They want this system so they can send attacking forces up without the Hun seeing them. Boys, we're taking the first step towards the shore."

Well, we started work three-quarters of a mile behind the front line. The first shaft was sunk at night and the exit was promptly camouflaged. It was a rush undertaking so all the men needed for the work were provided. When we got nicely under way, there were no fewer than five parties working at once. The system was to be an elaborate one, needless to state, the plans calling for barracks, dug-outs, mess rooms, Divisional Headquarters, etc. It was to be provided with ready means of exit in all directions and to be guarded by 28 machine guns, carefully placed so that they would command the whole sector. The plans had been carefully worked out but, owing to the extreme secrecy with which we had to proceed, it was a slow and laborious undertaking.

We worked during the day at excavating and at night we evacuated the bags on to a light railroad and hauled them back to a lake about three-quarters of a mile away. The earth was emptied into the lake because in this way the enemy would not be able to spot any spoil dumps, which would have given our plan away.

The work progressed well until the line of our main tunnel coincided with the old grave yard in Maple Copse. Here we encountered a veritable chamber of horrors. The line drawn for the tunnel went clear through the site of the burying ground where reposed the bodies of 100,000 brave men who had fallen in action—it was here that the casualties of the three battles of Ypres were interred. We were working on a six-foot level and every drive of pick or shovel seemed to bring us into contact with the decomposing remains of friend or foe.

I had read of the work of ghouls but never in my wildest flights of imagination had I conceived of anything to equal this. Yet we had to go on through. As fast as we drove the bore of our tunnel along we sprinkled the four walls with chloride of lime and creosote and hurriedly timbered it up. It became so bad that the men were not able to work for more than an hour at a time. We always wore our gas masks.

The human remains that we found it necessary to exhume were placed in a large trench, dug for the purpose, and the burial service was read over them. I do not know how many were thus disturbed but the number was large.

Eventually we got through that chamber of horrors and we were congratulating ourselves on the fact that nothing worse fronted us now than the ordinary discomforts of underground work, such as lack of air and noxious gases. We found, however, that we had figuratively jumped from the frying pan into the fire. Our line tapped a sewage drain—a main drain in which a man six feet in height could walk. It came apparently from some large town back of the German lines, running north and south and thus crossing our tunnel at right angles. Our odoriferous sufferings were not yet over.

The presence of this drain had not been ascertained before and it aroused misgivings. Suppose the Germans had used it to give them access beneath our lines? Or suppose they decided some time in the future to do so? An order came from H.Q. to investigate.

Knowing that the air would be bad, I got into a proto set [gas mask] and replaced my trench boots by rubber waders. Taking a canary with me, I cautiously set out on my tour of investigation.

I have not made mention before of the little feathered allies that we often took with us in our underground work. Canaries had been found invaluable in detecting poisonous gases in the galleries. They are very susceptible to carbon monoxide and at the first trace will fall to the bottom of the cage, thus giving us warning before our own senses had detected the danger. The use of the birds was not as cruel as may seem at first thought for they have a rapid heart action and soon recover when taken back to the fresh air.

The bird that I took on this occasion was called Bob. He was a great favourite with all of us and the hero of 18 tests. Despite this extended experience with the terrors of poison gas, Bob was still in splendid condition and a fine singer.

"Now see here, Bob," I remarked to him, as I swung his cage over my shoulder, "no singing this time. One solitary peep on this little jaunt and you may spill the beans for both of us."

Down we went into the sewer and I splashed my way in the southerly direction; first I flashed on a light every now and then to see how my little partner was taking it. As he seemed quite chipper and full of life, I concluded that the air was good. After going about 300 yards I reached the end of the drain where it dipped down and emptied into a stream. So I turned back and went in the other direction.

After passing the point where our tunnel had broken in and where I paused for a moment to speak to the sentry, I waded on for about three-quarters of an hour and finally came to what appeared to be a dead end. A stone wall faced me. Flashing on my torch, I discovered that there was a circular opening above my head and that iron rungs, imbedded in the clammy wall, provided the means of climbing up. I was just about to mount them when Bob, evidently pleased with the brilliant illumination of the torch after being so long in pitch darkness, raised his voice in song. High and shrill went up his cadence of gladness. I nearly dropped the cage, so horror-stricken was I at the untimeliness of his efforts. I judged we were at least half a mile behind the German lines by this time!

My first thought was to strangle the bird, but my next was better. I extinguished the torch and Bob immediately subsided into silence again. For a few moments I stood in frozen silence, waiting for sounds above to show whether we had been heard. No signs came, however, so I turned and started back.

It occurred to me then that the air could not be very bad since the bird had felt impelled to sing, so I decided to have as much comfort as possible on the way back. I turned off the oxygen and removed my mask. An odour that nauseated even my hardened olfactory organ enveloped me. I drew my mask back on again in a frenzy of haste. Bob was indeed a wonderful bird to be able to sing in that kind of an atmosphere!

Arriving back at our entrance I turned the canary over to his keeper and held a conference with my brother officers. They agreed with me that it would be necessary to find out what was above that hole and accordingly I elected to go back with a party of two to finish the investigation. My companions were an officer named Moore who had won the nickname of "Mopsy"—in our frequent hand-to-hand scraps underground with the enemy, his grimness in "mopping them up" had earned the name—and a sapper named O'Sullivan. The latter had spent part of his life before the mast and the other part delving in the bowels of the earth in a Cornish copper mine. His forte was wrestling and he had a genius for swearing in a conglomerate of the languages of the seven seas. Altogether they were a most suitable pair for the adventure ahead of us and I felt quite a bit of confidence in having such redoubtable comrades.

So we started off in ordinary dress and waders, armed only with revolvers. O'Sullivan carried the usual mobile charge of 25 lbs. of ammonal, for we did not know what an opportunity would arise to "blow." As we entered the sewer, he stopped and sniffed audibly. "'Taint exactly Ceylon's spicy breezes, sir," he remarked.

We gained the dead end of the drain and I proceeded to

mount the iron rungs, leading to the circular opening overhead. At this end the sewer had become deeper and the end wall was about nine feet in diameter. It was evidently part of a big drainage system. The work was very ancient but in a state of excellent preservation as it was built in Flemish bond.

I forced back the trap door that covered the opening without any difficulty, and, climbing through, found myself in a dark and musty upper chamber. The others scrambled through after me and we proceeded to examine the place warily. A further row of iron rungs sunk into the wall suggested that we must continue on up, so I went ahead, hand over fist. Another trap door, less easy to move, admitted me to small, low cellar filled with barrels. Here I stopped and waited for my companions. We exchanged uneasy whispers, for it was apparent that, if discovered now, we would be nicely trapped. I tipped one of the barrels and found it empty.

"Will we go on, sir?" asked O'Sullivan, in a hoarse whisper.

"Can't very well leave off now," I replied. "We've got to see what's above first."

At one end of the cellar was a flight of rickety-looking steps, leading up to still another trap door. I had mounted these steps and was just preparing to raise the door with my back when I heard hasty footsteps on the floor above. I crouched down into as small a space as nature would allow and held my breath. They came across the floor and stopped a few feet from where I waited. I expected to see the door raise above me and I gripped my revolver for action.

But nothing happened. The man above moved away. A moment later other steps sounded above and a rumble of conversation came to our ears. I motioned to Moore, who could speak German, to come up beside me. Very cautiously he negotiated the creaky steps and sat down beside me. He listened intently.

"Germans?" I whispered, after a minute or two.

He nodded. "Yes, officers, as far as I can make out."

As the conversation above proceeded, Mopsy gave evidences of excitement. He gripped my arm. "On with your torch," he whispered. "I want to make a note or two before I forget this."

I switched on my light and Mopsy carefully jotted down some of the things he picked out from the guttural murmur that reached our ears. I learned later that it was nothing very important he heard—some points with reference to the German positions and the names and numbers of some of the enemy battalions facing us. The most important point was that it showed the building above us to be the advanced divisional headquarters.

The conversation lasted perhaps half an hour. At the end of that time, a clatter of feet indicated the breaking up of the conference. After waiting to make sure that none of the Germans had remained behind, we climbed down to our friendly drain again and so back to camp.

The discovery was reported to Maj. Henry and, after another delay to allow him to investigate personally, it was decided to go ahead and load the cellar in readiness to "blow."

It proved the most delicate job we had attempted. Any noise would betray us to the occupants of the building above, so we had to work barefooted in the cellar, the cans of ammonal brought in bound in burlap and strapped on the backs of our men. This enabled them to carry them up the iron ladders without any handling, which would have been dangerous. Imagine transferring cans of deadly explosive up a ladder of iron rungs in pitch darkness.

Finally, we had our nest safely planted and wired. I was in the cellar when the last connection had been made and all that remained to be done was to put the "shores" in place. With me were Mopsy Moore and O'Sullivan. Below in the drain, the rest of our party were "tamping," building a wall of sand bags to close up our own gallery before letting a charge off and to make possible our own retreat in safety. They had been instructed to tamp for 50 feet, leaving a narrow passage at the top for us to wriggle out by.

Above all was silent for the time being, although we had had clear evidences just before of the building being occupied. We wanted it to be, needless to state. I was just ready to signal the retreat when a crash and a loud cry came up from below. We learned afterwards that one of our sappers had fallen, breaking his leg.

We stood stock still, Moore and O'Sullivan and I. If the noise had penetrated above, we were done for. A wall of sand bags blocked our retreat in the drain, for it would obviously be impossible for three men to crawl through the narrow passage left for us in the face of pursuit. There was nothing for it. We would have to stand and fight.

Overhead there was a sudden scurry. I sprang behind a barrel for cover and the other two rapidly followed suit. It was not a moment too soon. The trap door above our heads opened and a shaft of light cut the gloom of the cellar.

A guttural voice demanded to know in German who was there. Not a sound answered him. Further outcry had been stifled by the wounded man below and, as for us, we did not dare to breathe. The light wavered and we heard steps coming down. I glanced around my barrel and saw that this was an orderly, carrying an electric torch at arm's length ahead of him. Behind the orderly were two officers.

The party came down cautiously, stopping with each step to listen. They were nervous. One of the officers impatiently ordered the orderly to hurry up but did not himself show any eagerness for the investigation.

It so happened that Mopsy Moore and O'Sullivan had taken

refuge together on the opposite side of the cellar from me. The next development, therefore, came as a surprise to me. I had drawn my revolver, hoping that it would not be necessary to use it, and was crouching still more closely in the shadow behind my barrel. The three Germans had barely touched foot to floor when there was a rush, a scramble, a sound of falling barrels, the impact of blows and a jumble of breathless oaths in various languages. My companions had rushed them from behind.

I kicked the barrel from in front of me and stood up. The torch of the orderly had fallen to the floor and now sent up a slantwise ray of light which illuminated half of the cellar. But I could make out what had happened. So vigorous and unexpected had been the rush of my comrades that the three Germans had been swept over the open trap door. The orderly had, luckily for himself, fallen to one side, and there he lay, moaning softly. The two officers had gone through and down, not into the chamber immediately below us but, judging from the sound, clear through into the drain. It was a long fall. As a matter of fact we found their bodies later in the drain. Both had been killed in the fall.

Mopsy went over to the orderly and brought his wandering faculties into coherency with a vigorous shake. He first threatened the prostrate Boche with all manner of violence and then interrogated him as to things above. "We're safe, Tilly," he said, finally. "This chap says there's no one else above. I've got him talking at the end of my gat [gun] so I think it's the truth."

"Done for 'em!" exulted O'Sullivan. "Pretty clean rush, eh, sir?"

"Let's clean some of them up, above there as well," said Moore, whose fighting blood was aroused. "We might find a few generals or a mess of square-neck colonels up there. It's the chance of a lifetime!"

I could not dissuade him from climbing the stairs and looking into the room above. He came down a step or two and beckoned us. "Coast's clear," he announced in a hoarse whisper. "I'll stump you to see what kind of a place it is."

I don't know what impulse it was on which we acted. It was foolish in the extreme, nay reprehensible, for we were jeopardizing our enterprise by lingering there. Nevertheless we followed Moore up the stairs and into the room above.

The room in which we found ourselves was evidently used as an office. The windows were darkened with metal shutters and the only light in the room came from two small oil lamps. This evidently was by way of precaution for the building could not have been far from the front lines. We left O'Sullivan at the trap door to keep the prisoner below covered with his revolver and thus intimidate him into silence. In the meantime, Moore and I made a hasty examination of the room. We looked through the drawers of a flat-topped table that was being used as a desk and pocketed any documents that looked to be worthwhile. We were too excited to really examine the papers and took everything on chance. As it developed later, we were not lucky in our choice, for we secured nothing of any particular value, except some copies of recent general orders. Moore went about the work with more composure than I was able to summon. In fact, he seemed prepared to stay there indefinitely. Finally, after several low-voiced suggestions that we had better be moving on, I took him by the arm.

"Come on. Let's clear out," I quavered. "We have enough dope. The main thing is to get out in time to blow this place."

He assented rather unwillingly and we beat a hasty retreat to the cellar. O'Sullivan went right along with the prisoner and with instructions to the sergeant in charge of the party on the other side of the barricade of sand bags to wait for us. Moore and I then proceeded to put the shores in place. They had already been fitted so the work only took us about five minutes.

When we reached the drain, we found that the tamping had dammed up the sewage and—well, it was a case of wading through up to our armpits. Moore climbed up the barricade first and disappeared headfirst through the small opening that had been left. I followed and wriggled in after him.

To crawl through a close passage, 50 feet long, with barely enough room to move arms and legs in the effort to progress is an ordeal of the most severe kind. Several times I thought I would never make it. Moore was a smaller man than me and he was soon far ahead. I tried to call out to him but my breath failed me. To go back meant death when the "blow" came. To advance seemed impossible.

Once I stopped for several minutes in sheer desperation. Then, with strength renewed, I made a further effort. I found it possible to move along slowly. I struggled on by a series of jerks and contortions. It seemed as though that passage were miles long. But there is an end to everything; and finally I did get through; thoroughly tired and nerve-strung.

"What happened to you?" demanded Moore, brusquely. "Thought you were never coming."

"You had nothing on me there," I retorted weakly. "I began to think I wasn't coming myself. Close up that hole quick. We must blow now."

They filled the hole with sand bags. I took the exploder between my knees and pumped down. We heard a muffled roar and felt the earth shake. Our day's work was done.

Our observer outside reported to us later in the day that he had seen smoke and debris rise out of a small wood at a point coinciding with our calculations as to the location of the German headquarters. He also had noted that one of our aeroplanes, flying rather low at the time over the spot, had seemed to be seriously inconvenienced by our little eruption and, as soon as it had steadied, had fled from the scene of our wrath. The sequel to this was contained in a German communique which we obtained from the wallet of a German officer captured some time after.

"The ——th advanced Divisional HQ's of the Landsturm was completely wiped out on the morning of the ——st inst. by a direct hit from one of the enemy's bombing planes which was observed flying low in this vicinity."

Once more the much despised tunnellers were deprived of the honour done them. The early bird got the credit for the worm's stealthy work.

Gen. Arthur Currie leads the Canadians into
German territory, 1918

The Truth About the War

MAJ. GEORGE A. DREW
July 1, 1928

*In presenting Maj. Drew's article it is not the intention of
MacLean's to belittle in the slightest degree the part played by
the United States in the Great War. Nor do either the author
or MacLean's believe that the opinions expressed by the writers who are answered herewith reflect general public opinion in
the United States. The point is that the U.S. periodicals to
which references are made are widely circulated throughout
Canada. They are read by a considerable proportion of
the post-war generation. The perspective of that generation*

cannot but be affected by what it reads. And the absorption of misinformation concerning the part played by the British Empire from 1914 to 1918 must inevitably colour that perspective unless countered by facts. This article is a plain statement of facts.—The Editor

In February of this year, the *Cosmopolitan* commenced a series of articles under the heading "It's Time You Knew The Truth," by Brig.-Gen. Henry J. Reilly. In the course of one of these articles, Brig.-Gen. Reilly tells us that the lack of Allied success on the Western front was due to the British failure to enforce a draft law and their refusal to move their troops away from the Channel ports. This is but a sample of Brig.-Gen. Reilly's observations on the conduct of the British Empire during the World War, but it will serve to show the trend of his argument throughout the series.

An article under the suggestive heading "Who Won The War" appeared in *Liberty*, which told us that "a comparison by dates from entry into the war shows that we—the United States—put more troops more quickly in the face of the enemy than did the British, and that in the important last stages of the war we had more *facing the enemy* than they had."

Garet Garrett, in *The Saturday Evening Post*, says almost the same thing. "In the moment of declaring war we began to mobilize our fighting power. Eighteen months later we had *on the front against Germany* more men than any other nation, excepting only France."

These statements are absolutely false, and yet they are a fair and conservative sample of what is being produced for consumption by the readers of the U.S. periodical press. Unfortunately, we cannot ignore the fact that the thoughts and general information of a very large percentage of Canadians are being subtly moulded through the medium of U.S. films and reading matter. Many Canadians scout the idea that people in this country pay any attention to such statements, believing that their palpable absurdity must impress anyone who knows anything at all about the war. They forget, however, that the majority of those who read these articles and see the films know nothing whatever of the real facts of the war and that every year this majority will steadily increase. When one looks at it in that way, it is not comforting to realize that Canadians read a great many more U.S. periodicals than their own. It must be presumed that they read what they buy, and it is therefore a logical conclusion that a very great percentage of what Canadians read concerning the Great War comes from such unreliable sources as have been quoted.

It is time that an earnest appeal be made to intelligent Canadians to face the flood of mis-statement which is pouring into this country, and to keep alive the truth concerning the Great War; not with any idea of belittling the really fine effort made by American soldiers after they did come into the war, nor for the purpose of glorifying ourselves, but only that the vital lessons of the war, which cost us so much in men and money, may not be lost, and that Canadians now and in the future may feel the justifiable pride in the knowledge of a task well done which should warm the heart of everyone who calls himself British.

Stephen Leacock, who people sometimes forget is Professor of Political Economy at McGill, in a recent address in Montreal deplored the effect of U.S. war films in Canada and said that unless it was counteracted, children in Canada would grow up to believe that the United States was the only place where brave men were to be found and brave deeds done. In three recent pictures he had seen, the Great War had appeared as the Great

American War. In his characteristic style he summarized his impressions. "It was occasioned by a quarrel between Woodrow Wilson and a lot of nations living in Europe. Woodrow Wilson, whose only aim was to be good to everybody everywhere, found his efforts thwarted by a crowd of people in Europe. At last he declared war, invoking the blessing of God, of Abraham Lincoln, the Southern Confederacy and the Middle West.

"A vast American army invaded Europe. They first occupied France, where the French people supplied a comic element by selling cigarettes, waving flags and talking French, a ridiculous language, forming a joke in itself. Rushing through the woods, trenches, flames and trees, the Americans drove in front of them the Europeans. Exacting nothing in return, they went back to the Middle West, where they were met on the porch by their mother, the spirit of American democracy, and the inserted shade of Lincoln."

Even such a usually unsentimental civilian as Irvin Cobb, in the *Cosmopolitan* of March, 1927, said: "The debt of Lafayette was paid—with compound interest—in the first week after the first overseas contingent of the American Expeditionary Force landed on French soil."

Why was the A.E.F. in France at all?

The American Declaration of War is an unsentimental document. In clear and succinct terms it sets forth once and for all why the United States declared war. It commences thus:

"Whereas the Imperial German Government has committed repeated acts of war against the Government and the people of the United States of America: Therefore, be it Resolved by the Senate and House of Representatives of the United States of America in Congress assembled. That the state of war between the United States and the Imperial German Government which has thus been thrust upon the United States is hereby formally declared."

The wording is not susceptible to misinterpretation. There is no suggestion here of Uncle Sam entering the lists "for the rights of nations great and small," as Wilson expressed it.

The United States entered the war because it was impossible for her to do otherwise. War was "thrust upon the United States" by "repeated acts of war" on the part of the German government. Woodrow Wilson, in his address delivered at the joint session of the two Houses on April 2, 1917, summed up the situation in these words: "We enter this war only where we are clearly forced into it because there are no other means of *defending* our rights."

When we remember that the United States entered the war, not to pay any debt to Lafayette, not because of altruism, love of peace, or sense of justice, but because, in the words of Wilson, they were clearly forced into it by *repeated acts of war*, we realize that it was as much their war as our war, and that every sacrifice by any of the Allies which weakened the common enemy was as much a sacrifice in behalf of the United States as was any sacrifice of theirs a contribution to our cause. It was the same enemy, from August, 1914, to the end of the war, representing exactly the same principles which were ultimately as intolerable to the United States as to ourselves. Therefore, there is only one logical method of measuring the share in the ultimate victory of any of the Allied nations and that is in terms of their total contribution throughout the whole war. Toward that victory every life lost, every shell fired, every dollar spent was at least as much of a contribution in 1914 as it was in 1918.

In February of this year, as mentioned at the beginning of this article, the *Cosmopolitan* commenced a series of articles under the heading "It's Time You Knew The Truth," by Brig.-Gen. Henry J.

Reilly. The following editorial comment appears above the first article: "For 10 years, America has been waiting for someone to tell the Truth of our part in the World War. A year ago, *Cosmopolitan* selected Brig.-Gen. Henry J. Reilly as the man best fitted to do this. He was sent abroad to go to original sources to sift out the facts from the mass of propaganda, exaggeration and half-truths."

Now that is a fair method of approaching the question, and a Canadian naturally feels that facts presented in this impartial manner should be given due consideration. It is precisely this seemingly ingenuous method of approach which misleads, or is inclined to mislead, the majority of Canadian readers of such articles, who have neither the time nor the facilities to test the truth of the statements they contain.

The first of Gen. Reilly's articles, written after he had sifted out the facts from the mass of propaganda, exaggeration and half-truths, contains the following information: "When Gen. Pershing landed in Europe . . . the British had not yet adopted and enforced a real draft law to put all their available man-power in the army. Yet they had men to spare for expeditions to Greece and for a campaign in Turkey, neither of which could possibly win the war. The British thought only of protecting the French ports along the British Channel, these being on the shortest route to London from Germany. Their strategy consisted only in defending the ground they had or trying to get more ground in front of these ports. They had no idea of leaving this vicinity, no matter what arguments were advanced to prove that concentrations of troops on other parts of the Western Front would help whip the German Army." And then Pershing came.

Perhaps you will say, "Well, surely every Canadian knows that this is not true." Are you so sure that even the majority of those

Canadians who read the *Cosmopolitan* really know whether it is true or not?

In the second article of the series, in March, Gen. Reilly gives some of the fruit of his crusade for Truth by quoting an anonymous member of the German General Staff, chiefly in order to show what a very poor effort the British really made. As fiction it is interesting. A sample will do. "Britain had always kept at home, and in 1916 and 1917 was still keeping a considerable force at home." Gen. Reilly says, "If either is to make a criticism of the other, we are the ones entitled to do it." An examination of his articles reveals that their primary purpose is to compare British and American effort. Garet Garrett tells us that at the time of the Armistice, the Americans had more men on the front against Germany than any other nation, excepting only France. That statement appeared in *The Saturday Evening Post* which has a circulation of three million. Gen. Reilly said precisely the same thing. Let us examine the facts. The contribution of each nation is no mystery; it is a matter of cold dispassionate record. The figures were fixed for all time at the end of the war. Neither 10 years after nor 100 years after can they be changed by any amount of research or subtlety of argument.

Let us deal first with the last statement, repeated so often by different writers to millions of Americans and hundreds of thousands of Canadians, that the Americans had more men facing the enemy than the British at the date of the Armistice.

The United States did not have more men "on the front against Germany" than Britain and no one knows that better than any American officer who was in France. At the time of the Armistice the United States had 1,950,000 on their ration strength *in France* and the British had 1,718,000, but the United States did not have 1,950,000 *on the front* against Germany at that time. At the outset, the policy adopted by the American command was to send troops as quickly as possible to France to complete their training there, and less than one million Americans were ready to go into action at the time of the Armistice. The British troops who were in the same state of training as more than half of the Americans who were in France were still in England. Both principles were perfectly sound. As the men reached the point when they were ready to go into action, the British were sent to France to the combatant units as quickly as the Americans could be sent up from their training areas. It was the logical arrangement.

If the number of effectives in the war zone is to be considered, then let him add the British effectives in England who were preparing for service to those at the front, because they were just as available for service as more than a million Americans back in their training areas. He says there were 1,300,000 at the time of the Armistice in England. Adding this number to those at the front would give the British in round figures three million men as against two million Americans immediately available for service. But that is not a very satisfactory basis of comparison. The only satisfactory basis is to compare the number of men that were actually fighting, for as Gen. Reilly himself says, "A war is won by fighting."

The largest number of Americans engaged in battle at any time in the war was 896,000, and this included all combatant branches. This maximum was reached between September 26, 1918, and the Armistice, six weeks later, so that it will be seen that even that maximum number was engaged for a very short time, whereas the British troops actively engaged on the Western Front alone had been kept in the neighbourhood of 1,750,000 throughout the year.

Let us carry this comparison of men engaged still further. In April, 1918, one year after the United States had declared war, when the British were bearing the brunt of the German hammer blows and Haig had issued his memorable message, "With our backs to the wall and believing in the justice of our cause, each one of us must fight to the end," the Americans had only four divisions fit for battle. During all the heavy fighting that followed until the German offensive collapsed at the end of June, only five American divisions were in the line, and of these only three were actively engaged.

Much has been said of the American victory at Chateau Thierry, at the point of the salient formed by the German thrust on Paris between Soissons and Rheims, but, without detracting in any way from their effort, it is well to maintain a proper sense of proportion by remembering that only one American division was engaged in that battle.

When the German offensive collapsed at the end of June the Allies had won the war; Germany had staked everything and lost. It might be six months, it might be a year, but the victory was won. From then until the first of August there were a number of local attacks under which the Germans retreated to the lines occupied when the Allies commenced their great drive on August 8. There was no more question of a German victory. They had exhausted their reserves, and any possibility of a further attack on the scale necessary for success had disappeared with them.

The truth is that at no time right up to the Armistice did the Americans have more than half as many men in the face of the enemy as the British did in France alone. And remember, too, that up to the Armistice the British had suffered 3,679,264 casualties, as compared with 360,263 American casualties. And also do not forget that another British army had conquered Palestine and defeated the Turk; that another British army had advanced from Salonica against the Bulgarians and had been chiefly instrumental in their defeat; that they had also fought in Africa and were still fighting in Russia.

We have disposed of the gross misstatement that in the important last stages of the war the U.S. troops had more men facing the enemy than the British, whereas in fact most of the men being counted were still well back of the line in the training areas. But if a comparison is preferred even on the basis of men mobilized, the figures are still immensely in our favour. The United States with her draft law mobilized 4,165,483 while the British

Canadians capturing German officers after the battle of Vimy Ridge, 1917

mobilized 8,654,280, most of whom were volunteers and most of whom saw active service.

There is no better evidence of fighting ability than in the number of enemy prisoners captured. The fact that the British captured nearly four times as many prisoners and guns in the last three months as the Americans captured in the *whole* war perhaps tells in the most graphic possible terms who really did the fighting.

But that is not all. Gen. Reilly does not tell us that in the campaign against Turkey, which he criticized as a useless expedition, the British, in three weeks from September 18 to October 7, 1918, took, 79,000 prisoners, and the United States took 50,674 in the *whole* war. Were the efforts of Allenby and Lawrence of less use than those of more than a million non-combatant American soldiers in France? The answer is that Turkey surrendered.

"During 1917 to 1918, Britain's armies held the enemy in three continents and on six fronts, and co-operated with her Allies on two more fronts. Her dead, those 658,000 dead, lay by the Tigris, the Zambesi, the Aegean, and across the world to Flanders' fields. Between March 21 and April 17, 1918, the Germans in their drive used 127 divisions, and of these 102 *were concentrated against the British.* That was in Flanders. Britain, at the same time she was fighting in Flanders, had also at various times shared in the fighting in Russia, Kiaochau, New Guinea, Samoa, Mesopotamia, Palestine, Egypt, the Sudan, Cameroons, Togoland, East Africa, South West Africa, Salonika, Aden, Persia and the Northwest frontier of India." These are the words of another American, Owen Wister, who found his Truth in the official records.

Canadians are told that if any criticism is to be made, the people of the United States are the ones entitled to do it. For once let us forget the tactful reticence Canadians ordinarily exhibit when the question of U.S. participation is raised by some of our American friends. The fact is that any comparison between the fighting of the British and U.S. armies is manifestly absurd. Why, four Canadian divisions alone in those last three months captured 31,537 prisoners and 623 guns, as compared with 50,691 prisoners and 850 guns captured by the Americans in the *whole* war.

But perhaps the criticism is not of our fighting. It may possibly be directed against the equipment with which we fought. After all, guns, airplanes and tanks were of as vital importance as men toward the close of the war. What of the guns? Apart from the great naval guns mounted on railway trucks, and individual siege guns, the British at the time of the Armistice, after having lost thousands by shell fire during four years of war, had 6,993 guns of all calibres, from the 18-pounder to the 15-inch howitzer, organized in batteries, while the Americans had 3,008.

That does not seem a very large proportion of guns from the greatest industrial nation in the world, with all the wealth at her command to embark on an almost limitless production of the sinews of war. But the interesting fact is not the number of guns as compared with the British. It is the fact that so few of those were American guns. An authoritative work, entitled *The American Army in the European Conflict*, by Colonel de Chambrun, tells us that "Almost all artillery material and ammunition used by the Expeditionary Forces were procured in France and, to a much smaller extent, in Great Britain. Only a few heavy guns and 109 75-mm. were imported from the United States by November 11, 1918."

What of the air? Since the first successful flights of the Wright brothers, Americans had been pioneers in flying. Here we might reasonably expect to find them pre-eminent. Airplanes take a comparatively short time to build, and they had a great number of skilled flyers. When the United States declared war, they had the advantage of all the British and French designs being placed immediately at their disposal. Here at least the British had no advantage over the Americans, because during the war the last word in machines one month was almost obsolete the next. Yet what do we find? At the date of the Armistice the British had in action on the Western Front alone 1,758 battle planes and the Americans 740.

The first American combat group appeared at the front in June of 1918. To this was transferred the famous Lafayette Escadrille, a squadron of Americans who had been distinguishing themselves with the French since before the United States declared war. The American Air Force during the whole war brought down 753 enemy planes. To compare only the period of active American participation, British airmen, *on the Western Front alone*, from June 1 to Nov. 8, 1918, destroyed 1,837 enemy machines. During the whole war the British brought down considerably over 8,000 enemy planes as compared with 763 by the Americans.

Canadians have a particular interest in the record of the Royal Air Force. Thirteen thousand Canadians joined that branch of the service during the war and had a very considerable share of the 60,000 battles fought by British airmen. Gen. Seely said in the British House of Commons, "It is in a large measure due to the splendid quality of the manpower of the Empire, of which Canada supplied so large a proportion, that Britain became master of the air, and has raised her air power to a higher pitch than any of our Allies."

Tanks were the outstanding invention of the war. They were a British innovation of the greatest value. Ludendorff tells us that

"The best lines ultimately gave way before the tanks, which were able to overcome the greatest obstacles."

The tanks were comparatively simple to construct, and the United States, with its vast automobile factories, was in a peculiarly favourable position to turn them out in large numbers. The British Tank Corps had used this decisive engine of destruction to the limit of human endurance. From Aug. 5 to the end of the war they were in 96 days of almost continuous fighting, breaking one supposedly impregnable barrier after another, and in those 96 days, 2,000 machines were used. On the other hand, only three American tank units reached the battlefield, and at the date of the Armistice their material on hand consisted of 36 heavy tanks and 208 light tanks. The 36 heavy tanks were British. The 208 light tanks were French. The *first* American tank reached France one month *after* the Armistice was signed.

The facts and figures used are mostly from the respective official records and all are from authentic sources. On sea, on land, and in the air the story they tell is the same. Without attempting to go into details, they show what a silly and empty play on words is the statement by an American that, "If either is to make a criticism of the other as a result of the last War we are the ones entitled to do it." They show how equally silly and meaningless is the claim that, "A comparison by dates from entry into the War shows that we—the United States—put more troops more quickly in the face of the enemy than did the British."

Canadians and all other members of the British family will forever thrill at the recollection of the epic stand of The Old Contemptibles at Mons 14 days after the declaration of war. They were but 100,000, it is true, but that was many more than the Americans had *in action* at the time of their first battle at Chateau Thierry, 14 months after they declared war.

American achievement in science, medicine, commerce, and the arts, to say nothing of actual achievement in war, calls for our unqualified admiration, and thinking Canadians have ever been ready to praise, and to adopt the still higher flattery of imitating much that they have done. But when they have done so much which is really admirable, we can scarcely be accused of anti-American prejudice if we show our resentment of such wholly unnecessary exaggeration, particularly when the result of that exaggeration is a mischievous misrepresentation of British achievement to such a large proportion of the Canadian reading public.

There is no intention in this recital of British achievement to glorify war. The figures quoted serve to impress on our minds, more than anything else, that modern wars are not won by lofty sentiment alone, but by a colossal loss in human life and valuable material. Only an understanding of the truth of the last war in horror, misery and suffering, and some appreciation of what another war would mean with the intense post-war development in aircraft and mechanical transportation, will convince future generations how much peace is really worth.

This article is the first of several that George Drew, a lawyer and Ontario securities commissioner, wrote for Maclean's before beginning his successful political career. He had served in the artillery in the First World War and was severely wounded in 1916. Drew served as Ontario premier from 1943 to 1948, when he became leader of the federal Progressive Conservative Party. He lost both the 1949 and 1953 elections and later served as high commissioner to Great Britain from 1957 to 1964. Drew died in 1974 at the age of 79.

Capt. F. A. C. Scrimger

Canadian V.C.'s

W. W. MURRAY
November 15, 1928

I t is dawn at Ypres. A thin Canadian line is strung in narrow, surface-scratched ditches, back over the ridges from Poelcapelle toward the town, past Kerselaere to St. Julien, thence westward through Kitchener's Wood—into the blue. The roar and crash of high-explosive shells, the vicious bursts of shrapnel that sow the fields with death, the murderous, raking hail of rifle and machine-gun fire are an infernal chorus hymning the rising sun.

The poisonous fumes of chlorine gas hang heavily in the

morning air, dregs of the cloud which but a few hours before enveloped the French colonial troops and forced them to flee, leaving a four-mile gap in the line through which the Germans poured in their thousands.

Outnumbered, outflanked and at bay, the Canadians have fought the long night through. Their desperate efforts to buttress the shattered line, to stem the on-rushing tide, have brought into action every battalion of the 1st Division. And now with the coming of day, masses of field-grey infantry are on the move again, throwing themselves forward with reckless confidence.

Hour after hour, the Canadians, wearied but unconquerable, revitalized by the very nearness and sight of the enemy, gather themselves together and with supreme effort hurl them back. The line bulges here, gives there, for the strain is terrific; but it does not break.

Nearly 14 years have passed since the world thrilled to the epic of that modern Thermopylae. The old 1st Division had within its Spartan ranks many a Leonidas, and the four days of the second battle of Ypres, from April 22 to April 25, 1915, were filled with brave deeds. Since it is the purpose of a series of which this article is one to attempt again a recital of the story of those heroes upon whom was bestowed the most cherished distinction in the world, the Victoria Cross, inevitably the second battle of Ypres marks the starting-point.

Four members of the 1st Canadian Division had the honour conferred upon them for acts of bravery performed in this engagement. They were:

No. 24066 Lance-Cpl. Fred Fisher, of the 13th Battalion, Royal Highlanders of Canada.

No. 1539 Company Sgt.-Maj. F. W. Hall, the 8th Battalion, Winnipeg Rifles.

Capt. E. D. Bellew, machine-gun officer of the 7th Battalion, British Columbia Regiment.

Capt. F. A. C. Scrimger, medical officer of the 14th Battalion, Royal Montreal Regiment.

The award of the Victoria Cross to Fred Fisher was the first of the 61 that were presented to members of the Canadian Expeditionary Force (including the Canadian Cavalry Brigade) during the Great War, and the official citation that records the act for which the distinction was given, and in the performance of which Fisher yielded his life, is brevity itself—82 words. But back of it is a story of hardihood and bravery, of stubborn resolve and lofty courage.

The left of the Canadian line, comprising the 13th Battalion, had swung back from the neighbourhood of Poelcapelle during the night of April 22, and rested almost parallel to the Poelcapelle-Ypres Road as far as St. Julien. In the darkness, the support and reserve battalions of all brigades in the division had come forward and taken up some sort of defensive alignment on the flank of the Highlanders. A few hundred yards north by west of St. Julien and manning a hastily dug trench, out from the Poelcapelle Road, was a heroic remnant of the 14th Battalion. Immediately in rear and still in action, a battery of Canadian field-guns, commanded by Maj. (now Brig.-Gen.) W. B. M. King, had maintained its position throughout the long, uncertain night and well into the day of April 23. But the odds became overwhelming. Decimated by the merciless rain of bullets, of shrapnel and high-explosive that poured relentlessly upon them, the gunners were at last forced to make shift to withdraw the battery.

The enemy were advancing at point-blank range 200 yards away, intent upon the capture of the Canadian artillery. To man-handle the guns rearward in the face of this was a hopeless-looking task. But it is here that Fisher enters upon the scene.

In St. Julien that morning, detached from his battalion temporarily, Fisher trudged forward with his machine gun to join the 13th. He had gathered up half-a-dozen men from several units of the 3rd Brigade while in the village, and this little party essayed to run the gauntlet of death. They made their way forward, and the superhuman efforts of the artillerymen in striving to drag away the 18-pounders under the very eyes of the approaching enemy drew Fisher unerringly toward them. He took in the situation at a glance and acted immediately.

Doubling forward with his Colt gun, he set it up, amid a veritable tornado of shelling, between the battery and the advancing enemy. Exposed to the full blast, he sat and sprayed the Germans, emptying belt after belt into them. Willing hands replenished the belts but these became fewer and fewer as his little party withered under the concentrated rifle fire. One by one, its members fell until Fisher alone was left. But the enemy were checked. The 18-pounders were hauled out of danger, to take up a position from which they again came into action.

Still, Fisher was not through with the fight. He withdrew from his isolated post and staggered back to St. Julien where once again he picked up a number of men from the 14th Battalion. All set out for the front line, but only Fisher reached it. The remainder were killed or wounded.

Meanwhile, his own battalion—the 13th—were suffering fearful casualties from galling, enfilade fire that raked them from three sides. It was in attempting to subdue this that the brave youth lost his life. His officer, Lieut. J. G. Ross, called upon Fisher to accompany him to another post, located in a shallow trench, which gave observation over the area from which came the heaviest concentration. Together they set up the gun and the attack on the oncoming Germans was continued. But the pair presented too good a mark; their efforts were too destructive. Enemy riflemen levelled upon them a storm of bullets, and as Fisher lay with his eye along the sights of his Colt and his finger pressing the trigger, one missile out of that avalanche struck and he rolled over beside his officer, dead.

The massed attack on the Canadian line at Ypres developed on the morning of Saturday, April 24. It was then that the Germans, following up a hurricane bombardment of the entire area, projected gas which fell heavily on the northern arm of the triangle from Poelcapelle toward Gravenstafel Ridge. The brunt was borne by the 13th Battalion at the Apex, and the 15th Battalion on their right, with the 7th Battalion to the left receiving a large share. The 7th had been rushed into the breach east of the Poelcapelle Road, in front of and facing the ruined village of Kerselaere. Their position was on the forward slope of a ridge. Here it was that Capt. Bellew earned the Victoria Cross.

Exposed to the shelling, the British Columbians suffered tremendous casualties, blasted as they were out of the shallow holes which served them as trenches. The German infantry attack developed in strength, and on the flanks of the 7th Battalion some headway was made. But again and again the dogged resolution of the men from the Pacific Coast beat back the enemy. Capt. Bellew had two machine guns near the right flank of his sadly depleted battalion. From this point the story is best told from the official citation.

"The right company was soon put out of action, but the

Lance Cpl. Fred Fisher

advance was temporarily stayed by Capt. Bellew, who had set up his guns on the left flank of the right company. Reinforcements were sent forward but they in turn were surrounded and destroyed. With the enemy in strength less than 100 yards away, with no further assistance in sight, and with his rear threatened, Capt. Bellew and Sgt. Peerless, each operating a gun, decided to stay where they were and fight it out. Sgt. Peerless was killed and Capt. Bellew was wounded and fell. Nevertheless, he got up and maintained his fire till ammunition failed, and the enemy rushed the position. Capt. Bellew then seized a rifle, smashed his machine gun, and fighting to the last was taken prisoner."

This heroic officer spent years in a German prison-camp, and the award to him of the Victoria Cross was not announced until May 15, 1919—four years after the deed.

The same spirit of devotion, applied to a different situation, earned for Company Sgt.-Maj. Hall of the 8th Battalion the posthumous award of the Victoria Cross.

On the night of April 23, the 8th Battalion had extended its line on Gravenstafel Ridge, relieving a portion of the 15th Toronto Highlanders. A continuous hail of rifle and machine-gun fire harassed the operation. The front line trench lay about 15 yards in advance of a high bank over which the troops had to cross, and in so doing a number of them were wounded.

Checking up his company strength, Sgt.-Maj. Hall discovered a number of men missing. Groans from the top of the ridge indicated plainly what had happened, and in the darkness this warrant-officer climbed back on two separate occasions, returning each time with a wounded man. This did not, however, account for all of the casualties; and at nine o'clock on the morning of the 24th, the attention of Hall was again drawn to the moans of a wounded comrade, coming from high up on the bank.

It was broad daylight; the trench occupied by the 8th Battalion was being subjected to heavy rifle fire. But this did not deter Hall. Calling for volunteers, he was promptly joined by Cpl. Payne and Pvt. Rogerson. The trio began a hazardous crawl toward the wounded soldier. In full view of the enemy, who had settled down to steady and deliberate fire, they drew on themselves a veritable hail of bullets. Payne and Rogerson were wounded, but were able to return painfully back to what shelter the front line afforded. Hall essayed another attempt, this time alone. Unhit, he reached the man on the ridge, and manoeuvred cautiously to edge him into a position that would allow of carrying him down to the trench.

The whole of the German fire was now centred on the chief figure in this errand of mercy. The bullets zipped all around him. Squirming under the body of the sufferer, Hall finally worked himself into a position which might have permitted him to bring the wounded man back. He raised his head in order to survey the return route. In doing so he received a bullet in the brain. A few minutes later the soldier he had set out to rescue was again shot and his sufferings ended.

"Capt. Scrimger, during the very heavy fighting between April 22 and 25, displayed continuously day and night the greatest devotion to his duty among the wounded men at the front." This is the unvarnished conclusion of the 114-word citation that sets forth the reasons why the Victoria Cross was awarded to the medical officer of the 14th Battalion. Not all deeds of valour were confined to the forward area.

The evacuation of the wounded at Ypres was a grave problem; battalion stretcher-bearers worked till they dropped in sheer exhaustion or were killed beside the helpless men whom they were succouring. The wounded who were able to walk to the rear started off, but scores met their death in the heavy shelling that turned the region between the front line and Ypres into an inferno. Through the welter of death, however, hundreds arrived at the dressing-stations, and there received aid before being despatched "down the line."

In the outbuildings of a farmhouse near Wieltje on the St. Julien-Ypres Road, Capt. Scrimger has established his Battalion Aid Post, and thither came men from all the units engaged forward. The French Turcos and Algerians had crawled in, choking and dying, seeking relief on the afternoon of April 22; closely following them came the sufferers of his own and other battalions. The dressing-station was a conspicuous mark for the German gunners, and they exacted a heavy toll on the stream of wounded Canadians, stretcher-cases and walking-wounded who converged upon it from all points of the front. Within the farm-buildings, to the accompaniment of bursting shells and falling masonry, Capt. Scrimger laboured day and night. Rest was out of the question; the flow of sufferers was ceaseless. Not content with the devoted services he was rendering to the wounded passing through the Aid Post, this gallant surgeon made frequent trips forward to the advanced trenches to dress the wounds of men who could not be carried back.

In was on Sunday, April 25, that the dressing-station itself had to be abandoned. The enemy, in their swing south and east, were approaching close to Wieltje, and their gradual advance was heralded by an intense shelling of the stricken area. Every calibre of gun was used, and shell after shell burst upon the doomed farmhouse and its outbuildings, which took fire, and soon the whole place was a blazing inferno. Personnel and patients were got away with difficulty; the German infantry were within plain view, approaching Wieltje.

One badly wounded officer, Capt. Macdonald of the Brigade Staff, was the last man left in the doomed structure, together with Capt. Scrimger. At this stage the blaze reached a store of small-arms ammunition lying in the neighbourhood, and at once a crackle as of heavy musketry broke out. This was fortunate, it deceived the enemy and halted them. Taking advantage of the temporary lull, the medical officer carried Macdonald out of the dressing-station to the road. But there he was halted by shell-fire. Huge guns were blasting the route toward Ypres, and the bombardment had assumed the proportions of drumfire. In the midst of this were Capt. Scrimger and his patient, in imminent danger of being blown to pieces. With a devotion to characterize which words seem woefully inadequate, the medical officer laid the wounded man down in a roadside ditch and lay over him. Protecting him thus with his own body, with the shells crashing in ear-splitting detonations all about and rocking the whole area with their explosions, Scrimger stayed with his patient.

The gunfire subsided and the medical officer again took up his suffering colleague. "When he was unable alone to carry this officer further," says the citation, "he remained with him under fire till help could be obtained."

Capt. F. A. C. Scrimger was subsequently wounded, and he served as a surgeon at military hospitals in England before returning in late 1915 to the front in France. After the war, Dr. Scrimger returned to Montreal and joined the surgical staff at the Royal Victoria Hospital, where he became chief surgeon in 1936, a year before his death at age 57.

After the war, Capt. E. D. Bellew, a Sandhurst graduate, returned to his job with the federal public works department in British Columbia. Later, he went into ranching. In 1960, he travelled to London for a 100th anniversary party of the establishment of the Victoria Cross and shortly thereafter had a stroke. He died the following year at 78.

Bringing in the wounded, Vimy Ridge, April, 1917

Vimy V.C.'s

W. W. MURRAY
February 15, 1929

In the course of his recent trip to France, the Right Hon. W. L. Mackenzie King, prime minister of Canada, visited Vimy Ridge where, on the famous Hill 145, this country is erecting a monument to commemorate the achievements of the Canadian Corps on April 9, 1917, and subsequent days. The premier was also conducted to the subterranean cave, near La Folie Farm, "big enough to quarter an entire battalion," on the walls of which Canadian soldiers had carved their names, regimental badges and whatever else occurred to them as acceptable subjects whereon to exercise their art. The spaciousness of this tunnel astounded the prime minister who, following his visit, well understood why the Germans sheltering in such retreats had regarded Vimy Ridge as impregnable. The enemy excavated many similar defence works on the ridge, dug-outs far underground, capable of accumulating whole companies who could remain in perfect security from even the most devastating bombardment, emerging only to engage the infantry when the gunfire had rolled past.

One visualizes just such a place in recalling the incident for which Maj. Thain W. MacDowell, then a captain of the 38th Battalion, Eastern Ontario Regiment, was awarded the Victoria Cross. MacDowell, with his company runners, Kebus and Hay, behind him, gingerly descending the 50 odd steps beneath the surface of the earth and suddenly coming upon 77 men of the Prussian Guards, bluffing them into surrender and "getting away with it"—the picture is both inspiring and amusing. But the battle of Vimy Ridge was filled with inspiring events, and of these the story of how the five Canadians, upon whom the Victoria Cross was conferred, earned the distinction, stands out in bold relief against a vivid background.

There are several features connected with the assault and capture of Vimy Ridge which give it a character of its own in the record of the Canadian Corps. One is that the engagement was the first purely all-Canadian operation to be carried out on a grand scale on the Western Front. Another can be extracted from the speech delivered by Hon. J. L. Ralston, C.M.G., minister of national defence, to the Canadian Club of New York, at their last Armistice Day luncheon. Speaking on Canada's war effort, the minister said:

"It is probable that Vimy Ridge and its vicinity were the scene of more bloody fighting than any other section of the Western

Front, with the possible exception of Verdun. In 1915, the French made terrific efforts to secure the ridge and suffered appalling losses. They were only partially successful. Other Allied troops had taken over the ground from the French Army, and, in May 1916, by a surprise attack had been pushed off the portion of the ridge which afforded observation over the German lines.

"The Canadians not only retrieved the lost ground, but captured and consolidated the whole Ridge; and the offensive was carried across the plain to the very gates of Lens."

On April 9, deeds of heroism were performed which secured recognition for three Canadians—MacDowell, No. 427586 Pvt. W. J. Milne, 16th Canadian Battalion, and No. 53730 Lance-Sgt. E. W. Sifton, 18th Battalion. Next day No. 80887 Pvt. J. G. Pattison of the 50th Battalion earned the Victoria Cross, and on

Maj. Thain
MacDowell

May 3rd, Lieut. R. G. Combe, of the 27th Battalion, surrendered his life in the performance of an act for which he was given the coveted award.

To recount the deeds of the first three is to present a partial picture of the whole Canadian front on that Easter Monday in 1917 when, in a dismal mixture of sleet and snow, the four divisions of the Corps clambered out of their positions and fought their way from trench to trench over the crest of Vimy Ridge and down to the Plains of Douai. The 16th Battalion, in which Milne served, was a unit of the 1st Division which operated on the right flank of the attack; immediately north of it was the 2nd Division, of which the 18th Battalion that was distinguished by Sifton's bravery formed part. The 3rd Division continued the line until, on the extreme left flank, fought the troops of the 4th Division, in which MacDowell's unit, the 38th Battalion, served.

Zero Hour was at 5:30 in the morning—a sombre, overcast dawn. "Wheel to wheel" behind them, the Canadian infantrymen had the greatest concentration of guns that had up to that time flattened any portion of the Western Front in a deluge of metal. Amid an ear-splitting crash of explosions that rocked the whole country round, the 16th Battalion moved forward to its first objective. As it did so, a storm of snow, hail and sleet descended, turning the churned-up soil into a quagmire. It would have been perfectly proper to assume that the Canadian artillery had blasted every living thing off the Ridge, and without a doubt nothing above ground survived. But the deep dug-outs were the refuge of the enemy, and into these they had flocked as soon as the barrage dropped down on them. When the guns lifted to enable the infantry to press home the attack, the Germans reappeared with their machine-guns. And, whatever else may be said of them, the German machine-gunners were stout-hearted technicians.

The front of the 16th Battalion was swept by a leaden belt and the Highlanders dropped. Many casualties were suffered from a machine-gun that was being industriously served by a resolute crew. Pvt. Milne spotted the emplacement, and, on his hands and knees, he worked his way toward it. A bag of bombs was slung over his shoulder. The fire was low, bullets almost ricocheting off the ground, which forced Milne to hug the mud. By some saving grace he was untouched. He got within measurable distance of the emplacement and leaped to his feet. Into the middle of the machine-gun crew he hurtled his bombs, following these up by rushing the gun itself. This menace removed, his comrades dashed on to their first objective and continued to the next—the famous "Zwischen Stellung" (Intermediate Position).

The front of the Highlanders was raked by a vicious fire which came with particular ferocity from an old haystack directly in the line of advance. Milne's tactics having proved successful in the first instance, he elected to repeat them. Again crawling forward he discovered the haystack to be a concealment for a concrete emplacement, behind which a group of gunners were exacting a heavy toll. Milne's first missile knocked the gun out of commission. Taking advantage of the consternation among the crew, the gallant Highlander rushed the position and forced the surrender of the enemy. Of him the citation says:

"His wonderful bravery and resource on these two occasions undoubtedly saved the lives of many of his comrades.

"Pvt. Milne was killed shortly after capturing the second gun."

On the sector immediately north of the 16th Battalion, fronting Neuville St. Vaast, the feat of Pvt. Milne was almost duplicated by Sgt. Sifton of the 18th Battalion. This London, Ont., unit had made a clean-cut job of the first objective—the old German front-line; but when our men descended on the second they ran into grim opposition. It was the old story—machine-guns. Within their cement fortresses the Germans traversed the whole area, ripping a wide swath through the Western Ontario men. "C" Company of the 18th were badly cut up, and one gun immediately in front was causing most of the casualties. Sifton located it, the barrel peeping over the parapet and twitching jerkily as it vomited the contents of belt after belt.

Sifton did not hesitate. Bounding forward in the teeth of the murderous fire, he plunged into the trench, and with the courage of a lion took on the whole crew in a bayonet fight. It was soon over—and the Canadian won. But his daring brought on him an avalanche of Germans who closed in upon him. Undismayed the sergeant tackled them all. With bayonet and clubbed rifle he did deadly execution until "C" Company dashed up and closed the issue. The 18th Battalion were now safe at their objective and Sifton set his platoon to work consolidating the position and evacuating the injured enemy. Then took place one of those acts of treachery which still further stained the record of an already badly blotted war. Unobserved, a wounded German reached stealthily for a rifle, levelled it at the brave young Canadian, and pressed the trigger. Sgt. Sifton dropped dead.

"His conspicuous valor," says the official citation, "undoubtedly saved many lives, and contributed largely to the success of the operation."

The hardest fighting of the Vimy Ridge engagement during the first two days took place in the sectors immediately south of the Souchez River, in the vicinity of "The Pimple." The Germans fought stubbornly to retain their grip on this lofty eminence, and they were not dislodged until the evening of April 10. It was during the grim conflict waged in this neighbourhood that Capt. T. W. MacDowell, of the 38th Battalion, earned the Victoria Cross. MacDowell had a flair for capturing prisoners. Only five months previously he had been awarded the Distinguished Service Order for garnering three officers and 50 men on the Somme. At Vimy Ridge he exceeded this "bag."

With his two company orderlies, Pvts. Kebus and Hay, he found the footing over the ridge toward the first objective somewhat better than the men of his company, with the result that when they hit the front line of the German position, the trio were alone. The remainder of the company had worked somewhat over to a flank. In their stride, MacDowell and his two runners had destroyed one machine-gun and chased the crew from another. He was closely pursuing one of the fleeing gunners, when the latter scuttled like a rabbit into the dark entrance of a dug-out. MacDowell investigated. The shaft seemed to penetrate right into the bowels of the earth, for its descent was steep and pitch-black. A deep-lunged roar, demanding the surrender of whatever Germans might be sheltering below, met with no response; but that some of the enemy were there was beyond doubt. The officer decided to enquire. The steps were endless. Down and down he went until he felt that he must be hitting the very base of Vimy Ridge itself. But eventually he reached the bottom. A narrow tunnel led in from the foot of the steps, and rounding it MacDowell found himself crashing right into a phalanx of Prussian Guards. They were, as MacDowell said in his report, "all big, strong men who came in last night. They had plenty of rations; but we had a great time taking them prisoners."

His method was to turn back, quick as lightning, and shout orders up the dug-out stairs to an imaginary force. The bluff worked, and up went 77 pairs of hands.

The surrender of such a tremendous body was embarrassing. MacDowell was faced with the problem of getting his captives out of the dug-out and sent back to the Canadian line, with only two men to do it for him. He took the chance. He told off the Germans in parties of a dozen and passed each batch up the stairs where they were marshaled by Kebus and Hay. And then the expected happened. As soon as they saw how they had been fooled, the enemy were furious. One of their number snatched a rifle and shot at a runner, but he was summarily disposed of. And the lesson was taken to heart. Submissively this immense group were escorted back to swell the total taken by the Canadians on that stirring day.

The official citation tells the story badly in 95 words—little more than one word for each prisoner!

Thirteen months before the Battle of Vimy Ridge, a man presented himself as a recruit to the 137th Battalion, then mobilizing at Calgary. He was 41 years old, having been born at Woolwich, England, in 1875; and already he had a boy of 18 serving in that same unit. The father was J. G. Pattison, and his desperate bravery and unselfish devotion to his comrades furnish one of the brightest pages of the annals of those who have received the coveted Cross. Pvt. Pattison, Sr., had been sent as a reinforcement to the 50th Battalion in February 1917. Nine weeks later he performed the feat of signal gallantry that gave him his niche among the immortals.

On that memorable Easter Monday, the 50th Battalion had been held in reserve; but their turn came next day. The enemy had bitterly contested every foot of ground on the northern sector of the ridge, and the 10th of April found them still clinging firmly to the eastern slope. A daylight operation to dislodge them from their position was decided upon, and at 3:15 p.m. the 50th Battalion went over. Progress was slow and casualties were heavy. The enemy machine-gunners had a clear field of fire and laid an almost impenetrable belt of lead across the entire front. One strong-point stood in the way of the objective assigned to "A" Company, and time after time the Westerners attempted to force themselves through the storm. But they were as often beaten back, and they suffered grievous losses. "B" Company came up to buttress their attenuated ranks, and again the position was attacked; but this assault fared no better than its predecessors. The situation was critical. The men were scattered in shell holes fronting the strong-point, with bullets topping the grass, and there was every prospect of a definite check.

It was here Pvt. Pattison decided that if anything lay in his power to avoid it, such should not be the case.

Surveying the ground carefully, he advanced alone toward the machine-gun nest. Jumping from shellhole to shellhole, crouching flat as the gunners traversed over him, and gaining yards between each sweep, he reached within a long throw of the enemy. Thereupon he raised himself erect. Coolly, as if he were in the practice pits at Witley, he lobbed over three bombs into the position. One would have caused the Germans a great deal of distress; three were too much. The heavy grenades knocked the machine-guns out of action and did considerable damage to their crews. Before they could recover, the Calgarian was among them, rounding off his work with the bayonet. When the rest of

Pvt. J. G. Pattison

the company caught up with him, the 40-year-old hero had finished his job.

Pvt. Pattison survived this action, but met his death seven weeks later in front of Lens. As is the soldier's right, when his son joined the 50th Battalion, also as a reinforcement, in September, 1917, he wore on his right breast the ribbon of the coveted distinction won by his father.

The ferocious local actions in the Lens vicinity and on the plains of Douai—in the aggregate more costly than the actual capture of the Ridge—signalled the tapering away of the great offensive. With Vimy's lofty escarpment behind them, the Canadians pressed slowly forward, capturing a village here, a brickpile there, a trench somewhere else. The 3rd of May was the day set for an attack against the "Avion-Mericourt-Acheville-Fresnoy Line," an operation which did not meet with the success hoped for and which resulted in heavy loss of life. The attacking troops were caught by shellfire as they assembled in the pitch darkness; few reached their objective.

Lieut. Robert Grierson Combe, of Winnipeg, was an officer of the 27th Battalion. When the German barrage descended on his company in their jumping-off area it blasted their formation to fragments. Zero Hour—3:45 a.m.—saw only a pitiful remnant left wherewith to launch the attack. But Combe gathered this forlorn hope and, a hero leading heroes, he set off behind the curtain of Canadian artillery for the German trenches. The enemy fire withered them; when Combe reached the enemy's line, after an advance of hundreds of yards over open, featureless plain, five men alone out of his whole company were left. Undismayed they threw themselves on the packed position. With rifle and grenade this quintet, now joined by scattered details of other companies, hurled destruction among the enemy. They fought from traverse to traverse; dug-outs were bombed; Germans surrendered by the dozen as this devoted band of adventurers forced their way to the right and left. Eighty prisoners were taken; 250 yards of trench were captured.

"Lieut. Combe," says his citation, "repeatedly charged the enemy, driving them before him, and whilst personally leading his bombers, was killed by an enemy sniper. His conduct inspired all ranks, and it was entirely due to his courage that the position was carried and held."

Thain MacDowell, who ended the war as a colonel, was much celebrated in peacetime. He became an honorary lieutenant colonel of the Frontenac Regiment—MacDowell was raised near Brockville, Ont.—and his portrait hung in the National Gallery in Ottawa. From 1923 to 1928, he worked as private secretary to the minister of national defence, and he later served as a director and executive of various mining companies. He died in 1960 at age 70 in his home in Nassau, Bahamas.

William Barker

Canada's Fighting Airmen

MAJ. GEORGE A. DREW
May 1, 1929

There is no more dramatic story written in the annals of the Great War than the official record of the almost incredible exploits of Lieut.-Col. William George Barker. Of all the thousands from every part of the British Empire who served with the Royal Air Force on its many battle-fronts, only three were officially given credit for having destroyed more enemy machines, and two of these were Canadians. Bishop and Collishaw, Canadians, are officially credited with 72 and 60 machines respectively, while McCudden is reported to have brought down between 54 and 58 enemy planes. The lesser figure appears in his Victoria Cross citation. Barker is credited officially with the destruction of 50.

But even such a comparison as that does not convey the full import of Barker's contribution to the Allied cause, since it was only in the latter part of the war that he became essentially a fighting pilot. His earlier activities embraced practically every phase of the increasingly complex scheme of aerial warfare, and the official citations accompanying the announcement of his numerous decorations tell a wonderful story of bravery and skill in observing, reconnaissance, bombing, artillery co-operation, contact patrol, and photography. All this and the later days of strenuous fighting were only a prelude, however, to that last Homeric battle on Oct. 27, 1918, when he fought nearly 60 German machines, and, in spite of terrible wounds, brought four of them down behind the British line and lived to receive the Victoria Cross for one of the most remarkable deeds of the whole war.

Tall, lean, powerful and erect, Colonel Barker has more of the traditional appearance of the professional soldier than perhaps any of the great airmen of the war, although his military training was only that of the ordinary civilian enlisting in the ranks and going through the customary routine of a unit in the Canadian Expeditionary Force. His manner of quiet self-possession, his steady glance and keen eyes reflect the determination, quick decision and courage which were the outstanding characteristics of his astonishing career.

Barker was born at Dauphin, Man., on Nov. 3, 1894, when his famous wartime confrère, Bishop, was a baby of a few months at Owen Sound, Ont. He continued to live in Dauphin with his family until he moved to Winnipeg shortly before the war. He received the usual public and high school education and doubtless absorbed a valuable measure of that self-confidence and optimism which seem to spring from the very soil of the Prairie provinces.

Throughout his early life, he exhibited a love of shooting, and his subsequent success in the air may partly be accounted for by the experience he gained in handling firearms. Game was plentiful in Manitoba in those days and he did not have far to go for deer, moose and elk, while wild duck and prairie chickens were almost too plentiful for keen sport.

He was also a fearless rider and the sense of balance gained in the saddle probably contributed largely to the ease with which he later learned to fly. In the early days of the war, some of the senior officers responsible for the choice of prospective pilots caused much comment and some amusement because they apparently considered the only qualification required of any man who seemed reasonably sound in mind and limb was an affirmative answer to the question, "Do you ride?"

Shortly after the outbreak of war in 1914, Barker and a number of his friends who wished to join a mounted unit went to Brandon and enlisted with the First Battalion of the Canadian Mounted Rifles. There his name appeared for the first time on the records of the fighting forces of the Empire as No. 106074, Pvt. Barker, William George. Thus he began his military career at the foot of the ladder at the age of 19.

As a result of his knowledge of firearms he was attached to the machine-gun section where he remained until he left the battalion. He soon displayed the same skill with the cumbersome rapid-firing weapons as with a rifle, and quite unconsciously continued his training for the flying corps which had commenced on the rifle ranges of Dauphin and Winnipeg.

After some months of training in the severity of a Manitoba

winter, the 1st C.M.R.'s proceeded to England with their horses in the spring of 1915 and spent the summer in camp at Shorncliffe, in Kent. In another mounted unit nearby was Bishop, who was then a lieutenant, and had already decided that he wanted to fly. Barker's thoughts had not yet turned to the air, however, and on Sept. 22, 1915, he crossed with his battalion to France.

He and all of his battalion suffered a great disappointment before they went to the front. Static warfare having placed very strict limitations on the use of mounted troops, it was decided that all the mounted rifle battalions should go to France dismounted and serve as infantry. The ghastly reality of war was a startling contrast to anticipation in any case, but it was much more striking to men who had visualized their part in battle in the stirring rôle of mounted troops.

In the late months of 1915, trench warfare had reached its most stagnant point, and there was not even the exhilaration of real fighting to relieve the monotony of alternating periods in the front line, support and reserve. And with November the Canadians learned what mud could really be—bottomless, endless mud. The time spent in the front line in those wet months was a fairly miserable experience. There was little for the infantry to do but fill sand bags, keep under cover, vainly try to keep dry and hope that the next shell was not headed for their particular part of the trench. The machine-gunners at least kept up some measure of activity with occasional bursts of fire over the enemy trenches but even their work was impersonal and desultory.

During a particularly unpleasant spell of such enforced inactivity, Barker saw a fight in the air for the first time. As the machines manoeuvred for position far above the trenches, the distant rattle of their machine-guns could be distinctly heard. There at least was action and freedom from the awful filth of the trenches. But even more attractive in Barker's mind than the opportunity of fighting in a cleaner element was the thought of using a machine-gun on a visible target. What impressed him above everything else was the tremendous amount of ammunition they seemed to fire with no apparent result. Doubtless underestimating the difficulty of obtaining satisfactory results with the crude aerial weapons of 1915, he felt that he could have done much better himself if he once had an enemy machine under the sights of his gun. His mind was definitely made up that he was going to fight in the air.

Just at that time there was an urgent need for more observers and an opportunity was given to members of units at the front who had any previous experience which might qualify them for the work to transfer to the Royal Flying Corps. Barker immediately applied. Before receiving any word of acceptance or refusal he saw another fight—this time between a German and a French machine. There was nothing indecisive about the results on this occasion, however, for after a few rounds the French machine burst into flames and those below saw the ghastly spectacle of the occupants jumping from their seats and falling for thousands of feet.

Barker's enthusiasm for the air service had been considerably dampened, and when he received word a few days later that his application had been refused he was more glad than sorry. His active nature, however, began to revolt against the mud and monotony and he applied again, this time with more success, and with the rank of corporal, which he had held with his first unit, he was attached to the 9th Squadron, which was a Corps squadron operating on the Somme.

Barker was not long with the 9th Squadron before he established the reputation for marksmanship which never left him. He and his pilot were on a long reconnaissance in German territory in a slow-moving old B.E. 2C when they were attacked by a German scout. The odds were decidedly against them, but the pilot manoeuvred his cumbersome machine in wide circles in an effort to place Barker in a favourable position to engage their faster opponent. Finally, Barker got the momentary chance for which he had been waiting, and lining the sights of his gun with the same cool precision which had brought up the bull's-eye spotter so often on the Manitoba ranges, he pulled the trigger and a stream of bullets poured into the German machine just beside the pilot. Down it went completely out of control and in a few moments burst into flames. Decisive battles were still comparatively rare and this first victory against formidable odds while he was still very much of a novice meant more to Barker and his squadron than several such successes in the later days of the war.

On April 2, 1916, Barker was formally attached to the Royal Flying Corps with the rank of Second-Lieutenant. Up to that time he had been wearing the customary uniform of a Canadian corporal; so he was instructed to proceed to London to get his officer's uniform and equipment Five days later he returned to the front and was posted to the 4th Squadron with which he served until the middle of July.

The 4th Squadron was also on the Somme; in fact, practically all his flying in France was in that sector, and he came to know nearly every foot of ground for miles on both sides of the line. From the time he joined the 4th Squadron he commenced a period of intense activity which continued without cessation until the close of the mighty battles of the Somme in the middle of November.

The activities of the Corps squadrons such as the 4th embraced reconnaissance work, artillery observation, bombing, photography, contact patrol and general harassing of enemy troops on the ground. Perhaps the most important function of the air force was its rôle as the eyes of the army. In the past, cavalry had always been the means of obtaining information concerning the enemy's movements, but trench warfare had put an end to the use of cavalry for that purpose, and aeroplanes, in addition to the advantage of speed and greater vision, had the outstanding advantage of being able to communicate immediately any information they obtained by means of wireless.

Reconnaissance was difficult work and required skill, courage, perseverance and, above everything else, absolute accuracy. It entailed protracted flights over the enemy's line subjected to anti-aircraft fire from the ground and the constant threat of attacks by scouts in the air.

Something of importance would be seen on the ground, the observer would locate the spot on his map and then, perhaps, take a photograph of the arena to verify his observation. It was of little use taking observations unless the exact map location could be accurately communicated to headquarters.

During April, May and June of 1916, the British airmen became increasingly active in anticipation of the opening of the Battle of the Somme on July 1. Not only were the observers ranging the hundreds of newly arrived batteries on vital points behind the German line but they were also constantly on the lookout for any new target which might appear. Barker was particularly good at this and found co-operation with the artillery exhilarating work. There was an uncanny feeling of power in directing the fire of mighty guns and seeing the explosion of the shell thousands of feet below responding so mysteriously to the directing instructions which flashed from the wireless key under the observer's hand.

As July 1 approached, the Royal Flying Corps, which had been growing stronger and stronger, began for the first time during the war to dominate the situation. No longer was it a question of give and take as to which side of the line activity lay. Day in and day out, the British airmen "carried on" far beyond the enemy line and trained the fire of the colossal concentration of British guns on the German batteries which were being rushed in to meet the attack for which they were now prepared. Finally, on the day before the opening of the great bombardment, the British showed their full strength in the air when the word went forth to all the squadrons that the German airmen were to be swept from the sky.

All along the line on both sides, the clumsy-looking observation balloons floated at the end of their cables while the observers in each of them controlled artillery fire. So far they had been comparatively immune from attack and their chief concern was long-range shell fire. But on this last day before the storm finally broke, the British, in one great unexpected raid, brought nearly every enemy observation balloon on the whole Somme front in flames to the earth. It was a good omen for the test of strength to come, and from that day for many months the British and the French assumed complete mastery of the sky, with all that such means for the land forces in modern warfare.

Just a few days before the opening of the Somme battles, Barker was hit for the first time. He had been observing for the artillery and was attacked by a German scout. In the exchange of fire a bullet went through the fleshy part of his leg but did no serious damage, and he and his pilot were able to fight their way safely home without further injury. On landing it was found that the flesh was not badly torn and he did not even leave the squadron but was flying again in time to take part in the British attack on July 1.

During the attacks and counter-attacks of that awful summer, as the British and French drove the Germans back under such a deluge of shells as the world had never hitherto known, a new and vitally important task devolved upon the airmen. This was the contact patrol. From the close of the Battle of the Marne in the autumn of 1914 up to the opening of the Battle of the Somme in 1916, attacks had been on so narrow a front and penetration so shallow that there was rarely any doubt about the position of the opposing troops; but during the summer and autumn of 1916, as the Allies pushed forward, it was often found impossible to determine the position of the foremost troops except from the air.

Ingenious methods were devised for indicating to the airmen where the front of the line lay. By flares, smoke puffs, metal reflectors, cloth strips on the ground and other prearranged signals the foremost detachments would show where they were. The observer would then locate their position on the map and send the information to headquarters by wireless. It was very responsible work and called for absolute accuracy, as a mistake either in a map reading or as to the identity of the troops—a mistake easily made in bad weather—might result in the artillery shelling their own men or an infantry formation advancing into an area occupied by the enemy.

On July 18, he was transferred from the 4th to the 15th Squadron, with which he served continuously until he went to Italy 15 months later. By this time, the Canadian divisions were beginning to arrive at the Somme from the famous Ypres front, and exchange the mud of Flanders for the appalling devastation of the Somme battlefields which the summer had left strewn with a dreadful litter of human bodies and shattered material. By the middle of September, they were all in position ready to jump off in one of the greatest of the Somme battles.

On Sept. 15, 1916, Barker co-operated in battle for the first time with Canadian troops. With excitement and pride he saw his countrymen in their first attack on the Somme sweep over the ground he knew so well, capturing Courcelette and Mouquet Farm. On the very left of the Canadian Corps he saw his old battalion, the 1st C.M.R., advance successfully in the first line of the Canadian attack to their objective beyond Mouquet Farm.

Not only for Barker and the Canadians Corps, but for the whole British army, Sept. 15 was a red-letter day. On that eventful morning, the mysterious tanks waddled out of the low-lying mist for the first time into the vision of the fighting men. There had been vague rumours about them which even the enemy had heard, but no one at the front had the slightest conception of what they were really like, and when they came they spread terror in their path and new confidence in our men.

Flying high above the smoke and dust of battle, Barker saw these slow mobile forts make their cumbersome way through wire and over trenches, breaking down one defence after another until one of them at last found its way far behind the German lines into the village of Flers. While doing his usual work of contact patrol and observation a panorama unfolded itself before him of one of the most significant developments in modern warfare, which only the airmen were privileged to see in one broad picture. It was a sight which those who flew that day will never forget.

A few days later, he was detailed to photograph some new defensive works upon which the Germans had been particularly active. Such photographs were of the greatest importance. Upon being developed and printed, they showed the most minute detail, from which experts were able to determine the exact nature of the works and plot its position on the map. These were then handed to artillery officers who with the co-operation of aerial observers proceeded to destroy what the enemy had built.

Before Barker and his pilot had been able to take the necessary photographs they were attacked by two enemy scouts. In spite of the tremendous advantage which the fast scouts had over their slow machine, they did not turn back but assumed the offensive and were able to make things so uncomfortable for the Germans that eventually they flew away. Barker then took the photographs and started for home.

Their fighting, however, had only started. Before reaching their own lines they were attacked by four more scouts which dived, one after the other, pouring bullets from their fixed guns. Once more Barker showed his marksmanship and while he did not succeed in bringing any of them down, his bullets were doing so much damage that the scouts turned and left them to get safely home.

With the odds so much against them in the first fight, they would have been quite justified in turning for home without attempting to take the photographs, but it was typical of the high spirit of the Royal Flying Corps that Barker and his pilot should accept the odds and fight for their right to stay over German territory as long as they liked. Such a spirit and its results in observation gave our troops and particularly the artillery an inestimable advantage over the Germans at that time. The photographs turned out to be extremely valuable. This exploit, added to his consistent good work for many months, brought Barker his first of many decorations, the Military Cross.

Through September, October and November of 1916, Barker continued his good work as an observer, while the Canadian followed their brilliant victory at Courcelette on Sept. 15 by playing an increasingly important part in the great British offensive. During those months he saw an Empire being welded together as never before by the blood of her sons mingled in a common sacrifice on the plains of Picardy.

Day in and day out, in every kind of weather, Barker's squadron carried on its various duties. Contact patrols and artillery observation became more and more important. The first, because of the increasing difficulty of keeping in touch with the movements of our troops as the front became more confused, and the latter, because of the necessity of registering the guns every time there was any movement on the line.

During the Somme fighting, there came a new development in the co-operation between aircraft and artillery which greatly increased the offensive power of the guns and presented a new field of work for the airmen. This was an emergency message to artillery headquarters by wireless, then known as the zone call, which brought all the guns within range to bear on any important target which required prompt action for results.

Barker particularly distinguished himself at this work and, even in his later exciting experiences as a pilot, found nothing to compare with the extraordinary sensation of power felt in directing the concentrated fire of scores of batteries against some target far below.

On one occasion in October while ranging a battery on some enemy gun emplacements, correcting each shot by wireless, his pilot noticed several trains approaching a station. He pointed this out to Barker and flew toward them. By this time the trains had stopped and troops could be clearly seen leaving the cars and forming up nearby. Barker immediately located the position of the trains on the map, sent the emergency call to artillery headquarters, gave the code reference to the position of the target, and then waited for results.

Artillery headquarters, which was connected with all its batteries by telephone, instantly ordered those batteries within range
of the trains to open fire, giving the map reference and other necessary instructions. The officers at the batteries quickly calculated
the range and direction to the target, and in less than 10 minutes
from the time Barker had tapped out the message from his dizzy
height some miles away, the first batteries had opened fire.

In the meantime, Barker and his pilot had been anxiously
watching the troops rushing faster and faster from the train, has-
tened by the threat of the circling aeroplane. Already many of
them had left on motor lorries. Suddenly a shell burst near the
station. Others followed, quickly landing on the trains and among
the men. Presently shells of many sizes were pouring into the station, and trains, lorries and troops, were enveloped in dense
clouds of smoke. When the firing ceased and the smoke cleared
away, the trains were wrecked, the station had almost disappeared, shattered lorries lay scattered about and hundreds of dead
and wounded could be seen lying on the ground.

Apart from the loss of life and material damage, the main
result of the prompt action of Barker and his pilot was the complete disorganization of the relief force which would shortly have
been strengthening the German defence opposite some part of
the advancing British line.

It is impossible to give details of more than a few of Barker's
flights. Probably his greatest service as an observer came at the
close of the Somme battles. On Nov. 13, the village of Beaumont
Hamel, on the north-west bank of the Ancre River, with its network of caverns had at last been taken by the British after
repeated failures. This was an important capture, as it was of vital
importance that the advantage should be held.

As part of the general plan of closely watching enemy movements, Barker and his pilot were flying along the Ancre River the following day, keeping low above the water in spite of heavy rifle and machine-gun fire from both banks. As they approached Beaucourt, which was only a short distance from Beaumont Hamel and also on the north bank of the river, Barker observed at least a brigade of German infantry hidden in the valleys and sunken roads near Beaucourt, evidently preparing for a counter-attack on Beaumont Hamel. Had not the plane been flying very low Barker would not have seen the enemy as they were lying motionless and could not have been detected from any great height.

He immediately located their position on the map, sent in the emergency zone call to artillery headquarters and his pilot turned the machine to observe the results. In this case the fire of the batteries was controlled in such a way that shells of all calibres arrived together. When fire opened, Barker's machine was between the British guns and the target, and the rush of shells created so great an air disturbance that they almost capsized. This was a very real danger in observing zone calls and many machines were hit in flight by our own shells.

A dramatic spectacle followed. At one moment the valley was perfectly quiet and the hidden troops were unaware of any immediate danger. The next it was a seething inferno of bursting shells of every size from the smallest to the largest, and lay hidden under a dense pall of smoke. The whole area occupied by the troops was swept by shell fire, and when the smoke cleared away it was seen that the destruction had been terrible. A formidable force of some 4,000 men had been scattered with heavy loss of life.

There can be no doubt of the effect of the disorganization of such a strong force, for the enemy never counter-attacked and the high ground about Beaucourt was captured two days later by the British.

The "Blood Bath" of the Somme ended with these actions, and on Nov. 16 Barker proceeded to Narborough in Norfolk to train as a pilot. His period of training was amazingly brief. The experience of nearly a year as an observer had given him most of the technical knowledge necessary, and a thorough familiarity with the handling of a machine, although he had never operated the controls. As a result he had only two flights in a dual-control machine with an instructor before attempting his first solo. The first flight lasted 50 minutes, the second, a few days later, five minutes, after which his instructor allowed him to go up alone.

This seems almost incredible in these days of cautious training, but it must be remembered that time was precious and the sole test was whether a man could fly. He spent from four to five hours in the air every day for the next week, after which he passed the necessary tests and received his wings as a pilot. He went from Narborough to Netheravon on the Salisbury Plains for a few more days for the final touches and was then ready to return to France.

When he left France in November he had been the senior combatant officer with the 15th Squadron in point of service, but could not be promoted, as an observer could not command a flight. When he returned as a pilot he was immediately given command of C Flight and shortly afterwards promoted to the rank of captain.

For the next two months he went through the daily grind of observation, photography, bombing and patrols with few unusual incidents. One of the most exacting of the winter tasks of the Corps squadrons such as the 15th was the long reconnaissance. This particular phase of the airman's work was not spectacular but it was vitally important and it called for courage, skill and endurance of the highest order. These flights of perhaps three or four hours far behind the enemy's lines under the constant menace of anti-aircraft fire and fast fighting scouts were trying enough in summer, but in the depth of winter they were a severe test of endurance.

Such were the sort of "uneventful" flights which Barker and the other pilots in his squadron made regularly through the winter months. That was only one of the many arduous tasks performed day in and day out by the Corps squadrons which, because they lacked the sensational elements of actual combat, are all too little remembered in the stories of the Royal Air Force but which contributed immeasurably to the success of our armies.

On March 17, the British and French commenced to advance along the whole Somme front. Although there was no serious opposition it was an extremely difficult operation, as the advancing troops never knew when they would meet a withering burst of machine-gun fire from some hidden strong point. The result was that the whole front was in a constant flux, now one part now another advancing with greater rapidity.

In this confusion the various staffs in command were almost entirely dependent upon the air force for information as to the location of the advancing troops as well as of the enemy. It was during this advance that Barker won his second decoration.

During the winter there had been a change in the operation of the reconnaissance machines. In 1916, the observer had done all the wireless work and had carried on the control of artillery fire. In the spring of 1917, it was decided that the pilot should do this work, leaving the observer free to do general observation and operate his machine-gun. Barker therefore found himself still doing the actual fire control for the guns as well as flying, and with more than a year's experience in this work behind him he now had ample opportunity to make full use of his skill.

Just before the British reached the Hindenburg Line an incident occurred which had far-reaching results in the future handling of zone calls, and illustrates very forcibly the appalling responsibility which rested upon youths like Barker—he was then 22.

During a reconnaissance he discovered a very strong position, well hidden, about two miles north-west of Bullecourt and about one mile in front of the Hindenburg Line. He could clearly see a considerable German force occupying a sunken road and a series of hastily constructed trenches directly in the path of our advancing troops. Knowing the proximity of our own troops he flew so low over the position, in spite of intense rifle and machine-gun fire, that he could see the colour of their uniforms. Having made absolutely certain that they were German troops he flashed the zone call back by wireless and waited to observe the fire. Nothing happened. Presently he realized that for some reason the call was not going to be answered and flew back to Division Headquarters where he landed. Here he located the officer in command of the artillery, reported what he had seen, the message he had sent, and asked why there had been no response.

He was told that the guns had not been ordered to fire, as they had reports from the infantry that the area in question was occupied by our troops, and that Barker must therefore have been mistaken in his observations.

Barker immediately telephoned to Gen. Longcroft, who was in command of the Corps squadrons, and told him what had occurred, pointing out that in addition to his having clearly seen German uniforms he had the fairly conclusive evidence that his machine was riddled with bullets fired from the trenches supposed to be held by our troops.

Gen. Longcroft from past experience had great confidence in Barker's observations and asked to speak to the artillery commander. He pointed out to him the impossibility of effective co-operation unless zone calls were promptly answered and insisted that Barker's observation be accepted in spite of the contrary information in their hands. Finally the artillery commander agreed to fire on the observation given and Barker was returning to his machine to observe the fire when his report received effective confirmation. A runner arrived with a message sent several hours before that the British advance guards had been forced to

With H.R.H. The Prince of Wales, after the war in Surrey, 1919

retreat from the area in dispute and that it was now held in considerable force by the enemy.

A few minutes later Barker was once more over the position and this time saw the enemy driven out under a crashing storm of high explosives. This incident was the subject of considerable discussion and in future it was only in the most exceptional cases that the zone call was not immediately answered.

Often during the advance Barker found it necessary to land to get any information concerning our troops. Frequently he was not certain whether he was behind or in front of the Germans. He would come down, leave his engine running with his machine pointed into the wind for a quick getaway, and then look around for some signs of our troops. His splendid service during the advance won him his second decoration, a Bar to the Military Cross.

On Aug. 7, he was again slightly wounded, but this time it was a very close shave. He had been ranging a 9.2-inch howitzer battery on a German battery position and had just reported the complete destruction of the target when the anti-aircraft guns suddenly found his range and he was surrounded by the coal-black puffs of high-explosive shells. Holes began to appear in his wings as he employed the usual tactics of diving and banking to deceive the gunners. Just as a particularly vicious burst appeared near the machine, he was struck under the right eye by a steel splinter which was fortunately deflected by the cheek bone and passed over his eye without injuring it. He was soon back over the lines, landed without further incident, and immediately had the wound dressed. The bone had not been damaged, and while it was necessary to wear bandages over the wound for about two weeks, he did not leave the squadron and was flying again next morning.

In the beginning of September, he received orders to return to

England and proceeded once more to Narborough where he was to be attached for six months as an instructor. By then he had been flying almost continuously at the front for more than a year and a half and it was considered good policy to send pilots back before they "cracked" under the strain.

Now he was tasting the joy of handling the agile Sopwith Camel, and after the slow, clumsy machines he had flown in the past, he felt the liberation of a completely new experience and wanted to express that freedom in loops, rolls and spins, which were decidedly not a part of the training programme as conceived by Maj. "Grumpy" Lee Smith.

He had only been in England a few weeks before he decided that he would very much prefer to be back in France with a fighting squadron, and asked to be transferred. This was at first refused. He then adopted another course. He continually "stunted" his machine in the most conspicuous manner, and made life miserable for the headquarters staff by zooming over their huts at all hours of the day. Finally, after a particularly daring stunt which very much disturbed some visiting senior officers, he was hauled before the camp commandant and told in no uncertain way that this could not continue.

Barker replied that there was a very simple way out of the difficulty as all he wanted was to be sent back to France. This was something new. Men did at times devise various ingenious methods to get away from the front, but here was an officer frankly insubordinate for the purpose of getting back into action. Major Smith saw the humour of the situation and agreed to his transfer. He was immediately given command of A Flight in the 28th and on Oct. 2nd flew to France again with his new squadron. They landed at Saint Omer in Flanders where so many Canadians detrained on their way to the Ypres Salient. From there they flew to a new aerodrome assigned to their squadron not very far away.

The great Flanders offensive was at its very height. Thousands of British guns were churning the Flanders clay into a picture of the most hopeless desolation, just as they had done with the chalk fields of Picardy a year before, and in the midst of this waste of mud and water in which no building or tree survived to give the land the appearance of human habitation, the Canadian Corps was once more plugging steadily along toward victory in the closing battle of the year at Passchendaele.

On Oct. 15, information was received from spies of the arrival of a large number of German troops, who were to relieve immediately the exhausted battalions on both sides of the Ypres-Menin Road. Barker received orders to take his flight of six machines and attack the relieving troops along the road.

At this time the pendulum had swung back to the German side in the matter of fighting scouts. The Fokker F 1 triplane had just reached the front, and one of the first squadrons to receive it was Baron Manfred von Richthofen's famous Jagdstaffel 11, which was then operating along the Flanders front. Richthofen, himself, was away on leave at the time with 61 victories to his credit, but his squadron of picked fighters was a formidable group at any time, and particularly now that they had received their new machines. With this knowledge Barker called his flight together and outlined his plans.

He and his companions would fly low over the lines and then directly along the Ypres road toward Menin. If they were fortunate in finding troops on the road they were to come down to the tree-tops and use their ammunition with the greatest care, firing only when sure of their target, as he was certain that with such an important relief in progress, German scout machines would be prepared for such an attack, and it was important that they have some ammunition left for the fight that was bound to follow. If they did get into a fight they were to drop as low as possible, as the Camels could manoeuvre better and take chances over the trees and hills, which would be suicidal for the faster Fokkers.

The six machines of his flight crossed the lines early one afternoon with Barker in the lead. The day was dull and the clouds lay in a dense mass little more than a thousand feet from the ground. The visibility was so poor that they were well over the shell-torn earth held by the Germans before they were even seen. Thus they escaped any serious rifle or machine-gun fire, and they were flying too low to be seriously bothered by the larger anti-aircraft guns. Flying straight along the tall double row of poplars which marked the Menin road, Barker presently sighted at least a battalion of infantry standing motionless under the trees in an effort to avoid detection by the aeroplanes which had been seen approaching. Down he went till his wings were barely clear of the trees, followed by the other five machines in single file. As they dipped down, a deadly stream of bullets poured into the hiding troops as their twin Vickers came to life with a chattering roar. Once clear of the end of the column Barker wheeled and they repeated the attack. After they had passed over them the second time the Germans on the ground who had not been hit were so scattered that Barker saw that further firing would be a waste of ammunition, so he re-formed his flight and started for home.

They had not gone far before they saw another formation of 10 machines approaching in the opposite direction. At first in the dull light they could not tell whether they were friend or foe, and they had almost met before the distinctive red markings became visible. Evidently the Germans had also been in doubt, as the two formations passed through each other without a shot being fired.

Then as they both wheeled, the bitterest fight in Barker's long experience started.

The enemy machines were all Albatross D 5's, faster and more powerful than the Camels, but much slower in turning. Immediately the Camels followed Barker's instruction and took the fighting literally down to the tree-tops. It was a dogfight of the wildest order, each pilot fighting his own battle with every nerve strained under the constant tension of watching machines, targets, and the ground all at the same time.

The first to draw blood was Malloch, who shot down one of the Albatrosses into a clump of trees where it burst into flames. Malloch was easily the most picturesque member of the 28th Squadron. An East Indian of high caste, he had graduated from Oxford before the war, was European in his speech and tastes, but always wore his turban even when in the air. He was a man of great courage and a splendid fighter.

A moment later one of the British machines went down, also in flames, and now to add to the wild confusion two sickening tongues of flame flickered 30 or 40 feet up into the milky air from the burning machines.

Barker had been diving to the assistance of the British machine, which had just crashed as he saw it attacked by two of the Albatrosses, when suddenly a burst of bullets ripped the fuselage beside him, and turning he saw that one of the enemy was "on his tail." He kicked his machine to the right and discovered that he was able to keep just clear of the fire from the fixed guns of the slower-turning Albatross by continuing to circle. Finding that his circling tactics had saved him from what would ordinarily be a fatal position he now decided to change the position. He knew that the Albatross with its heavy Mercedes engine could not loop so close to the ground as the Camel with its light rotary Clergy engine, so he circled lower and lower till he knew the German could not possibly loop, and then suddenly pulled his machine over in a loop, and in less time than it takes to tell, was over and behind his enemy. The German could do nothing now but fly straight away, trusting to his speed for escape. But it was a clear shot, and as he crossed Barker's sights a short burst of fire sent him down in flames.

Barker was just turning to rejoin his comrades when he found another German machine diving to attack him. The programme which he had coolly calculated in the heat of battle to deceive his first victim had worked so well that he decided to repeat it on his fresh opponent. He permitted the enemy to get close behind him and again started to circle. Once more he looped, and once more as the German found himself trapped and started to fly for home, he brought his enemy down in flames.

By this time he had lost the remainder of his flight and decided it was time to return. He began to climb and before the new enemy machines which had arrived during the fight could intercept him, had disappeared into the low-flying clouds. He had climbed to 10,000 feet and was not yet clear of the clouds, when suddenly he noticed by the action of his instruments that he had gone into a spin due to the lack of any sense of direction while flying in clouds.

He cut off his engine and did his best to right the machine. The altimeter showed the dizzy descent although he scarcely felt it himself. Nine thousand, 8,000, 7,000, on down to 1,000 it read in a few minutes before he was once more clear of the clouds. Finally, with the sense of balance restored, he righted the machine only a few hundred feet from the ground after falling for more than 9,000, got the engine started again, and began to fly by compass for home.

It seemed to take him a surprisingly long time to reach the line, and when he finally did, he found that he was behind Arras nearly 40 miles south of Ypres where he had intended to cross. After refuelling at the first aerodrome he found, he flew back to his own squadron where he was greeted enthusiastically as they had given him up as lost.

On his return he found that the only other officer of the six who had returned was Lieut. Fenton, so things looked rather blue for his flight. Later in the evening, however, they learned that two of the others had landed safely behind our lines, Malloch, who was badly wounded in both legs during the fight, having created a disturbance by knocking over a tent filled with Canadians near Caestre while making a forced landing. Fortunately the occupants of the tent were not injured. Malloch's wounds put him out of action for some months. The two remaining pilots of the flight had been killed.

The flight had given a good account of itself, however, against odds which were considerably increased by the arrival of new machines during the fight, for they had completely destroyed four of the enemy, two falling under Barker's guns, while Malloch and Fenton had each accounted for one.

The following day events took place far away at Caporetto in the Isonzo Valley separating the Austrians and Italians which had far-reaching consequences for Barker and his comrades in the 28th. When news of the collapse of the Italian army trickled through to the Western Front it conveyed very little to the British airmen other than the thought of possible disaster to a staunch ally. None of them dreamed that in a few days it was to change the whole course of the war so far as many of them were personally concerned.

The fight over the Menin Road on Oct. 16, in which Barker

won his first double victory, was his last decisive encounter on the Western Front for nearly a year. Barker was preparing for his third winter in France. The first he had spent as an observer, the second as a pilot with a Corps squadron doing reconnaissance, artillery observation, photography and bombing; and now as a scout pilot he was looking forward with keen interest to the prospect of a winter of fighting against the famous Jagdstaffel 11 under Richthofen which was operating on the same part of the front. But all their plans were suddenly changed in the last week of October.

On Oct. 26, before the public was aware that anything serious had happened, the British and French general staffs met and decided that the plight of the Italian army was so critical that, in spite of the urgent need for troops on the Western Front, they must send assistance to Italy without delay. Each army agreed to dispatch immediately five complete divisions and four squadrons of aeroplanes. The next day the 28th Squadron received orders to proceed to Milan by train.

The wings were removed and their faithful Sopwith Camels placed in box-cars with their wings beside them. Then, almost before they had time to realize what had happened, the whole squadron with its pilots, mechanics and machines started south in one train, leaving behind them the Flanders plain which they knew so well for a type of fighting which none could visualize. For Barker it marked the beginning of one of the most romantic chapters in the story of aviation, and for the whole squadron the threshold of a great adventure.

As it proceeded through Italy, the 28th Squadron was hailed with an enthusiasm which its members found a little difficult to understand. To the overwrought nerves of the Italian people, who were suffering from the strain of a great catastrophe, these British youths, drawn from the four corners of the globe, were not merely doing their allotted military task. They were liberators come to help in freeing Italy from the heel of the invader.

Their new surroundings were in striking contrast to the level mud of Flanders which they had left a little over two weeks earlier. Instead of the long, level plain ending in the modest row of hills which stretched back from Mount Kemmel they now found their landing field dominated by the snow-capped ranges of the southeastern Alps, and in place of the substantial metal hangars and orderly rows of huts they now had canvas coverings for their machines and tents for living quarters.

As they rose from this aerodrome above the Piave River a wonderful scene presented itself. To the north lay endless piles of snow-capped mountains, in front of them the beautiful Venetian Plain and to the south-east, some 40 miles away, the blue waters of the Gulf of Venice.

Christmas 1917 was a red-letter day for Barker. There were strict orders at this time against unauthorized flights, as the shortage of machines and parts made causal flying with its resultant losses a serious handicap to the efficiency of the units. This fact had an important bearing on what followed. He was leaving the mess hut on Christmas morning with two young English lieutenants of the 28th Squadron when they saw an Austrian balloon hanging just under the clouds far back near the mountains. In the clear morning air the balloon looked attractive quarry and, either from the holiday spirit or mere desire for adventure, they decided to carry out an offensive of their own and remove the enemy balloon from the landscape before proceeding to see what else luck would bring in the way of a target.

The aerodrome was some distance away, so Barker got his car and drove over to their machines without the rest of the squadron knowing anything of their plans. They were soon in the air and on their way over the Austrian lines, taking advantage of the clouds to hide their approach from the balloon. Its destruction was only a matter of seconds. Diving out of the clouds Barker raked it from end to end with inflammable Buckingham bullets and it instantly burst into flames. This was his second balloon. Barker then rejoined his companions and they flew farther still into enemy territory with his machine in the lead.

Presently, Barker observed an enemy aerodrome in which there was considerable activity, but there were no machines on the landing field. This was a situation which he had frequently considered and had a plan ready for the occasion. He had decided that the ideal way to attack a hangar was to be low enough to fire through it and not down as this would give the inflammable bullets a larger target with more chance of setting the enemy machines on fire, but this was only possible if the landing field was clear.

Diving steeply toward the landing field he skimmed along, scarcely clear of the ground, and poured Buckingham bullets into the hangars. At the end of the field he rose into the wind and circled back to repeat the procedure. The other two machines which had followed him down imitated in turn what he had done, and then, almost before the amazed pilots and mechanics who had been working on their machines inside had time to real-ize what was happening, the three Camels were down at them again. The hangars took fire and were soon burning fiercely.

In the meantime, the Austrians had rushed to a trench dug along the side of the aerodrome as a shelter from bomb splinters. Barker now turned his attention to them and, flying the length of the trench, he sprayed it with a withering machine-gun fire. Again the other machines followed. Turning, they swept over the trench a second time and then flew home without meeting any enemy machines in the air. They had not, however, escaped without damage. A number of the Austrians had carried machine-guns and rifles to the trench and had maintained a heavy fire as the machines passed over, riddling their wings with bullets but fortunately hitting no vital part.

Their arrival at the 28th aerodrome was not observed by the other members of the squadron, who were busy celebrating Christmas at their huts some distance away. The three adventurers rejoined them without comment on what they had done as their expedition had been clearly contrary to orders, and now that

Barker in front of a damaged Sopwith Camel, Italy, 1918

it was over they were none too sure what the official attitude would be in spite of its success.

Christmas passed with as much evidence of the holiday spirit as possible and a cheerful dinner in the mess at night. The next morning, however, was far from peaceful. Shortly after daybreak the pilots of the 28th were awakened by the alarm signal, and as they rushed to their machines could hear heavy bombing to the south. As they rose into the air they could distinguish a large number of enemy machines bombing a neighbouring aerodrome. The Camels had a high climbing speed and were soon level with the enemy machines. Before long they were joined by some Italian scouts and, presently, by far the greatest aerial battle that had yet taken place in Italy was in progress. There were 22 Austrian machines in the first formation they encountered—all two-seaters. During the fight that followed—which resembled the massed aerial battles common on the Western Front during 1917 and 1918—12 of the enemy were destroyed by the British and Italians and fell behind the Italian lines. One of these fell under Barker's guns. The raid had been a costly failure to the enemy.

The survivors had scarcely crossed their lines when Barker sighted another formation of 10 machines approaching. Climbing up to them he discovered they were German Gothas, the first which had appeared since his squadron went to Italy. These were great twin-motored biplanes similar to those which bombed London and were very heavily armed, usually carrying at least two gunners in addition to the pilot. He knew that it would be foolhardy to dive into this formidable group of machines, as their massed fire power all directed at one target was almost certain to be fatal if it be closed in to the usual short range before firing. He therefore decided to change his tactics and, circling far ahead of them with his faster machine, waited until he was directly in front of the middle of the formation and on the same level, and then flew straight at them.

As they approached with terrific speed, he manoeuvred his Camel until he had three of the Gothas in direct line, then, taking careful aim, he opened fire at nearly 300 yards, hoping to damage one of the three machines in the line of his bullets. Meeting at the rate of over 100 yards a second, he only had time for a momentary burst of fire before he dived under the leading machine, but he could see that his tracers were finding their mark. As he flattened out from his dive, he saw that the second machine of the trio he had fired on was in trouble and had swung out of the formation. This was exactly what he hoped would happen and he now climbed rapidly above the disabled Gotha.

Diving like a flash before the other machines could come to its rescue, he poured lead into the great bomber which was fighting back vigorously from its two rear guns, and then, as he passed below it, zoomed up and finished his drums through the floor of the fuselage under the pilot's seat. Immediately it went into a steep nosedive and burst into flames, falling like a huge torch on the Italian side of the Piave. By this time more British and Italian machines had arrived and the remaining Gothas turned for home.

It was not long, however, before Barker was recommended for his third decoration. By the end of the first week of January he had destroyed two more enemy machines in flames bringing his total up to five in the two months he had been in Italy. Shortly afterward, he received word that he had been awarded the Distinguished Service Order.

During January, February and March, Barker continued his aggressive fighting, sometimes in the mountains and sometimes over the Venetian plains. By the middle of March, after many strenuous battles, he had destroyed four more machines and two more balloons. He also established a high reputation as an escort and inspired great confidence in the reconnaissance machines he accompanied because he would never be drawn away by some inviting target in spite of his recognized desire to meet the enemy. This was a weakness of many of the best fighters, as in their eagerness to fight they would dive after any enemy machine they saw and leave the slower machines unprotected.

His continued good work brought him his next decoration late in March, of which the following official citation appeared in September.

London *Gazette*, No. 30901,
16th September, 1918
War Office

His Majesty the KING has been graciously pleased to approve of the following Awards to the undermentioned Officers and Warrant Officers in recognition of their gallantry and devotion to duty in the field:

AWARDED A SECOND BAR TO THE MILITARY CROSS

Captain William George Barker
D.S.O., M.C., Gen. List and R.F.C.

For conspicuous gallantry and devotion to duty. When leading patrols he on one occasion attacked eight hostile machines, himself shooting down two, and on another occasion seven, one of which he shot down. In two months he himself destroyed four enemy machines and drove down one, and burned two balloons.

This was equivalent to a third award of the Military Cross and was his fourth decoration.

Early in April he carried out a particularly daring daylight raid on the Austrian Army Headquarters at San Vito. His squadron had excellent photographs of San Vito, and through prisoners he learned the exact location of the buildings occupied by the Headquarters staff. They were a conspicuous group in the centre of the town easily located from the air.

As there were several enemy aerodromes nearby, he decided that he would not be able to carry out his plans if he flew straight over the line to San Vito, which was some 40 miles up the Venetian Plain, as the Austrian scouts would be warned of their approach. Leading his patrol of six machines to the coast behind the Italian lines he flew out to sea just north of Venice, up the coast until he was opposite San Vito, and then straight inland until they reached the town. By their circuitous approach they had escaped detection, and the first warning the Austrian Headquarters had of their arrival was the concentrated roar of six engines as the British machines swept down toward their buildings. They were certainly not prepared for what followed.

Descending to the level of the windows, which were just above the surrounding buildings, Barker and the others after him fired through the windows of the Headquarters buildings. This they repeated several times; then one by one they circled overhead and dropped their four bombs. By this time several Austrians were in the air and Barker led his flight straight home across the Piave. They were continually attacked and fought intermittently a great part of the way but reached their aerodrome without losing a machine. The damage inflicted was considerable but the moral effect was a great deal worse. That British machines could come 40 miles behind the lines and fire in the very windows of their building was not a comforting thought to Army Headquarters.

On another occasion, while flying alone he observed several scouts diving to attack a flight of French Salmsons returning from a reconnaissance up the Brenta Valley. Without a moment's hesitation he shoved the nose of his machine down and dived after them. Just as the Austrians arrived above the French machines and were preparing to open fire from their commanding position, they were startled by the staccato roar announcing Barker's simultaneous arrival. In their anxiety to get above the French they had not observed his wild dive, and his opening burst of fire had been a dead shot at less than 100 yards. The enemy machine which he had singled out fell in flames after his first fusillade. As he zoomed up and dived again, the enemy lost heart and flew away, leaving the French machines to proceed safely home.

This incident, added to the good work he had already done with the French, won him his next decoration, the Croix de Guerre.

As the spring advanced, the reconnaissance patrols reported increasing activity on the part of the Austrians, and several railroad spurs which were being pushed toward the front indicated preparation for another great attack. It became increasingly important, therefore, to obtain information of the enemy's movements. In France the spy system was highly organized on both sides, one of the methods adopted being to drop the spies from airplanes behind the enemy's lines. This had not, however, been attempted on the Italian front.

The adjutant of Barker's squadron was Capt. Wedgwood Benn, recently appointed Secretary for India in Ramsay MacDonald's second Labour Cabinet. Barker and he decided that there was no reason why spies could not be dropped from airplanes in

Italy and offered their services in the enterprise. Their plan was submitted to Italian General Headquarters by the 14th Wing Commander and was approved. They were then instructed to go to Verona and choose a machine suitable for the work. Barker, who was to do the flying, chose an S.V.4 built by Caproni. This was a large twin-engined biplane with a boatlike body which protruded well in front of the wings, giving the observer a wide field of vision. After a short test flight which convinced Barker of the steadiness of the machine, he and Benn flew it from Verona to the squadron aerodrome.

Busy days followed preparing the bomber for its task. The most important change was to make the necessary provision for carrying and dropping the spy. A circular compartment with a trap door which could be opened by a lever in the pilot's seat was constructed. The spy was to sit in this compartment with his parachute folded below him and then, as the machine reached the proper place over the spot where it was intended that he should land, the pilot would pull the lever and drop the spy through the trap door.

A volunteer had been obtained for the hazardous undertaking. He was an Italian whose home was in that part of Italy then occupied by the Austrians. His wife and mother still lived there, and the plan was that he should land in the darkness near his home, hide with them, and then through them and their neighbours obtain information of the Austrian movements which would be sent back across the line by carrier pigeons which he would take with him when he dropped from the plane.

Once the machine was ready, their next step was to rehearse the whole programme carefully beforehand, as the success of the adventure depended wholly on accuracy of judgment in dropping the human projectile so that he would land close beside his own home. Any error in calculation and he would probably fall among Austrian soldiers; which meant the absolute certainty of his being shot.

The most important thing at the outset was to locate the exact spot where the spy was to land. After Barker and Benn had flown over the area several times in daylight and become thoroughly acquainted with the country surrounding the house, their next step was to make the trip at night and pick up some distinguishing features which could be recognized with accuracy in the darkness. As a single airplane flying low at night with no apparent objective might arouse suspicion, they decided to carry a load of bombs and give the flight the appearance of an ordinary night raid by bombing some town or supply centre after a careful survey of the area had been made.

Capt. Benn devised an elaborate method of signals with the different British aerodromes. Upon calling any of the squadrons by wireless, the aerodromes were to show a certain number of searchlight beams, thus indicating clearly to those in the air the exact location of each aerodrome. In this way the two airmen expected to be able to pick up their position if they should become lost while flying low over the enemy country.

Waiting for a favourable night when there was practically no wind to carry the parachute out of its course, they took the spy on board and prepared for the flight. His rôle called for the greatest courage, not only after he landed but during the flight. He sat in a smooth cylindrical compartment from which he could not observe the country over which he was passing, and his seat was part of a trap door which would drop him into the darkness without warning when the pilot and observer decided they had reached the correct place. This was necessary, as his descent must be timed almost to the fraction of a second, having regard to the direction of the wind, the speed of the airplane and the length of the drop.

The spy was dressed as an Italian soldier, but carried on his back a sack containing a peasant's costume such as he wore in the fields at home. He also had an ordinary entrenching spade to dig a hiding-place for his clothes, and, most important of all, a cage of carrier pigeons with which to send his messages to Italian head-quarters. The parachute was folded below his seat and the para-chute straps in place, so that it would open automatically as he fell from the machine.

The reason for his going over in uniform was that if he landed near Austrian troops and was unable to get away, he had some chance for his life if he was in uniform and could get rid of the peasant's costume, as he would be an ordinary military prisoner; whereas if he came down in a peasant's costume, he was marked as a spy and would be shot without question.

The trio crossed the Piave on a clear moonless night, and Barker flew without difficulty to their destination and hovered low over the farm he now knew well. When he and Benn were perfectly satisfied of their position, the trap was drawn and they could see the parachute open and the spy fall slowly toward the ground. They then continued at the same level, bombed an Austrian supply centre nearby and returned without incident, picking up the four searchlights of their own aerodrome without any difficulty.

They now waited with excitement for news of their adventur-ous passenger. In a few days they were elated to hear that the first pigeon had arrived at headquarters with valuable information. The spy had landed in a field adjoining his home, had changed his clothes without interruption, dug a hole and buried his uni-form and the parachute, and within a comparatively few minutes after he dropped from the machine, entered his own house to the utter astonishment of his family, dressed as any other Italian farmer of the district. There he remained in hiding for some days until the troops in the neighbourhood had changed, but in the meantime he was able to pick up much information from his family owing to the boastful conversation of the Austrian soldiers about the impending offensive. As soon as he had any information of value, he dispatched one of his pigeons with a message which was the first knowledge the airmen had of his fate. He soon used all the pigeons he had carried with him, and twice Barker and Benn carried fresh cages which were dropped with a small parachute in the same place as the spy had landed, he being warned of their approach by the sound of the engine.

The enterprise had been a complete success; the information gained, particularly as to the movement of troops, was extremely valuable, and very shortly afterward Barker received word that the King of Italy had conferred on him the silver medal for valour for his gallant services on the Italian Front. This is the highest honour awarded by Italy to any but her own soldiers.

That summer, during the great Austrian offensive, Barker had two very narrow escapes from death. After a long fight in the Brenta Valley, during which his machine was hit several times, he made a forced landing in Lake Garda and was rescued by a rowboat. Only a few days later he found it necessary to make a forced landing in the Alp foothills because of engine trouble and his Camel turned a complete somersault on landing; but in neither case was he even scratched.

During this period he was adding steadily to his list of victories but it is impossible to describe each of these in detail. On June 15, 1918, the Austrians launched their great attack after the most elaborate preparations. But this time the Italians were prepared from the information given by airplanes, prisoners and spies, and after limited local successes the attack was thrown back, except on the Montello. The British on the Asiago and the French on Mount Grappa had thrown the Austrians back of their original lines with heavy losses, and farther to the south the Italians had done equally well, but at Montello, which was the most critical point in the whole line, things were going badly.

Early in the day the Austrians succeeded in pushing several pontoon bridges across the Piave, and just before noon on the 15th, Barker, patrolling alone over the river, was amazed to see thousands of Austrian troops on the south shore and the bridges loaded with a steady stream of men and transports. No word had gone to the air forces of what had happened and this was the very place where they were needed. He immediately flew back and dropped messages stating what he had seen to several aerodromes along the line before rejoining his own squadron. They were soon in the air, loaded with bombs and machine-gun ammunition.

When they arrived, a number of the Italian squadrons which had received Barker's message were already there and were furiously bombing the bridges and the troops who had crossed. Austrian machines had arrived to protect their troops and soon a great aerial mêlée was in progress with nearly every available machine on both sides involved.

Barker led his squadron down over the river, where they raked the pontoons with machine-gun fire and then dropped their bombs among the infantry and mounted troops. As soon as their supplies were exhausted, they returned for more. This was continued almost without interruption for the next 24 hours. From 4:00 p.m. on June 15 to 4:00 p.m. on June 16, the British squadrons dropped 10,000 pounds of bombs and fired 31,000 rounds of machine-gun ammunition at troops on the roads and bridges. The damage they did was appalling. Sweeping in massed formation over batteries waiting along the wooded roads for their turn to cross the bridges, they would sometimes almost wipe them out with machine-gun fire and bombs. They broke the bridges with their bombs and then returned to shoot down the engineers who attempted to repair them.

A few days later, the Austrians were forced to withdraw their troops, as they found that it was utterly impossible to maintain their bridges. Once more the Piave was in flood and the Montello was saved. While the rising waters had much to do with the ultimate withdrawal, there is little doubt that the Italian line would have been broken before the rains began if the airmen had not so effectively interrupted the movement of troops and supplies across the bridges. If the Austrians had retained their air supremacy or had remained on anything approaching even terms, the battle of the Piave would have been a very different story.

For his services before and during the Piave fighting Barker received a second silver medal for valour, bearing the proud inscription "Protector of the Air." This medal was pinned on his breast shortly afterward by the King of Italy.

The last two weeks of June, 1918, were busy days for the British squadrons in Italy. The great Austrian attack, which commenced on June 15, was pressed with unremitting vigour against the Montello Plateau until the end of the month, and Barker and his companions were in the air during most of the daylight hours, bombing aerodromes, sweeping down to attack troops on the ground, and fighting Austrian machines wherever they met.

The work of the one flight of new Bristol Fighters attached to the 66th scout squadron, which Barker now commanded, had been so good that for some time the desirability of having a complete squadron of this type had been apparent. The request for a new squadron was granted and on July 14 the new Bristols arrived and the 139th Squadron was organized, with Barker in command. He was promoted to the rank of major on the same day. A most unusual concession was made to Barker in his new squadron. He preferred the single-seater Sopwith Camel and asked to be permitted to lead the Bristols in his old machine. Doubtless due to the fact that he stood head and shoulders above any other British, French or Italian pilot in Italy at the time, his request was granted. He sometimes flew a Bristol on reconnaissance patrol but most of the time led the squadron in his Camel.

The 139th was a real Imperial unit. Barker the Squadron Commander was a Canadian and the three Flight Commanders came from Australia, New Zealand and South Africa. It did not take them long to get into action. On July 15 an offensive patrol of three machines met eight of the enemy over Mattarello and destroyed two of them. Then on July 18 Barker and one of his Bristol two-seaters, in co-operation with a patrol from his old squadron the 66th, made what might be called a perfect score on five of the enemy.

Further fighting on July 29 brought Barker's total of confirmed victories up to 33 enemy machines and nine balloons, and he was awarded a Bar to the Distinguished Service Order.

Barker now had the Distinguished Service Order and Bar, the Military Cross and Two Bars, the French Croix de Guerre and the Italian Silver Medal for Valour, twice awarded, a total of eight awards for bravery.

Toward the end of July, Barker began to fly his Bristol a little more, for a reason that throws an interesting light on the character of another very gallant soldier. The Prince of Wales was attached to the staff of the British Headquarters in Italy during the summer, and took the keenest interest in the activities of the British airmen, but particularly in Barker's outstanding work. It was not long before he arranged a flight over the British lines in the observer's seat of Barker's Bristol, and from then on he was a frequent visitor to the 139th Squadron. During the war the Prince displayed always the keenest anxiety to see conditions as they really were, and he was anxious to see something of the disposition of the enemy forces behind the Piave.

Unknown to Headquarters he arranged with Barker for the flight and they crossed the enemy's lines alone, flying back to Vittoria, which was an important centre of Austrian activity about 20 miles from the front in the foothills of the Dolomites. On their way back they were subjected to heavy anti-aircraft fire, but met no enemy machines. It was not long before the staff learned of the flight, largely through the intimate knowledge of the enemy back country which the Prince displayed in discussions of campaign plans. So further flights of a similar nature were stopped, but the Prince had proved, as he so often did before and afterward, that he was a soldier of rare courage and anxious to know everything possible about the front on which he was located.

On Aug. 8, the day on which the great British offensive opened in France with the Canadian Corps as the spearhead of the attack, Barker carried out a particularly daring daylight bombing raid on the aerodrome at Pergine, about 30 miles up the Brenta Valley. As the four Bristol Fighters of the patrol approached Pergine, they were surprised to see a number of Austrian machines rise to meet them, for they had become accustomed recently to seeing the Austrians immediately drive for their aerodromes. The enemy was in a fighting mood, however, and they soon met. After a short fight two of the enemy went down in flames almost into their own aerodrome and the rest flew away, while Barker and his companions dropped their bombs before turning for home without any casualties.

A few weeks later, they learned from an enemy airman who had been taken prisoner that their fight had been most unfortunate from an Austrian point of view, as they had arrived while the Emperor Carl, together with the Archduke Joseph and General Arz, were inspecting the Pergine Aerodrome. The fighting spirit shown by the Austrian airmen was meant to impress the Emperor but the results had been most disastrous, as he had seen a perfect demonstration of what usually happened when the British and Austrians met.

Barker continued to pile up one dramatic exploit after another until he finally left Italy early in September 1918, having received orders to take command of an instructional school for fighting pilots at Hounslow. On arrival in England he surprised the Air Ministry by asking to be permitted to go to France for a few weeks before taking over his new command. He contended that he should have an opportunity of meeting the new German machines, which were a great advance on the Austrian, and of learning the latest aerial tactics on the Western Front before being properly equipped to instruct pilots who would be fighting in France. After considerable argument his request was granted and he started fighting again after little more than two weeks' rest.

He was given one of the new Sopwith Snipes, which was a combination of the best features of the Sopwith Camel and Sopwith Dolphin. They were tremendously fast and had a "ceiling" of about 24,000 feet. Only a very few of these machines reached the front before the Armistice.

Before the arrival of the Snipe, the Germans had been able for some weeks to cruise about in their latest airplanes well above the highest point which any of the British machines could reach.

When Barker reached the front with one of the first Snipes, he found himself in the fortunate position of having a machine that could climb above the highest Germans and frequently take them by surprise, as most of them were not yet expecting to meet any British machines above 20,000 feet. He had a few very successful weeks during the rapid Allied advances of October, 1918. Once more he saw the tide of battle sweep across the Somme plains over which he had flown for nearly two years, and then out beyond into country which none but the most optimistic had imagined they would ever see.

When he received orders that he must report at Hounslow to take over the squadron to which he had been appointed on Oct. 27, he had raised his total of official victories to 46, and the only living British aviators with a higher record were Bishop, Collishaw and MacLaren, all of whom were Canadians. Barker prepared to leave the front, however, with considerable regret. He knew that the command of an instructional squadron meant the end of his active service, and in spite of the fact that he had probably flown longer at the front than any pilot then alive, he had no desire for the comparative safety of instructional work. No one as yet dreamed that peace was only two weeks away.

The morning of Oct. 27 dawned clear and bright. Having packed all his equipment, which was to be sent by rail and boat to England, he said goodbye to his friends of the squadron to which he had been attached, climbed into his Snipe which had become well-known at the front in the past few weeks, and started for Hounslow. But fate had decided that he was not to reach his destination. As he rose rapidly into the clear morning air he saw a large white German two-seater soaring over the British lines in fancied security far above the height at which it expected to meet any British scouts.

Barker was now on his way home, had said farewell to the war and had every reason to be satisfied with his record at the front; but here was an enemy who could only be reached by a machine like his own, and without a moment's hesitation he decided to attack. He climbed to a height of 22,000 feet and engaged the enemy over the Mormal Forest. As they manoeuvred for position at tremendous speed Barker found that the German pilot was exceptionally good and handled his machine so well that it was impossible to get close without running directly into the fire of the enemy observer, who was shooting with deadly accuracy and had hit the Snipe several times.

Once again Barker trusted to his shooting skill. He had removed the standard aviation sight on his guns and had replaced it with an ordinary peep sight. Circling at the same height until he was several hundred yards away, he turned again toward the enemy machine and took careful aim at the observer. At about 200 yards he pulled the trigger and the German observer collapsed in his seat. Barker now closed in and a short burst from his deadly guns shot away some vital part of the two-seater and it broke up in the air.

He had been so intent on the battle with his skilful opponent that for perhaps the first time in all his fighting experience he was taken completely by surprise. During the fight, a Fokker biplane had climbed above him, and he only became aware of its presence when his right thigh was shattered by an explosive bullet just as his first enemy went down. Although his right leg was now useless he immediately turned on the Fokker, and after a short flight in which both machines lost considerable height, his unerring eye found the enemy under his guns for the vital fraction of a second and a stream of well-directed bullets sent it down in flames.

He now found himself in the middle of a complete German "circus" of nearly 60 Fokkers, according to the estimate of observers on the ground who saw the whole course of the amazing battle. They attacked from every direction and thousands of bullets streamed at him from all sides. His machine was riddled and once again he was severely wounded, this time in the left thigh. He continued the apparently hopeless fight, however, and drove two of the enemy machines down in a spin, but whether or not they crashed the spectators on the ground did not see.

He then fainted from loss of blood and his machine fell completely out of control for several thousand feet with the engine wide open, and it seemed to those on the ground that his plucky fight had come to an end; but the rush of air revived him and he succeeded in regaining control of his machine, only to find that he was still being attacked by the Fokkers. It evidently seemed to him that he had no chance of surviving, and so, turning on one of the enemy in front of him, he deliberately charged it with the obvious intention of crashing it with his own machine; but he was still firing, and just as it seemed that the two machines would crash, his bullets found their mark and the German went down in flames.

During this last fight his left elbow was shot away by an explosive bullet and he again fainted, his machine circling at full speed, completely out of control. Just when it seemed that nothing could save him he regained consciousness and again commenced to fight. Although both legs and his left arm were now practically useless, he succeeded in controlling his machine and dived on the tail of the nearest German, shooting it down in flames.

He then attempted to dive for the British lines but was intercepted by another formation of German machines. He fought these new machines as few able-bodied pilots could have done, and although he could now scarcely sit up from weakness he broke up their formation. He turned again toward the British lines just as one of the German machines shot his gasoline tank completely away from under his seat. It was only by the rarest chance that his machine did not take fire. Just as he was losing consciousness again, he mustered sufficient strength to turn on a small auxiliary tank which carried enough gasoline for a few minutes' flight.

By now he had practically no control of the machine, and there was no possibility of reducing its speed for a landing. He came down just behind the British lines at terrific speed and the machine turned completely over as it crashed. Some Highlanders who were the first to reach the wreck were amazed to find him still alive. The only additional injury he had received on landing was a broken nose.

He did not regain consciousness for some days and his life hung in the balance for many more, but his rugged constitution pulled him through and he was moved back to No. 8 General Hospital at Rouen.

The story of this great fight, which has no parallel in the official records of any of the armies in the war, brought letters and messages from all parts of the battlefront as well as from England and Canada such as few of any rank were fortunate enough to receive.

Toward the end of November he received word that he had been awarded the Victoria Cross. For once the official statement lost a little of its cold formality and the following announcement of the award was published on Nov. 30th:

London Gazette No. 31042

30th November, 1918

His Majesty the KING has been graciously pleased to confer the Victoria Cross on the undermentioned Officer of the Royal Air Force, in recognition of bravery of the highest possible order:

Major William George Barker, D.S.O., M.C.

No. 201 Sqn., R. A. Force

On the morning of the 27th October, 1918, this officer observed an enemy two-seater over the Forest de Mormal. He attacked this machine and after a short burst it broke up in the air. At the same time a Fokker biplane attacked him and he was wounded in the right thigh, but managed, despite this, to shoot down the enemy aeroplane in flames.

He then found himself in the middle of a large formation of Fokkers, who attacked him from all directions, and was again severely wounded in the left thigh, but succeeded in driving down two of the enemy in a spin.

He lost consciousness after this, and his machine fell out of control. On recovering he found himself being again attacked heavily by a large formation, and singling out one machine, he deliberately charged and drove it down in flames.

During this fight his left elbow was shattered and he again fainted, and on regaining consciousness he found himself still being attacked, but, notwithstanding that he was now severely wounded in both legs and his left arm shattered, he dived on the nearest machine and shot it down in flames.

Being greatly exhausted, he dived out of the fight to regain our lines, but was met by another formation, which attacked and endeavored to cut him off, but after a hard fight, he succeeded in breaking up this formation and reached our lines, where he crashed on landing.

This combat, in which Major Barker destroyed four enemy machines (three of them in flames), brought his total successes up to 50 enemy machines destroyed, and in a notable example of the exceptional bravery and disregard of danger which this very gallant officer has always displayed throughout his distinguished career.

The hopes expressed in the letters and messages were speedily realized and, in January, 1919, Barker was able to be moved to England, where he completed his convalescence.

Shortly after arriving in England, his meteoric war career was rounded out by promotion to the rank of lieutenant-colonel. Later in the year, Barker returned to this country and with Bishop organized one of the first commercial aviation companies in Canada. The venture did not prove profitable, however, and in 1920 he rejoined the Royal Canadian Air Ministry. While on duty in England he went on a particularly interesting expedition and flew for months over Iraq and Palestine, choosing flying routes for the Royal Air Force in the East.

In 1924 he returned to Canada, resigned his commission and has since then been engaged in the tobacco-growing industry near Simcoe.

Barker's record of 50 machines and nine balloons places him third among Canadians and fourth in the whole Royal Air Force, but above the mere numbers of official victories stands the even more amazing record of nearly three years' continuous flying on active service. Combined with almost unexampled courage were patience and devotion to the task in hand, which marked this young Canadian as one of the greatest airmen in the war. There was reason for the Latin enthusiasm which inscribed on his second Italian Cross of Valour, "Protector of the Air."

William Barker's legs never fully healed, and he spent the rest of his life somewhat disabled and in pain. After the war, Barker hooked up with fellow V.C. winner Billy Bishop to run a charter air company that soon went bankrupt. Toronto's Canadian National Exhibition once hired the duo for a stunt performance that caused a stampede when they buzzed the stands. Legend has it that a woman miscarried as a result and the two aces had to forgo their fees to pay the damages.

In 1930, Barker, then 35 and suffering from depression, died in a plane crash while testing a new Fairchild aircraft. Since he was such an experienced pilot and the plane had been problem-free, there was speculation that Barker killed himself, although eyewiteness pilots blamed the crash on an over-confident flyer at the controls of an underpowered aircraft. His funeral procession in Toronto attracted 50,000 people.

*The unveiling of Canada's Vimy Ridge memorial
by King Edward VIII, July 26, 1936*

What Price Vimy?

WILL R. BIRD
April 1, 1936

Ask the wizened, grey-headed old man who lives in a cottage near Watling Crater, guarding the relics of battle that lie where they were left in '17. He will peer at you and shrug his thin shoulders; then he will point to the Vimy Memorial, to the Beacon of Light on Notre Dame de Lorette at the white-stoned cemeteries. "No one will ever know what Vimy cost," he will tell you, "but this I can say: 'It was too much.'"

Can you imagine yourself being told that this is your last day of life, while around you stand men with rifles, and a stern voice tells you you will be shot at six o'clock? That old man at Vimy who peers at you with war-weary eyes had such an experience three times.

When the Germans came, his master, the owner of the immense estate known as La Folle Farm, was in Arras. The German officer in charge of the advance patrol seized this chap, who was head gardener, and demanded the proprietor. He was told, quite truly, that the gardener did not know where his master had gone. Seething with rage, the German had the man's arms bound, had him thrust against a wall, gave him one hour to prepare for death.

The man stood there, watching the grim soldiers who waited, their rifles ready. He was too frightened to speak. Another German officer arrived, asked questions, had the man loosed. Suddenly he altered his decision, had him retied, and said he should be shot two hours later.

Again the gardener went through an agony of apprehension. There seemed no hope, and the soldiers muttered about him, wishing that the first sentence had been carried out. A third officer arrived and asked questions. The man was again released from his bonds and questioned. His ignorance about his master's absence enraged the newcomer as it had the others, however, and for the third time the Frenchman was sentenced to die within two hours.

This time he had no hope at all, and tried feebly to repeat his prayers. An hour passed. Another half hour. The firing party was assembled, and he was being led to a post to which he was to be tied, when his master arrived. The Germans listened to the proprietor as he told them that his gardener was absolutely truthful in what he said, and he talked with such eloquence that the man was released. But his hair had gone white in the eight hours!

Then he was taken back as a prisoner, and for four and a half years his existence was a hell on earth. What price Vimy? He can tell you plenty.

The proprietor of La Folle Farm was a wealthy man and he had buried 100,000 francs in his garden before going to Arras. After the war, he returned to the ghastly waste and wreckage that had been his estate, and dug patiently to find his money. It was gone. Some soldier, probably by accident, in a hasty digging of a trench or through a shell upheaval, found the treasure— what a find!

What price Vimy?

Vimy Ridge, says a French historian, is the famous hill that runs in a S.S.W. direction between Lens and Arras, and is crossed by the main road connecting the two cities. It rises to a height of 475 feet above sea level, sloping gently into the Scarpe Valley near Arras, but falling sharply on the eastern side to the Douai plain. It is nine miles in length, and dominates the entire area, forming a natural rampart in the richest coal fields of France. The Ridge was one of the most important strategic positions on the Western Front.

In early 1916, Gen. Joffre, who commanded the French armies on the Western Front, wrote:

"In the last days of April, the French 10th Army, acting in concert with the British 1st Army, will undertake an important attack north of Arras with a view to piercing the enemy's line. In order to carry out this attack the 10th Army will be strongly reinforced."

The British Official History of the war states:

"In front of the centre of the French line, between Notre Dame de Lorette and Roclincourt, and at an average distance of 5,000 yards from it, lay Vimy Ridge, which forms the eastern edge of the plateau. Here the ground falls to the plain of Douai even more abruptly than it does from Notre Dame de Lorette, on the northern side, to the plain of Flanders. The main attack of the French Army was to be delivered on a frontage of four miles, with the crest of Vimy Ridge, between Farbus and Souchez, as its objective. The occupation of the Ridge was to be the first step in breaking the German line, and preparatory to an advance into the plain to the line Cambrai-Douai."

The attack was postponed on account of misty weather until May 9. The French attack in the centre was brilliant. The Moroccan Division, flinging away all heavy equipment, depending largely on the bayonet, advanced between La Targette and Carency, 2 1/2 miles in less than three hours. No other attack ever made at Vimy was so fierce, so overwhelming. But when they had reached Hill 140 and sent patrols into La Folle Wood, the French reserves to take care of such an opportunity were 7 1/2 miles away.

Four German divisions had been holding Vimy. By night they had two more. By May 15 they had 13 divisions in the Vimy sector.

The Moroccans, minus support, were driven from the Ridge after three days' occupation. You can see their Memorial today, at Hill 140. On May 15, the French attacked again, at Neuville St. Vaast, the Labyrinthe and Souchez. They made but small house-to-house gains. They attacked again June 7, and secured both the Labyrinthe and Neuville St. Vaast. On June 16 they made a final effort, but were repulsed.

French losses for this battle for Vimy Ridge from May 9 to June 16 were 35,008 killed; 65,062 wounded; 2,463 missing; a total of 102,533. The Germans published their losses as 49,466 of all ranks, but have admitted the loss of all records of those who died of wounds. The French captured 7,441 prisoners.

This was the result of the first attack.

What price Vimy?

On Sept. 25, the French attacked again, and made very slight gains. This was to be a grand attack, and the British attack at Loos was to divert the German attention and make more sure of the anticipated grand French success. Instead, the French reserves were this time brought too near the front and suffered terrible losses from early shell fire, while the constant delays in their assaulting gave the German forces ample time for preparations in defence. Gen. Joffre, after being advised of the losses, gave Foch the following instructions: "Stop the attacks of the 10th Army, taking care to avoid giving the British the impression that we are leaving them to attack alone, or the Germans that our attack is slackening off. Economize ammunition."

French attacks had begun at noon and accomplished little. During the night of the 27th-28th, the French 33rd, with part of the 3rd Corps, advanced 2,000 yards and captured La Folle Wood, and Foch was granted permission to carry on. At 3:00 p.m. on the 28th, the 6th Division, of the 3rd Corps, gained Hill 140, which had been the German third line of defence.

They could not, however, retain what they had gained, as the flanks had not kept up with the central attack. By Oct. 15, they were back to the original German front line and held there. Their losses, to that date, were 48,230. The Germans had lost during that period a total of 30,024 in all ranks.

What price Vimy?

The British took over in March, 1916. On Feb. 8, the Germans had made their first attack on Vimy and had driven the French from half a mile of trench systems. On Feb. 21 they attacked again and captured the "Pimple."

The British found that the entire front line was being mined.

Ten British and five French tunnelling companies worked desperately in countermining. On April 26, 1916, the first mine on Vimy went up, forming the first crater. On May 3, Momber, Love and Kennedy Craters were blown. Broadmarsh had been blown April 29. On May 15, at 8:30 p.m., five craters were fired, known afterward as the "Crosbie Group." Fourteen officers and 93 other ranks were lost during the consolidating of these craters, all being members of the Pioneers. In five weeks of holding the line, the 25th British Division had 1,274 casualties.

At 7:45 p.m., on May 21, the Germans made their third attack on Vimy and carried the 25th British Division halfway down the Ridge. The Germans had 80 batteries firing on a frontage of 1,800 yards with "200 shells per hour per battery." Three German divisions had attacked the frontage of one British brigade.

The British tried to counter-attack, but all their reserves had been taken to the Somme and they were not recalled. They had lost, in two days, 2,475 in all ranks. In the two days, the Germans admitted losses of 1,344. The net result of this German attack was that they occupied a portion of what had been the old French front line.

In October, the Canadians came to Vimy. They carried on extensive raiding throughout the winter. On April 9, they attacked and captured the Ridge. Various figures have been given regarding their losses. It is generally admitted that 75,000 Canadians opposed 140,000 Germans. Canadian Medical Service records state that 5,976 wounded Canadians were handled in the first 22 hours. Seven hundred and six German wounded were treated.

The complete Vimy fighting extended from April 9 to June 6.

During that period the Canadians lost 912 officers, 20,461 other ranks.

In the 38 days of fighting known as the Arras battles, 20,834 prisoners and 252 guns were taken. Sixty-one square miles of territory were captured. The total British casualties were 146,586 all ranks. The German casualties were 132,000 all ranks.

Casualties of British airmen were highest in April, 1917. They were higher than that of any other month during the war, with 316 killed or missing. Yet only 29,500 hours were flown. The average was 92 hours per casualty, which is the lowest average made during the war. There were 3,151 planes engaged in France for the four weeks previous to April 27.

From April 9 to May 16, 4,261,500 rounds of ammunition were fired, or 109,800 tons.

"The Canadian casualties at Vimy," stated a newspaper report, "were very light."

Read extracts from battalion records:

"Every officer save one in the 10th Battalion was killed or wounded."

"Eight officers of the 16th were killed, 13 wounded."

"The 87th Battalion lost 60 per cent of its men in a short time."

"Every officer of the 102nd Battalion was killed or wounded, and command of the unit fell on a company sergeant-major."

"How desperately the 73rd Battalion fought can be judged from the casualties. Every officer in 'A' Company was killed or wounded; only 14 other ranks were unharmed. One officer and 12 other ranks were left in 'B' Company; 15 other ranks survived in 'C' Company; 18 other ranks in 'D' Company."

The entire 4th Division suffered very heavily.

What price Vimy?

No one will ever know. Visit the German cemetery at La Targette. There are 41,000 graves in that one alone, and they are still finding plenty of German dead.

Go over to Notre Dame de Lorette and see the French National Memorial. It has four features; the Cemetery, the Beacon, the Ossuary, and the Basilica. In the Cemetery, there are the graves of more than 18,000 identified dead; 12,077 were given to relatives for burial in home cemeteries. There are more than 16,000 unknown dead.

The Ossuary is formed of four-storied groups of oak coffins tinted in ivory, over 25 vaults. Under there is a room 10 metres square containing the remains of nearly 40,000 unknown warriors. The French themselves do not know how many of their men died at Vimy. One grim sentence in their war diary is enough. "Each night, at Souchez and at Carency, the death carts were heaped full."

The British cannot tell you how many of their men actually died at Vimy. But go into the cemeteries around the Ridge and you will find 17,291 British graves—men of the United Kingdom only—without visiting the smaller burial grounds.

As for Canadians, just around Vimy: 666 Canadians buried at Aubigny; 828 at Ecoivres; 347 at Ligny-St. Flochel; 1,009 at Villers Station; 721 at Cabaret Rouge; 492 at Bully Grenay, and 171 in the Communal Cemetery as well; 163 at Ablain-St. Nazaire; 677 at Barlin; 226 at Nouex-les-Mines, and 71 at the Communal Cemetery there; 77 at Estree Cauchy; 276 at Bruay; 306 at Etrun; 296 at La Targette; 93 at Zouave Valley; 446 at Bucquoy. This list does not include the smaller cemeteries, or the one on the Ridge.

Canada's Vimy Memorial, by far the most beautiful thing of its kind in all Europe, will cost about $1,250,000. That would not be enough to pay for more than half a day's shelling at Vimy.

Will Bird spent most of the war in the trenches. Afterwards, he returned to Southhampton, N.S., near where he was born, and ran a general store, and then worked for the post office, while developing a writing career. Maclean's commissioned him in 1931 to return to the battlefields of France to write a series called "Thirteen Years After." Bird died in Halifax at 93 in 1984.

German soldiers captured with gas masks, 1915

Unheeded Warning

KIM BEATTIE
May 1, 1936

It was 4:45 on a blue April afternoon. Behind flimsy front-line parapets weary Canadians groused in monotony, and cursed the indolent *poilu* who had left his dead gruesomely protruding from the redoubt walls.

In calm and orderly Canadian Division Headquarters in the Chateau des Trois Tours, just off the Brielen Road, a heel-clicking signaller handed a message to "Q"—"Have you got any playing cards and mouth organs?" The St. Julien garrison was bored.

Time ticked on.

Beyond the French-held section of the line, grey-clad engineers in gargoyle masks tested valves of strange iron tubes. Big-booted infantrymen exulted, "They will be helpless."

Time struck!

A hurricane of shells from the 183 German guns ringing the Ypres Salient hurled down in screaming concert. They obliterated the strong points, pummelled the roads, lingered on the crossings, smashed into dozing St. Julien, Wieltje, Langemarck, Keersalaere and Boesinghe, and heralded a historic madhouse.

From the German front line at the break of the wild *strafe*, a strange green-yellow vapour began to rise and float and spread. It crept slowly forward on a lazy wind, bellied and ground-clung, rolling relentlessly. It sagged into the gullies, monstrously mounted the earthworks of Algerian and Trailleur, heaved over and blotted them out.

On their right, the only Canadian Division yet in France—the 1st—saw the creeping fog of death, and watched the French black troops break. Those on high ground could see them fleeing in awed panic from this uncanny agony that clutched suddenly at their throats until they dropped and choked and died. Survivors reeled back, babbling and gasping, pleading in pitiful gutturals for the aid posts that could not aid them.

They cluttered the Canadian support positions, stumbled back to the Yser Canal and were drowned, or swarmed into the old Flemish walled city to transform spreading terror into mad panic. As twilight dropped over the dead-dotted fields, order slowly began to come out of chaos. In their terror-stricken wake, the French colonials had left a 4,000-yard gap, through which Duke Albrecht of Wurtemburg meant to cut off the Ypres Salient and march his troops to Calais. Only the untried Canadians with a gaping flank stood fast to thwart him.

So broke the Second Battle of Ypres that heads Canada's glorious Cavalcade of Courage in the Great War. It sent her name ringing around the world and startled the nations with the word of poison gas in battle; that Germany had added the concoctions of the chemist's stink-pots to the guns of Krupp.

Thus were the Canadians blooded. Here in the stricken, chlorine-soaked lowlands about St. Julien, the citizen soldiery who had been called "an undisciplined mob"—even by their own newspaper correspondents—laid the foundations of courage and determination upon which the great Canadian Corps was built.

That the raw but gallant Canadians were badly handled by other than their own and left to hold on, and fight on, while the French dawdled and British bickered with them, has long been known to students of military history and to many veterans. Many historians have deplored that mishandling.

But that the British and French leaders knew the gas attack was coming for days before catastrophe cracked down and still took no action will be startling news to the bulk of the survivors, even at this late day—the 21st anniversary of the famous battle.

That this is true was only revealed, completely and indisputably, through a French general's resentment 17 years after the battle. In attempting to give his name its just due in history, he divulged that not one warning, but an ominous series, was in Allied hands long before the tubes of chlorine were hissing hideous death.

As a matter of fact, German history discloses that the gas attack was planned as early as October, 1914. It was well on its way by February, and by March 10 there were 6,000 yards of German front line in the Ypres Salient holding tubes of chlorine. Unfavorable winds caused delay on delay, with discovery always imminent. Finally it was decided to change the area of attack. The tubes were taken out and moved one army corps sector to the north, to the northerly curve of the Salient line. They were installed and again ready by April 11 on the front of the 26th German Reserve Division, between Poelcapelle and Steenstraat.

All this movement and preparation, plus the issuing of gas masks, made even the German private aware of the waiting attack. It was inevitable that rumour and report should cross the two lanes of barb wire. But the excuse that it was "too inhumane to be believed"—that was given them, and is still generally understood as the reason for the "surprise"—is first of all ridiculous in the light of the fact that Germany used gas in battle nearly three months before that fateful April 22.

On Jan. 31, 1915, General Hoffman, of Hindenburg's staff, squatted in the belfry of a church in Bolimov to observe the effect of 18,000 gas shells hurling into crowded Russian trenches. The cold weather killed much of the lethal sting and there were few gas casualties. But what killed that 11-week warning?

It was not too inhumane for the Germans in January; why should it be in April?

Following that, and surely confirming it, came the capture of German shells holding deadly gas during the battle of Neuve Chapelle early in March. Here was proof actually in Allied possession on the Western Front! There was still more than a month to prepare to make use of it. But research does not disclose a single precaution! Certainly no effort was made to provide the obvious defence—a gas mask.

Warnings of the coming deluge of gas in Flanders now were heard in swift succession. Late in March, prisoners captured by the French 10th Army on the slopes of Vimy Ridge disclosed that the trenches in front of Zillebeke—in the Ypres Salient—held many gas cylinders awaiting a favourable wind. Their stories were disbelieved and dubbed scaremongering propaganda.

On the night of April 15-16, a week before the roof fell in, two warnings came into Allied hands. A former German N.C.O., bitter over being reduced to the ranks for striking a superior officer, gave himself up to the 11th (French) Division astride the St. Julien-Poelcapelle Road. But he remained loyal. Questioned about the gas mask he was carrying, he insisted it was issued "in case the British use gas." He was believed despite the fact that a few hours later a Belgian spy whose information had been described as "generally reliable" sent a message over the lines to expect a "German attack with asphyxiating gas."

Then, on April 18, there was a strange German official communique: "Yesterday, east of Ypres, the British attacked with shells and bombs with asphyxiating gas." As the British had yet no thought of using gas, that, plus other evidence in Allied hands, should have been enough to launch desperate measures to meet this new menace. But the Allies had still much to learn about German military mentality. It, too, was dismissed as alarmist propaganda.

Next came ominous activity on the new Canadian front. Sentries of the 16th Battalion Canadian Scottish, now in the line south of Poelcapelle Road, reported "peculiar pipes" being installed or handled in the German front line. But even more conclusive and startling evidence was known to the Allies before the German ex-N.C.O. surrendered, before the Belgian spy sent his ominous word, before the German H.Q. issued its astounding communique and before the Canadians saw those "peculiar pipes." And when it is remembered that this most specific warning of all followed the Russian gas shelling in the East, the capture of the gas shells in the West, and the information from prisoners taken on Vimy Ridge, it is inexplicable why Doom was allowed to march on unhindered.

This proof that a large-scale gas assault was preparing came into the H.Q. of Gen. Ferry, commanding the 11th (French) Division, as the Canadians were preparing to move up from the South to take over from his battalions in front of St. Julien. On the night of April 13, Pvt. August Jaegar, 234th Reserve Infantry Regiment (51st German Division), crawled cowering into the French line near Langemarck, hands high and yelling "Kamerad."

The man, a former chauffeur and an intelligent soldier, had a gas mask made of tow [cloth] and soaked in some chemical. Under interrogation he revealed the entire plan of the coming gas attack!

Gen. Ferry interviewed him personally next day, April 14. He learned that gas cylinders, 1.4 m long, had been dug into the Boche parapet in batteries of 20 tubes every 40 metres along the line. Jaegar even gave approximately correct limits of the proposed assault.

He described the tubes; he explained that a rubber hose was attached to discharge the gas beyond the German parapet. He gave the signal for release of the gas for five minutes—three red lights sent rocketing into the sky from an artillery position. Men of the Royal Highlanders, Montreal; of the 48th Highlanders, Toronto; and of the 8th Battalion (Little Black Devils) of Winnipeg, saw that same signal of choking death from their doomed front-line redoubts eight days later.

Stressing the extent of attack preparation, the betrayer also stated that 24 airplanes, a captive balloon, many reserve machine-gun units, light and heavy guns, had been newly brought into the forward area. Increased aircraft activity and heavier machine-gun and artillery fire were noted in many Allied reports and, in the end, everything Jaegar told was proved true.

Almost every detail was thus known to the Allies eight days before that fateful zero hour!

Only Gen. Ferry read the signs correctly and believed the momentous information. He pleaded to have the guns turned on to smash the deadly tubes of chlorine. Prompt bombardment could have prevented the assault or blasted away the worst of its effect. But Gen. Balfourier, his Corps Commander, called him a "credulous fool!"

Despite his superior's attitude, Gen. Ferry warned his flanks. He advised Gen. Bulfin, commanding the 28th (British) Division, next to him, on the right, in the Salient line. But Gen. Bulfin was too busy preparing to blow up Hill 60 trench-works with five mines on April 17 to be perturbed.

Gen. Sir Hubert Plumer, commanding the British V. Corps (28th, 27th and Canadian Divisions) passed on Gen. Ferry's invaluable information "for what it was worth." A later V. Corps order held apprehension of German assault and even advised the three divisional commanders where to assemble in the event of the Salient having to be abandoned. But apparently there was still no real credence placed in the warnings of a wave of poison fumes.

Gen. Ferry, also on his own initiative, warned Gen. E. A. H. Alderson, the British officer who commanded the Canadians, as he came up to his relief. Brig.-Gen. A. W. Currie (later Sir Arthur Currie, Commander of the Canadian Corps) was first to relieve part of the 11th (French) Division with his 2nd Brigade. He was urged by Gen. Ferry "to provide some means to prevent inhalation of the gas." But it was too late now to think of gas masks. All Brig.-Gen. Currie could do was urge his battalions to take all precautions and stand to.

The 2nd Brigade units thus expected, or watched for, a gas attack, and in their inexperienced enthusiasm were even a little disappointed that the line stayed monotonously quiet. The 1st Brigade were in reserve, and the 3rd Brigade, on the left flank, which was to bear the brunt for many hours, came into the line after Gen. Ferry's warnings had passed through, and few of the units commanded by Brig.-Gen. R. E. W. Turner, V.C., had a hint of the grim fate preparing.

Rumours were rife, but apprehension was so slight that no effort was made to provide a gas mask. It was not until April 24, in fact, two days after the main discharge and the day that the Canadians directly faced gas, that a belated start was made to improvise something to help fight the deadly fumes. On that day, Lieut.-Col. Wingate, No. 10 (British) Field Ambulance, secured a German mask from a prisoner in Vlamertinghe Dressing Station. Col. T. H. J. C. Goodwin rushed it to Sir John French's G.H.Q. at St. Omer and chemists at last went to work. When this second gas attack was made—on the 15th and 8th Battalions—it was found that moisture seemed to relieve the irritation a little, but the water carried by the men was soon gone.

Still acting without his Corps Commander's knowledge, Gen. Ferry took the only precaution he could without the backing of his superiors that would give him the artillery action that might well have smashed the German plan. He thinned out the men he still had in the line to a skeleton defence, the usual disposition when there was danger of a mine being blown.

Had every commander in the threatened area done the same—believed his report, or at least taken the cautious course and followed his example—thousands of the 60,000 casualties of the battle that lasted until May 24 would have been saved. With the bulk of the holding troops secure in the rear, a swift and strong counter after the deadliness of the gas had been dispelled could have retaken all lost ground in a single stroke.

But apparently both British and French staffs were too deeply rutted in the rule-of-thumb tactics of their outdated training to either imagine such a departure from existing weapons or devise a counteracting plan. All they could see was "alarmist propaganda," and their only action was to seek to dispel apprehension.

Joffre's liaison officer came back from Ferry's H. Q. saying: "The gas attack is a myth." The British liaison officer also visited Gen. Ferry and apparently believed likewise; he certainly brought back no word to cause nervousness. The French Grand Quartier-General topped the disbelief by officially reporting: "All this gas business need not be taken seriously."

In later days of the war, any trained intelligence officer, with a better knowledge of German mind and method, would have quickly linked that series of warnings and seen certainty of the intention by the enemy. But even considering the limitations of these early days of war, and the fact that the British were concentrating on the operations at nearby Hill 60, it is still difficult to see why some action was not taken other than merely to urge vigilance.

All the while, Ypres and the back lines were under a steadily growing bombardment while the Germans waited for a slow, favourable wind. There was no threat seen in this increased gun work as it was considered retaliation for the British assault on Hill 60 on the 17th, or perhaps preparation for an ordinary counter-offensive.

Then came historic April 22 and catastrophe. And now the astonishing sequel. Gen. Ferry, the only divisional commander, or officer of higher rank, who had sought to avert what would have been a major Allied disaster but for the stubborn courage of the

Canadians, and which was a major Allied defeat despite their gallant sacrifice—was relieved of his command!

In the history of the Great War such injustices were not uncommon. But Gen. Ferry's resentment over the injustice rankled until he could no longer hold his peace. He decided to make public the pre-battle secrets of the Second Battle of Ypres. In 1932, he finally divulged the story and laid bare the chain of gas-attack warnings to an interested France, the warnings that both British and French Headquarters fatally ignored.

Gen. Ferry's intention was to wash out the undeserved stain on his cut-short military career. He gave all details, names and dates. His story at once proved that the "surprise" of the Second Ypres was a false impression, obviously fostered and encouraged to cover a blind intelligence and a short-sighted staff. It also had one of the most unusual of all the strange sequels of the Great War that followed men back into civilian life.

Gen. Ferry's account reached Germany and inevitably the ears of Adolph Hitler. The German dictator ordered an investigation. It was followed by a search for the traitor who had betrayed Germany's plans for the poison gas atrocity in the long gone and bloody April of 1915.

And ex-Pvt. August Jaegar of the 234th Reserve Infantry discovered how far-reaching are a man's threads of destiny. He faced the Reich Supreme Court in December, 1932. His only defence was that the gas mask in his pocket had warned the Allies of the coming wave of poison fumes in any event. On the 17th of December—17 years after his betrayal that profited the Allies nothing—Jaegar was sentenced to 10 years penal servitude and lost his civil rights.

There is one more little-known aftermath to those fearful fumes that left men lying with death darkly mantling their faces or drove them back to linger out their lives in military hospitals. The scientist who perfected chlorine gas likewise lost his civil rights. Fritz Haber, a German Jew, who also perfected mustard gas, lost his job as Director of the Kaiser Wilhelm Institute for Physical and Electro-Chemistry at Dalhen, during the Nazi revolution.

It may have been resentment over this ingratitude for his grim addition to the science of killing, or it may have been a tortured conscience; but it was assuredly a strange reversal to find Fritz Haber described as "a worker in the cause of peace and internationalism" when he died in 1934.

As for our memory of the immortal stalwarts who fought the Second Battle of Ypres, this story that suggests "what might have been" can only bring a greater admiration for the men who suffered because great generals had failed to read those ominous signs correctly; for the men who, face to face with disaster, resisted to the end.

Second World War

Canadian tank division arrives in English army camp, 1941

Over There

WALLACE REYBURN
December 1, 1941

Through the misty Midlands dawn a long line of camouflaged army lorries and carriers rolled into the market place of a sleepy town, turning down a narrow road to the outskirts. Each camouflaged vehicle bore a great yellow "X" and its complement of tired, disconsolate, tin-hatted soldiers—"enemy" troops bound for the prisoner-of-war cage. Directing the stream of prisoner traffic, a French-Canadian corporal with a Tommy gun sat on a Canadian-built carrier, shouting: "*Par là*—that way!—*va-t'en*—go!—to the prison camp!"

Along the narrow streets, troops of a Quebec infantry regiment of the 1st Canadian Division searched for stragglers, chattered excitedly of their unexpected bag, greeted wide-eyed townsmen popping half-dressed from doorways and windows. By piercing strong enemy lines in an unbelievably fast plunge ahead, the French Canadians had short-circuited an "enemy" column moving over a presumably safe route. Within two hours the busy Quebeckers, foiling every effort to inform "enemy" headquarters of the trap, were outnumbered by their own prisoners, had more than they could feed. A few hours later the town was circled by "enemy" forces, but the Canadians held out until the main advance came through to relieve them.

This Midlands-town battle in October's massive British Army manoeuvre northwest of London was just one aspect of a mechanized manoeuvre in which 300,000 troops—some 50,000 of them Canadians—fought for a week on a front from the Chilterns to the Fen Country. But the spectacular showing of the historic Quebec unit typified the energy and eagerness of the Canadian Corps thrown into a bitter encounter with heavy "invasion" forces. Returning home after an exhausting week on the move, every man in the Corps was in high fettle, enthused by the manoeuvre's close approximation to real battle.

This Canadian Army in England, borne overseas in an almost ceaseless stream of ships these last two years, is a self-contained, mobile striking force of unrivalled power and excellence. Three infantry divisions, an armoured division and an army tank brigade—plus Corps troops for emergency use with any formation in any situation—plus special complements in several branches, notably artillery and engineers. This is the picture of the Canadian Corps at the end of 1941—a force perhaps not equal in numerical strength to the old Corps of 1916–1918, but far greater in actual striking power. Back of the Army in the field is the complete administrative organization of Canadian Military Headquarters.

The Canadian Corps, which Winston Churchill has earmarked for the highly important, but so far none too exciting, job of helping defend England, has been one of the key units in General Headquarters Reserve. This is Commander-in-Chief Sir Alan Brooke's "ace-in-the-hole"—a fast-moving, hard-hitting force ready to be thrown into battle in any sector where the invading enemy may threaten to gain a foothold.

The Canadians know Southern England from the Dover Straits almost to Land's End better than many know the roads and topography around their own home towns. In getting to know the country they have come to know its people; and interest in "free-and-easy Canada where people really *live*" has boomed to a point not even achieved during Canada's peaceful invasion of England in the First Great War.

How do the Canadian troops live in Britain? Because it makes a good news story and shows the way Canadians and the people of Britain are fraternizing, most of the picture stories and articles dealing with living conditions of the Canadians show the troops billeted with families. This must give the average Canadian the impression that for most of our troops Army life over here consists of days with the Army on manoeuvres and training, and evenings among civilians living the home life of the everyday Britisher. But the proportion of soldiers billeted on families is very small. The great majority of them—almost two-thirds—live in barracks. Perhaps a sixth live in tents or huts which, in the summer at any rate, have a much bigger appeal for the troops.

When detachments are stationed near villages or towns, a large proportion are quartered in empty houses, and about a quarter of all our troops over here are living in this way. To the local people, Canadian soldiers who move into empty houses in a community are just like any other newcomers. They're welcomed by the neighbours, who lose no time dropping in on them to see that they're comfortable. Most of the soldiers I've talked to can't praise their civilian next-door neighbours highly enough. They're swell, say the troops, and go out of their way to make things as pleasant as possible. Naturally the furniture for these houses, being supplied by the Army, isn't overluxurious, so the local people often step in and augment it with spare furniture from their own homes.

One soldier told me of moving into an empty house, with three other soldiers, at nine in the morning. The house was bare when they arrived, but the neighbours rallied round and contributed beds, chairs, tables, curtains and other furnishings. By five o'clock the house had been completely equipped and looked thoroughly "lived in." Another soldier told me how a lady couldn't bear the thought of their living room having no curtains and, not having any spare curtains available, cut up her wedding dress and made it into lace curtains for the windows.

And the soldiers themselves are eager to play their part in the community life. Most of them take a pride in the appearance and upkeep of the house they live in. A good example of this is the case of a group of officers who were moved into a large house on the outskirts of a certain town. Before the war it had been a lovely house with beautiful gardens. For a time it had been used to house a party of evacuees from London and the gardens and hedges had been allowed to become overgrown and untidy. Despite the fact that they knew they were due for another move and were going to be there for only a few weeks, the Canadians took it upon themselves to put the place back into shape. They borrowed mowers and clippers from the neighbours and went to work, and in a fort-night had lawns and hedges looking as well kept as ever.

This summer Canadians living in empty houses joined in Britain's "Dig For Victory" campaign and converted many a spare plot into a vegetable garden. Just like any other good neighbour they yarned over the garden wall to the folks next door and competed with them in growing the biggest cabbages and most succulent marrows. Those who haven't gardens of their own frequently drop round to a neighbour's and give him a hand with his digging and the tending of his vegetables.

Living side by side with the Canadians like this, the people in the districts in which they're located are naturally coming under the Canadian influence, from learning to sing "Alouette" to absorbing Canadian slang in their conversation. The Canadians over here are all self-appointed publicity agents for the Dominion and, as earlier stated, British people are now probably better informed about Canada than they have ever been.

Of course on their arrival most of the Canadians were amazed at the ignorance of the average Englishman regarding Canada. Those who didn't think that practically the whole country was under a foot of snow for most of the year were of the opinion that Canada was still a colony and that when Britain declared war we were brought automatically into it, having no say of our own. The troops soon explained pretty clearly that Canada is a self-governing Dominion and broke English people of calling Canadians "colonials," an epithet that makes many Canadians fighting mad.

An interesting side light on this Canadian influence is to be found in one town where an Ottawa Army Service Corps is stationed. Not long ago they organized a barn dance, something quite new to the local people. It was such a success that now they stage a dance every Friday night, with a full complement of square dances.

When a Canadian goes on leave he never has any difficulty in making friends. The English have always been notoriously bad mixers, but the war has changed all that. Wherever the soldiers go they are eagerly greeted, asked into homes, taken to shows and given a good time generally. An increasing number of the troops are marrying girls they have met over here. The total of Canadians who have married in Britain now runs into several thousand, but to make sure that none of the soldiers rush into an ill-advised marriage, a senior officer or the unit padre always has a chat beforehand with the girl a soldier wants to marry. Many a newly-married soldier brings his wife to live in the town near where he is stationed. From his unit he can get a "sleeping out" pass, which allows him to go home each night after the day's work, and to soldiers who have been living in barracks for the last two years this home life *and* home cooking is a real boon.

Canada's lads overseas, many of them, have been for two years in Britain, training incessantly for the invasion they will meet— or make. So far as they are concerned the day can't come too soon. The 1st Division, which sailed from Canada in an armada of peacetime luxury liners three months after war broke, has run the gamut of the training manuals. Under command of Maj.-Gen. G. R. Pearkes, V.C., its personnel has gone down the line from heavy artillery gunnery to unarmed combat, the jujitsu of the Army, which may prove of inestimable value in the hand-to-hand struggle that will come with invasion.

Marshalled under somewhat less pressure and just as truly a crack formation, the 2nd Division under Maj.-Gen. V. W. Odlum has followed a similar training schedule. Now both are woven perfectly into the Canadian Corps texture. The two divisions have worked side by side on Corps manoeuvres in all parts of England from the Midlands south. In the monster October manoeuvre, when England's Southern Army defeated the "invading" forces of its Eastern Army, the Corps was split in two, the 2nd Canadian Division being suddenly placed under British command to meet a tactical crisis. Meantime, the 1st Canadian Division went into victorious battle alongside a British division put under the command of Lieut.-Gen. A. G. L. McNaughton.

For every formation and unit, training in England is extensive and varied. Artillery units trundle their guns to ranges to fire on moving and stationary targets. Reconnaissance scout cars and carriers dash over twisting roads and unmapped trails until their drivers know every turning in Southern England. Tanks plunge through streams and over ditches, firing as they go. Infantry march over winding roads, paddle across rivers in rubber boats, deploy through furze and gorse, blanket themselves beside hedges for the night. Selected officers and other ranks are hardened and trained in the rugged tactics of independent operations. Every man who wears the "Canada" shoulder badge gets as close as can be to modern warfare short of actual battle.

Aside from the Army in the field—which is the Canadian Corps—the Canadian Army numbers many thousands of troops manning hospitals, operating training schools, compiling the mountains of records needed for a force far past the 100,000 mark, and generally maintaining a close liaison between Headquarters at Ottawa and the formations overseas.

Not every Canadian unit concentrates on training alone. Some are making a permanent mark on the face of the United Kingdom. Canadian foresters, from almost every province, sound their tearing saws from dawn to dusk through the island's most heavily treed areas. Canadian tunnellers, mostly from Northern

Ontario, were assigned to secret operations throughout England almost on arrival—and are engaged with British units in improving the fortifications of Gibraltar. A road-construction company from Northern Ontario, using materials and plans supplied by civil authorities, built by-passes around two key towns in southern England—broad traffic lanes that will be as much of a boon to the postwar motorist as to a fast-moving army on wheels in event of an invasion attempt. One of these by-passes is called "Canada Road," the other "Young Street"—a sly reference to Toronto's Yonge Street and a tribute to Maj. E. J. Young of North Bay, Ont., commanding the road construction company.

The spirit of the Canadians overseas is best expressed in a three word quotation: "We want action!" These boys left their homes and their jobs, hockey games, football finals, strawberry shortcake and a lot of other things they scarcely knew they lived for—and they want to get back as soon as they've done their job. They impatiently feel that the sooner they are in action the quicker they'll see their home country again.

It has been a major problem of the "brass hats" to keep the boys in khaki from getting bored. They have developed special training schemes and arranged educational courses which are surprisingly popular. With the co-operation of the four auxiliary services—Salvation Army, Y.M.C.A., Knights of Columbus and Canadian Legion—sports meetings, concert parties and movie shows are organized for the troops and other recreation facilities provided. Because a change of scenery improves morale, units and formations have been shifted from area to area. This has the dual purpose of helping them to get to know every road well in case of an invasion attempt. In the successful campaign against boredom the higher-ups have been aided by the open-armed hospitality of the English people, especially in the unbelievably beautiful country spots of the South.

The demand for action was heightened by the disappointing—though doubtless fortunate and well-advised—changes in orders that halted Canadian expeditions embarking for Norway in April and for France in June. A few troops reached the continent as France collapsed, but the main expedition did not leave the English port where they piled aboard ship. The expedition to destroy Spitzbergen's coal mines as a Nazi supply source gave a fillip to Canadian morale, and without a casualty. Every officer and every man who got to France or "Spitz" is envied by those who watched them go. Every mention in the newspapers of invasion—whether of Britain or of the continent—is hailed by the troops with delight.

There is no question but that they are aching for action, anxious to get on with their job.

Wallace Reyburn covered the Aug. 19, 1942, raid on Dieppe and wrote a book about it, Rehearsal for Invasion. *After the war, the New Zealand–born writer moved from Canada to Britain, where he continued to contribute to* Maclean's, *wrote a column for the* Toronto Telegram *and published 25 more books, including* Flushed with Pride, *a biography of Thomas Crapper, the purported inventor of the flush toilet. He died at age 87 in England in 2001.*

HMCS Skeena off the British coast, January, 1941

Fighting Ships

CHARLES RAWLINGS
March 15, 1942

This is a Navy tale of convoy. The ensigns of a dozen nations fly and some of them go down in its action. Its setting is outside, in the middle longitudes of the North Atlantic Ocean, but it is a Canadian story.

A thin screen of Canadian ships faced Hitler's undersea wolf pack attacking in great force out there and brought their convoy through; battered, decimated, bloody, but on the course, steaming home in line of convoy still. It is known, where such things can be known and talked about, as *Skeena*'s story—*Skeena* the destroyer. She was not alone. She had supporting corvettes, those plump, small, tumbling ship clowns in the Battle of the Atlantic's grim circus, and they fought like lions. She had S.C.X. under her lee, Slow Convoy X, and it was a brave convoy manned by brave men who kept their weary merchantmen plodding on through more than two days and two nights of sustained *Rudelsystem* attack, as the Germans call it. But it is *Skeena's* story as you will see, and we must begin with her, at the beginning.

Skeena was weaned on no bitter milk. Thornycroft built her in 1931 for the peacetime Canadian Navy. She came of Beagle class lines with modifications appropriate to Canadian conditions and approved by N.S.H.Q. She turned out to be a splendid example of the destroyer type which, as you know, has been evolved for great speed and flexibility. She is 321 feet overall, and 32,000 horsepower hurry her 1,337 tons ahead at better than 30 knots. She made 37 knots in her trials. They named her *Skeena* after the river the Siwash named, and the present Naval Attaché in Washington, Commodore Victor G. Brodeur, brought her over. All hands pitched in and gave her chromium-plated rails—because they could not see her shine enough.

In 1939, she was chosen to be the first North American voice, out of all the millions of voices that were waiting, to swell into a roar like the shout of a planet welcoming Their Majesties, the King and Queen, to Canada. They were inbound on the *Empress of Australia* and *Skeena* was ordered to meet her at sea. Slicing precisely through a calm, rose-coloured evening ocean, using her range finder to judge the closing yards, *Skeena* kept the rendezvous at the precise second of scheduled meeting, which was at 18.00—a Navy way of saying six o'clock p.m. Later, she carried the royal party to Prince Edward Island and the King lived on her bridge for hours at a time, his Royal Standard above him at her gaff. You can see that regal bunting now as you go down into her wardroom for a pink gin. It is furled under a glass case screwed to a bulkhead.

War found her of course very fit. The battle paint of the northern water, that hue that resembles nothing so much as the shade of lead coffin sheathing slightly grave-weathered, but which bears the name North Atlantic grey, covered the chromium rails and her other bright work. She took on her camouflage like a trim, hard little dance star pulling on a Navy boy's jersey and went out to the eastward to help Britain in the narrow waters about the Isles.

She arrived in England the first day of Dunkirk and lived through action there for a year, which has no place in this story but which will make gripping material for someone's typewriter someday. Then, as war-seasoned as plates and tubes and guns and turbines and officers and destroyermen can be and remain whole, she came back to Canada to help guard the western buttress of that great overseas bridge of ships known as the Western Ocean Convoy.

Along about harvest time last fall, as she led her corvettes out of a northeastern station and cleared its granite headland and turned her face to sea to make rendezvous with Slow Convoy X, eastbound, her roster read like this:

Lieut.-Comdr. James C. Hibbard, R.C.N., Halifax; Exec. Officer E. E. Boak, R.C.N., Victoria; Lieut. W. Willson, R.C.N., Calgary; Lieut. J. S. Horam, R.C.N.R., Vancouver; Lieut. F. Wilcox, R.C.N.V.R., Montreal; Lieut. J. A. McAvity, R.C.N.V.R., Saint John; Surgeon-Lieut. C. Oake, R.C.N.V.R., Oakville, Ont.; Sub.-Lieut. J. MacDowell, R.C.N., Ottawa; Sub.-Lieut. J. A. Mitchell, R.C.N.R., Victoria; Sub.-Lieut. F. E. Barlow (Gunner-T), Halifax.

Twenty-five chiefs and petty officers.

One hundred and fifty-five ratings.

A typical destroyer's list they read, written down like that. They were better than a typical list last harvest time. The typewriter tapping out their names cannot show you their eyes, squint-crinkled and cold and level from a solid two years and a half of war. Nor can it depict for you their lean hardness, or how they moved about their ship knowing her every corner and angle and camber of deck and creak and lift and pitch. Or how they knew her weapons and her speed, and how she could stop and knife and thrust. They knew all that because they had been small fighting parts of her great fighting whole through black nights of fight and gales filled with fight and fights in the snow and fog and blazing noons of running battle. They eased *Skeena* outside, running slow to let the corvettes keep station, and stood their watches and caught their sleep and ate as they always had, in action or safe jogging like this, down to the bottom of the cook's last pot.

They made rendezvous with S.C.X. and saw that it was a big convoy, 60-odd bottoms. They studied it quietly, unemotionally, marvelling mildly, if at all, at its size in contrast with their own. It was like all the other convoys of the past war years—a trifle more weather-beaten, possibly, for each one as it came to them was a little older. It was stretched out as far as a hoisted signal could be seen, and there were flush deckers there and three island freighters, and tankers and squat-rigged modern hulls all gear and hatches, and tall rigged old coasters, and a snub-nosed laker with her funnel seeming to pop up out of her very transom like a shanty stovepipe. They were weary ships, grey and dun with rust and soot and labour, unwashed, unpainted, unknown almost, unsung. They wallowed slowly ahead rolling out their vulnerable, thin-plated, heavy bellies.

Making those bellies heavy was a half-million odd tons of precious stuff to nurture and strengthen Britain in her island fortress. In the cold greasy forecastles, or manning their faithful engines and their decks, were men like themselves, men of the sea, enough of them to people a small village: 2,500 more or less, officers and men of the merchant navy.

Where they were at this particular moment does not matter, for the whole North Atlantic Ocean was preparing right then to be exactly the same all over. A gale struck. In three hours it hove them to, escort and convoy alike. They lay, heads tucked under wing or heads tucked under stern, whichever way their widely different hulls could best lay to. With engines just holding way they tussled with an old and honourable enemy, an autumn south-easter. In 36 hours it decided they had had enough and could go on. They had remained so well together that all but five ships and one corvette had been constantly within visual signal touch and these five, just over the horizon, were quickly located. All ship-shape and on station, the great caravan set off on a course that carried them north and east until they sighted a bold headland of basalt mountain and glacier and stark shore cliffs. It was a bright day with a long dead following sea heaving them along, and all hands came up into the morning sunlight to stare at the strange cold cape.

Surgeon-Lieut. Oake has written some verse for *Skeena*'s wardroom scrapbook. He dwells on the scene.

The day dawns fair and cool, the sea is blue,
As this land's icy mountains come in view;
Bathed in the Arctic air, sunlit, serene;
Their bleak serrated peaks, an awesome scene.
"But look! a foamy wake approached now

The right wing of the moving convoy's line;
A lookout shouts, "Torpedo! Starboard bow!"

It was the first shout of all the shouting that was to follow. The first warning cry. *Skeena*, far ahead at the front of the fleet, closed at 24 knots.

"That way!" the right wing ships cried to her. "Periscope! Torpedo! Something! It sank and is gone."

She followed their pointing arms and searched and listened with those long mysterious tentacle ears called Asdic that can hear beneath the water farther than any shark can hear or eavesdropping cod down on the bottom mouthing his thick lips. Nothing! *Skeena* turned and surveyed the convoy drawn ahead. It had no vacant station, no limping ship. The alarm might have been nerves, a bonita school knifing their fins. She pretended that was what she thought and stormed back into the line and scolded one ship who had lost her head and broken radio silence.

"Break silence only if you see and are sure of what you see," she ordered. "That, why, that was nothing."

Nothing it remained for an hour. A short crisp message broke the air. It came from the Commander in Chief, Western Approaches.

"Enemy in your vicinity," it said.

The commodore heard it and could read its official code. *Skeena*, too. Together they decided to change course, and the great flotilla, still unaware, made its swing and settled down due north with the icy coast abeam, 40 miles. The evening, late and lingering in those latitudes, came drifting down. At 9:37, just good dark, a warhead blew the belly out of the fourth ship in the port wing and she went down in the moonlight, like a stone, with all hands. The next ship in the line signalled the attack with white rockets. *Kenogami*, one of the corvettes who was nearest, carried out a sweep in the rear of the convoy and at 9:42 she was heard to drop a single depth charge. At 9:48, she sighted a torpedo track that passed her starboard bow, and at 9:50 she sighted a U-boat at 1,000 yards steaming away at high speed. She opened fire with her four-inch gun but she needed more light on the target and at 10:00 she lost all contact.

Skeena, near her now, illuminated the port side of the convoy by star shell, and realizing *Kenogami* had lost contact ordered her to search for 10 minutes and then come back. When returning herself, the commodore far in the front of the convoy reported to her that he had sighted a U-boat on his port bow very close to the time of the opening explosion. He thought there must be two Huns attacking. At 10:10, two merchantmen sighted what was considered to be a third submarine, and within a few more moments four ships were crying out by megaphone and firing machine-gun tracer at a U-boat that was inside the convoy running down between the seventh and eighth column. *Skeena* thought of ramming, but this proved impossible owing to the number of ships in the way. She again fired star shell and closed the position and dropped depth charges. After 20 minutes, another sinking called her away and one minute later a tanker exploded. The corvette *Orillia* reported that out of the three ships, she had rescued 95 survivors.

The moon was still aloft but hard and white now, coldly staring down. When the star shells shone, an answering glow that was thought at first to be distant fire from big guns showed ahead. It was a pair of icebergs coldly reflecting back the light from their sheer ice. All warmth had left the sky, had left the world. It was what it had been all the time, a battle place, and the enemy was not one, or two lurking submarines. It was the wolf pack. Naval headquarters estimates the attacking force at this time at 12 submarines.

Shortly after midnight, a cloud bank mercifully moved in from the northeast and covered the mocking moon. The aurora flickered and went out. In the first of the darkness that seemed like the blackness of a pit, there were shouts and then suddenly the jangle of machine guns spitting white hot tracer.

"Here!"—"Here's the swine!"

Skeena was close enough to hear and she swung into the convoy and raced down lane to ram. The submarine crossed her too far ahead and, like a ki-yi-yi-ing dog in flight, it skidded around a corner and raced up the next lane over. They passed going in opposite directions and *Skeena* could see the wet conning tower of the Hun shining in the darkness, and, as she watched, it slid under in a crash dive. At that moment the convoy, acting on orders from the Commodore, made an emergency turn to port and *Skeena*, caught in the changing traffic, was suddenly surrounded with danger of collision.

Her people say that it was the direst moment of all the night. In the absolute darkness, where to turn? She knew one thing sure—she of all of them must not be put out of action that night. Without her there could be no hope. The corvettes alone could not hold off the wolves. If she went down or out, nothing remained for days but a slow relentless slaughter of the helpless, and here she was in horrible danger from the very ones she had to live to protect.

A black hulk leaped out of the darkness—one of the merchantmen—and just in time the 32,000 horsepower in her engines reared her back and away in full reverse. Then she wheeled and drove on and on until at last she was free and the convoy was inside of her and outside was nothing but darkness and sea and enemy. While she was still sweat-soaked and panting from the terror, the ship nearest her, a tanker carrying fuel oil, exploded. It shot an orange geyser of flame a hundred feet into the black sky. Around the base of the column of flame was billowing smoke and at its top was a downy smoke cushion.

"Why I could sit on it," Gunnery Lieut. Wilcox remembers he marvelled to himself.

The blast blew a hot wind in their faces on *Skeena* and they blinked their eyes in the glare. Wilcox remembers he reached up and snatched off his earphones and from behind him on the bridge came a voice, a young rating's voice filled with stark, wide-eyed awe. "If my folks," it rasped as if talking to a ghost, "could be here to see me now."

At last they brought up morning and the sun. U-boats with anything against them do not like the light. They draw off to horizon where they can see, yet cannot be seen themselves, and run the surface there paralleling their prey in truth like wolves stalking a timbered trail. This time there was but one horizon, for inside to the westward gloomed the ice-covered coast.

In the convoy there was the creak of bunks as men flopped down in their boots. The eternal smell of breakfast coffee scented the air as it will on judgment daybreak at sea. Tobacco blued the forecastles, for now relaxed nerves could suck it down in a deep inhale and it would taste. The steady engines beat away the yards, the cables, one by one the slow, slow knots. Before the sun had burned away the morning clouds, the herring gulls that flew out from the coast and wheeled overhead to look down with black shoe-button eyes for garbage saw an orderly convoy, staunch in station, running well.

Skeena's commander slouched down in his chart-room chair, boots stretched out, and stared far away into the coming night. But they had given the Hun a pounding. They had hurt him down deep, bruised him with the ash cans. When water was as thick with U-boats as it had been last night the mere sum of ash cans that his morning report had told him had been dropped was guarantee of that. They could have been dumped blindly and some of them would have found a mark. And they had not been blindly dumped. They had been carefully laid on good targets that signal had proved. Even if there had been no certain killing hits, sub crews could only take so much ash-can strafing. In Britain it was a mandatory two weeks' leave for sub crews who had been ash-canned no matter how ineffectually. Their nerves needed two weeks' rest just because they had been in the same neighbourhood with ash cans.

British sub crews were as tough as the Hun. There were some Hun nerves on ragged edge out there on the horizon. But still—he wished there could be more than just the thought of unnerved Huns to comfort his boys. A convoy cheered and forgot its troubles when it learned a Hun had died. He'd relish the smell of some Hun oil himself, enjoy watching it opalescing, rainbowing as the sure slick rippled and spread and proved the kill.

At noon he killed. The wolf pack teased a hard-luck ship, or made a bet, or, in their humourless way, ordered a single U-boat to try a desperate sneak attack. The single sub sneaked in. It caught a ship named *Thistle Glen* and hit her amidships with one powerful warhead. And then, not satisfied at the mere sound of the well-aimed shot going home, it stuck its periscope out to have a gander. Curious! Greedy! It wanted the name and size of its victim for some swagger.

"Periscope!" raised the cry. "There's the b——!"

Skeena closing fast was close enough to look. It was a light grey periscope, sneaking slowly under. There was no need for instruments to divine range and depth. Pounce attack! Ten depth charges, 5,000 pounds of TNT with shallow fuse settings, blasted the water into geysers which sloshed back to make a hellish patterned doily of foam. *Skeena* drew off to 1,700 yards and those long mystic ears, the Asdic, groped and found the fool. He was on the bottom frozen with terror, wounded more or less. This time slowly, with check and countercheck of every move, with engines slowly turning and the detection routine going on as still and studied as in an examination drill, the exact spot where he lay on the sea's floor was found. The German could hear the hunt, count the slow beat of *Skeena's* heart, her engine. The sound of her pulse came down through the water to him and his whole hull was like an amplifier magnifying it.

"Round! Round! Round!" He could hear the big flywheel turn as she idled, making her computation. "Around! Around! Around!" it talked to him as she slowly gathered way, her mind made up. Then "aroundaroundaround—" She came up to 14 knots and held that beat as true as fate's watch ticking, and he could hear that rhythm coming closer—closer. He closed his eyes and stopped his ears with the heels of his palms, trying to shut out the sound, but it came on until it was straight overhead and then—"*Gott*"—it seemed to blur. And at that instant the depth charges were in the water and plunging, turning, falling, streaming silvery bubbles of air that floated back up into the light and sun that he would never see again and they plummeted—straight—down—on—HIM.

On the surface *Skeena* turned and, very sure, or she would not have dared to make a sitting target, she stopped her engines. The Asdic, like a doctor's stethoscope confirming death, went out and pressed against the corpse and there was no life for it to hear. A large air bubble appeared, then smaller air bubbles for 10 minutes and then a small patch of oil.

"When this good news," says the Surgeon-Lieutenant's verse, "through *Skeena* was announced"—

The whole ship's company broke out in cheers;
Tired eyes and bodies did appear revived,
Their fighting spirits soared, their nerves were steeled.

At midnight came another cheering break. Two newly-commissioned Canadian corvettes, the *Chambly* and the *Moose Jaw*, had been sent sometime earlier up into the northeastern water on a training cruise. They had been contacted by the Admiralty or by their own superiors back in Nova Scotia and ordered to move at once to reinforce S.C.X. This order they were hastening to obey.

Shortly before midnight two merchantmen in the convoy sighted a U-boat on their port bow and a moment later another was sighted by a third vessel 3,000 yards away. *Skeena* coming up fired star shell. At that very moment the two corvettes were within sight of the convoy and, according to the surgeon, this is what they saw.

Gunfire and rockets belching from convoy,
Star shells and flares descending from the sky,
A merchantman ablaze, torpedoed, doomed,
Its killer speeding by into the gloom.

They were young, these corvettes, and green if you will, but what they saw—the sky rosy with violence ahead and then suddenly, close alongside, that "killer speeding by into the gloom," did not scare them in the least. They co-ordinated well and closed the startled Hun, who certainly did not expect to find them there. He

was one of those sighted in the convoy and, frightened away by
Skeena's star shells, was fleeing for his life. He made a crash dive
like a startled frog and the two young corvette clowns closed over
his water and dropped a shower of ash cans right on top of him.

Up he came gasping for air, completely at bay. He was so close
to *Chambly* that in two lengths she was hard alongside and the
first thing anybody knew the Hun *oberleutnant* came flying
through the air like the young man on the flying trapeze. He had
made a long desperate leap for *Chambly's* decks and safety. His
crew followed him, 30 hands, and forgot the ignominy of defeat in
snarling their rage at their *kapitan*. He wanted to shake hands
with them in mutual congratulation on their escape, but they
turned their backs and spat in hatred and disgust.

Chambly, crowded with Germans, and *Moose Jaw*, empty and
envious, continued on and joined the escort under *Skeena*. The
wolf pack, reduced to nine effectual submarines now, according
to Naval estimate, still pressed the attack. A merchantman
sighted a U-boat on her starboard bow, steering a reciprocal
course. The merchantman altered course to ram, at the same
time opening fire with her total armament of three machine
guns. The master estimates that 70 rounds found their mark and
the U-boat dived. It was the third time in 24 hours that this same
ship had engaged an enemy.

A rescued master aboard a corvette observed red lights in the
water and heard voices. He asked if a boat might be lowered. The
corvette's boat was lowered with the master and an officer and
four ratings from the corvette. Despite a nasty swell nine men
were rescued. Others were seen in the water but the small boat
could hold no more. It regained the corvette and unloaded and
went back for the rest. The area was searched for two more hours
but no further survivors were found.

Aboard *Skeena* that night, empty star-shell cases made a drift of blackened brass around her forward gun. She was counting her depth charges and her star shells now with worried surmise. Her fuel gauges made her commander and her engineer lieutenant grim. A day, a night, another day of solid action and now this night that seemed to have no end, had taken a heavy toll of stores and fuel. She was getting a bit thin, a bit drawn. Not her men, mind. Her men were still top-hole. You can shoot away star shells and dump your last depth charge and burn up the fuel, but you can't wear down good men, not in two days' fighting.

Lieut. Wilcox had the bridge and Cmdr. Hibbard settled slowly into his chair in the chart house and stretched out his boots again. It was another morning and this was the time to do the thinking. To plan! He could go on fighting them with star shells—as long as there were star shells left. It hadn't worked so badly, shining the light down on them, lighting up the *Rudel-system*, the wolf-pack system. The devils were going to sneak in and get inside the convoy, there was no avoiding that. But he could light them up before they could get set. Let the convoy see them and rattle the machine guns against their slimy hides.

"Object sighted ahead, sir," a seaman saluted standing in the doorway.

What is it? he almost said, the *Deutschland*? The way things were going it should be the *Deutschland*. Instead he simply nodded and stood up and pulled on his hat and hurried to the bridge.

"Object bearing red 45, sir," said Lieut. Wilcox, binoculars fast to eyes. "Appears to be a destroyer. Yes! A destroyer! No! Two destroyers! Three destroyers, sir! Four destroyers! Five destroyers!"

They were fanned out wide on the horizon, sweeping westward. As he watched, the outside specks closed in, for the flotilla had sighted him. They changed from black to grey. Their leader closed with *Skeena* and hailed through the loud-hailer. It asked questions of technic. What screen had they been using? It asked that. What night technic? Quickly it asked and seemed to jerk the answers inboard as if they were something sprawling scandalously in mid-air. There was no compassion, no mercy in that bloodless, nettled voice.

"When did this begin?" it snapped.

Skeena told him.

There was a pause. The air, the strip of sea between the two ships seemed to hold still for a long eloquent moment. Then the voice, human now, gentle with understanding, said,

"I did not know that it had been as bad as that."

Charles Rawlings, the first husband of Pulitzer Prize–winning author Marjorie Rawlings, was an American short story writer and journalist who served briefly during the First World War. Rawlings wrote extensively for the Saturday Evening Post, *particularly on nautical themes. He died at 79 in Maine in 1974.*

The Skeena *was on escort duty for D-Day and then returned to North Atlantic convoy duty until she ran aground off Reykjavik harbour in October, 1944. The vessel sank in 1952 while being towed from Iceland to England.*

Bombers arriving in England from Canada

Bomber Ferry

D. K. FINDLAY
April 15, 1942

The German raiders had been busy over the British coast. Out of the clouds and the smoke of a burning city another black shape appeared and the anti-aircraft guns opened up again. Pinpoints of coloured light dropped from the shape and the battery fire ceased. A weary A.A. officer had his glasses to his eyes. "It's a ferry bomber from Canada. Pass, friend."

That bomber was a pioneer of the Atlantic run. Now they come in a steady stream—twin-engined Lockheed Hudsons and the new, big, four-engined Consolidated B-24, called the Liberator, armour-plated cockpits, a range of 3,000 miles and a speed of more than 300 miles an hour.

The Royal Air Force Ferry Command which delivers these aircraft to Britain is an odd mixture of the services and civilians. Its Commander in Chief is Air Chief Marshal Sir Frederick Bowhill, with incredibly sweeping eyebrows and a heroic row of ribbons, who learned to fly with the Navy. Senior Operations Officer—until he left recently to take over a new job with the C.P.R. airlines—was the famous 43-year-old Canadian pilot "Punch" Dickins, who won the D.F.C. in the last war, mapped great areas of the Canadian north from Edmonton to Aklavik, N.W.T., flew prospectors and fur traders over it and got the O.B.E. for his work. And the Controller of Operations, now Senior Air Staff Officer, is Group Capt. G. J. Powell of the R.C.A.F., who flew the *Cambria* over in 1937 and pioneered the Cape to Cairo route for Imperial Airways.

Headquarters of the command is at Dorval, near Montreal, where there is a field as big as a prairie and, besides the usual offices, a wireless school, an inn, a skating rink and a cafeteria. The cafeteria is like something out of Hollywood. Here are to be seen airmen in the various uniforms of the Empire, the United States and most of their allies; pilots in leather jackets and sheepskin boots; "Waffs" (W.A.A.F.) of the cipher department; people in ski clothes from the field and the hangars, policemen and ordinary citizens.

"When the first flights were made in November, 1940," remembers "Punch" Dickins, "no one knew whether an Atlantic bomber ferry was practical or not. But ships were scarce and shipping was slow and risky and meant dismantling the aircraft. Fifty experimental flights were made before it was decided to go ahead. We didn't have enough navigators then—we sent the first group of seven planes off with only one completely trained navigator to lead them. He lost track of most of them in a short time, but they all turned up on the other side."

The ferry command has several hundred pilots now—the exact number is a military secret. Most of these are civilian pilots and about 75 per cent of the civilians are Americans. One reason for this is that a great number of experienced Canadian pilots are in the R.A.F. or the R.C.A.F. Whether American or Canadian, they were usually co-pilots with the airlines, flying instructors or bush pilots. Average age of the group is about 30 and they all have one thing in common—experience.

The North Atlantic with its fierce gales and icing conditions is no place for a novice. A candidate for the ferry service must have a minimum of 750 hours in the air, a transport licence or its equivalent, and instrument rating. The command takes in about eight pilots a week and washes out a third of them. They have thousands of applications on hand, a good many of them from crackpots.

When a pilot comes to the Ferry Command, no matter how good he is, he goes back to school. For the first week he studies navigation, mostly dead reckoning; the second week, navigation and instruction in the use of oxygen equipment, automatic pilot, de-icers, emergency landing procedure. The third week he tries an examination and the fourth week—if he's still with the Ferry Command—he gets to fly a bomber. He will be given 10 to 25 hours' flight instruction, the idea being not only to make him familiar with the controls but to teach him the exact technique required of him for transatlantic delivery. Dorval is one of the few places which give instruction on four-engined aircraft, and it is probably the most exacting school in the world.

Capt. W. C. Siple, young and tough-minded, who is in charge of civilian instruction, has been across five times himself. "When one of our boys lifts a ship off the runway here," says Capt. Siple, "you can count that one delivered."

The pilot usually makes his first trip over as a co-pilot. Then he makes his first trip as a captain-pilot in charge of a Lockheed Hudson. The pilots give a cynical reason for this. A Hudson, they say, costs about $50,000; a Liberator costs $350,000 and up. A pilot is physically capable of making three trips a month. After five trips he is given a rest. He has to take an oath of secrecy and sign articles which bind him to fitness and obedience. Civilian pilots (captains) get $1,000 a month, co-pilots $800, navigators $800 and radio operators $600. Most of them feel keenly about the cause for which they are flying. One pilot, who was killed in a crash, used to turn over to the Red Cross $800 of his $1,000 pay. Service pilots get service pay.

The pilots are usually returned by air, either by Clipper or in one of the Command's Liberators. Sometimes they come back by boat, and they hate it. If you ask a pilot for a story of heroism in the Ferry Command he will probably tell you about some pilot who took 29 days to come back on a tramp steamer.

Besides the North Atlantic ferry, the Command flies Consolidated flying boats—the PB-Y's—from Bermuda. The PB-Y, known as the Catalina, won world-wide prominence when one of them spotted the *Bismarck*. They cruise along comfortably at 112 miles an hour, and with the usual tail wind make the 3,000 nautical miles to England (the route Mr. Churchill took) in 24 hours. More than a hundred of these have been ferried and not one has been lost, though one arrived with its ailerons torn off.

Bombers for the northern route are flown across the United

States from the American factories by American crews. Canadian crews go to work on them in Canada. The Liberators carry five— captain, co-pilot, navigator, flight engineer and radio operator. Empty, this big aircraft weighs 32,000 pounds; loaded, 56,000 pounds—and every one of them takes off fully loaded. For these bombers are carriers too, helping to conserve shipping space. There is a freight office at Dorval stacked with packages, each marked with a priority number. Besides passengers and mail they carry templates, spare parts, blueprints, radio parts, food, vitamin pills (especially vitamin "A" which helps the night fighters to see in the dark), secret things and things needed in a hurry. They have carried radium, live frogs—for research purposes—and something which smelled so bad the pilots still wonder what it was.

The Ferry Command is not keen on carrying passengers, because a passenger means 200 pounds less freight capacity, but they have a distinguished clientele. Persons carried are usually senior officers and people on government business. They flew Prime Minister Mackenzie King across last fall. Some of the names which have appeared on their passenger list are Lord Beaverbrook, Lord Douglas Hamilton, the Duke of Kent, American Ambassador John Winant, Air Marshal Breadner, Col. J. L. Ralston, Geoffrey Shakespeare, Capt. Harold Balfour, Malcolm MacDonald, Brig. Vanier, Harry Hopkins, Robert Sherwood, Robert Riskin, screen writer, and Robert Montgomery.

The service is free but to be taken as a passenger you must be recommended by one of the Allied Governments and okayed by the Commander in Chief.

In an office at Dorval there is a table covered with bronze plaques. Each one has a legend:

In Honourable Memory of . . .
Pioneer of the North Atlantic
Killed in line of duty
In Memory of his achievements.

There are 54 of these and they all bear one of three dates.
They commemorate the worst three days of the Ferry Command
when in quick and tragic sequence three aircraft, carrying returning personnel, crashed in the British Isles. Twenty-two were killed
on Aug. 10, 22 on Aug. 14 and 10 on Sept. 1, 1941. The enquiries
found that the cause of the crashes was pilot error. The number of
bombers lost during actual ferrying operations has not been made
public but it is less than 1 per cent of the bombers flown across.

The scene is an airport in Newfoundland. Flight LX12, a Liberator, is waiting, ready. Her engines have been rechecked, her fuel
tanks "topped"—filled so full that not a bubble of air remains—
and now she is ready for her 2,200-mile hop. Her captain is Alec
Lilly, born in Moose Jaw, Sask., ex-mounted policeman, aged 29,
with 3,500 hours in the air. He used to fly government officials
and the crisp new treaty money to the Indians in the north. This
will be his sixth trip across. His radio operator is an English civilian, his navigator a sergeant of the R.C.A.F. going to join a
squadron in England.

The ground crew moves away from the aircraft.

"All set, Captain."

The noise of the motors sets the echoes clanging among the
hangars. It moves off, belly-low, turns and faces into the western
wind. The captain turns in his seat to look at his crew. All are in
their places. Across from him the co-pilot has buckled his belt

and is staring straight ahead. It is his first trip across. Everyone feels tense. The bomber is heavily loaded. She carries 1,800 gallons of gasoline. A swerve on the take-off may mean explosion and disaster.

"Let's go."

The four motors rev up, the bomber hurtles down the field. The buildings stream past, the boundaries flash below. It holds on into the west, inching up into the sky, then begins a wide careful turn which brings it on course, heading out over the Atlantic. In the aircraft, the pilot and co-pilot are busy with retraction gear, stabilizers, fuel adjustments, a dozen things that must be done at once. The radio operator begins to take bearings on known radio beacons. An hour later, Captain Lilly takes his sheet and compares it with the navigator's chart. He is on his course.

"Radio silence."

From now on the operator will send only pre-arranged signals, at intervals, so the Canadian base may follow their progress. Sometime during the night a station on the British Isles will take them over. Sometimes the captain will ask for bearings. He will not ask unless he needs them, for other people are listening too. An enemy station intercepted a request for bearings and obligingly gave them—false ones, which brought the bomber over the coast of France before she discovered her position.

The three great menaces of the North Atlantic are bad weather, icing conditions and carburetor icing. The pilots watch unceasingly the temperature of the outside air. If it changes before the weather map predicts a change, then there has been a change of front, a change in the wind. Probably a storm is blowing up. Sometimes ice will form so quickly that the de-icers cannot break it off. One bomber got back to Newfoundland with 6,000 pounds of ice on it.

Flight LX12 is flying between layers of overcast now. The stars have disappeared, there is nothing but darkness above and below. There comes a sibilant crackling against the windows, the windshield turns grey and shimmering.

"Frost crystals. We'd better go up."

As the aircraft climbs, the pilots watch the gauges which measure the temperature of the carburetors. A drop might mean condensation and ice which would stop the motors.

"Temperature falling."

Capt. Lilly increases the manifold pressure which increases the heat around the carburetors. The pilots keep an eye on the wings. There is a sheen on them, some rime is forming. The bomber slants upward to the higher, drier air. In spite of the cabin heaters, it is getting cold. At 12,000 feet the captain orders oxygen masks for everybody.

At first, pilots were not always careful about using oxygen— but not after they saw some experiments in the McGill University laboratories which showed them what the lack of it would do. The captain tells the co-pilot to take over and slips from his seat. He stops beside each one of the crew, talks for a moment. It is part of his job to know if they are alert—or if the altitude is taking too great a toll.

He remembers a thing that happened on a bomber. One of the crew left his place to go to the toilet in the tail, the aircraft ran into icing conditions and had to climb. Some time later the crew member was found unconscious on the floor with one hand against the skin of the aircraft. Part of his hand had to be amputated for it was frozen.

Now they are approaching the famous "point of no return." Four hours and a few minutes—depending on the wind—off the coast lies the critical meridian for the Lockheed Hudsons. Once across this line they must go on, no matter what storms or mishaps they encounter, because they have not enough gas to get back. The line is less definite for the Liberators with their greater range, but for every loaded bomber somewhere over the empty ocean there is still a point of no return.

They are well over halfway now, the weather is good and the air dry. LX12 drops down to 9,000 feet. The crew take off their oxygen masks. They relax, talk, drink mugs of hot coffee. The radio operator tells of an incident of the last trip. They had a passenger aboard and they had put him to bed in a cot in the tail. Later they had to climb to escape icing conditions, and afterward strange noises began to issue from the tail. They found their passenger sitting up, singing and trying to get up. In his sleep the oxygen mask had slipped off, now he showed all the symptoms of a happy drunk. They had to tie him down until he recovered.

The crew see they are flying over a floor of white cloud—and cloud is a very handy thing to have around when you are coming into the patrol area. The tail wind has pushed them steadily. They are nearing the coast ahead of schedule. The crew members act as lookouts. There is little danger of interception by enemy fighters—they are too far north—but there is one chance in 10,000 of being spotted by one of the big Focke Wulfe Kuriers (German patrol bombers).

"Aircraft on the starboard beam!"

Everyone has a look. It is a long way off, it is not much more than a black dot, but it suggests the hornet look of a fighter.

"Might be one of ours. Might be a German weather plane . . ." The Germans send out fighters stripped to the last essential, even of their guns, to collect data for their weather maps. "Guess we'll go downstairs anyway. It's time we were getting under this ceiling."

They find a hole and LX12 drops through. Now they are in the clear with wisps of mist about them. There is a land below them, grey-green from their height, with the grey water all around it.

The new members of the crew crowd the windows, they can't see enough of it. They fly on toward a line on the horizon. The line on the horizon is Britain. One of the crew stands ready with the Aldis lamp. They are challenged off the coast and reply with the signal of the day. They are in a prescribed area protected by anti-aircraft batteries and balloon barrages, and they must fly strictly according to orders. Movable balloon barrages, with the balloons hidden in the clouds, put beads of sweat on a pilot's brow.

They see the patchwork of an old civilization, houses and church spires and meadows and clear winding roads. There is a field below them so well-hidden that they do not recognize it until they are right over it. The faithful motors change their note as they are throttled back. LX12, her long flight over, lets down. *Bumbledy-bumbledy-bumbledy* go her three wheels on the runway.

Another bomber for Britain.

D. K. Findlay wrote for Maclean's *from 1935 until the end of the Second World War. He also wrote short stories and later published several novels.*

Capt. Bob Keefer and F.O. Jack Calder (right) in England, 1941

I Flew into Trouble

FLYING OFFICER JACK CALDER
August 15, 1942

A hand fell on my shoulder and I turned away for a moment from the job of destroying maps, documents and instruments at the navigation desk. Keefer stood at my elbow, still carrying the hatchet with which he had chopped the rear gunner out of his jammed turret. "I guess this means a long rest for us," he shouted above the noise of the big bomber's motors. "I never thought we would end up in Ireland."

"Maybe we'll get out of it yet, Bob," I ventured, tongue in cheek. "We've been in tougher spots."

Keefer, captain of the aircraft, went forward and took over control from the second pilot. The wireless operator fired off another Verey signal cartridge, hoping to attract attention from some airdrome. I finished clearing my desk and went up beside Keefer to peer into the darkness.

"I always wanted to make a parachute jump anyway," he said over the phone.

"But not under these circumstances," I replied. "It's a long walk home."

For four months the two of us had been flying, rooming and eating every meal together. In those four months, attached to a Royal Air Force squadron in England, we had attacked shipping and inland targets from Brest to Bremen, from Boulogne to Berlin. Now we were running out of fuel over the west coast of neutral Eire on a chilly morning. Seeing that we couldn't reach Northern Ireland or England, Keefer had picked out a hole in the thick layers of icing cloud, and we were circling above it, so that when we jumped we would be sure of coming down on land.

"Check the petrol again, will you?" he asked.

"There's enough for about five more minutes."

"Okay," he ordered. "Line up the crew. You and I will jump as close together as possible. I'll yell at you in the air and we'll try to get out of the country together."

I shook hands with the four sergeants as I herded them to the escape hatch. The rear gunner, who was on his first operation, was bleeding a little about the face. He said he was all right.

The starboard engine cut out. The front gunner kicked open the escape hatch on the captain's order and dropped through. The second pilot, rear gunner and wireless operator followed.

Jumping was easy. As my feet went out, the slipstream caught them and I was speeded through by the rush of air. I pulled the rip cord; in a moment my head was jerked back as the chute opened and I felt as if I were being sawn through. The sensation ended quickly and the first thing I noticed was the desperate quiet after eight hours of listening to the buzz of the engines and the crackling of the telephone.

I shouted for Keefer and got no reply. Then I heard the low whirr of our aircraft—old "C for Charlie"—gliding to her finish. Bob had planned to head her out to sea, but now she seemed to be coming around. I learned later that Keefer had headed her for the sea, started to jump and then had seen she was turning inland. He returned to the controls, pointed the machine for the Atlantic and jumped. The aircraft came around again and finally broke her back in a pasture.

For a long time I seemed not to be falling at all, just swaying a little in the breeze. I turned around to make sure that I wouldn't be carried out to sea and I inflated my "Mae West" just in case. Suddenly I realized the ground was near and I relaxed for the impact. Nothing happened. I bent my knees. My feet hit the ground and my knees hit my chin.

I got up, released my chute and tucked the folds under my arm. In the darkness I could see absolutely nothing but the stars and a couple of lights on the coast. I decided to start north and try to find Keefer. I stepped out smartly and immediately went to my hips in water. I retraced my steps and headed south; this time I sank to my knees in ooze and goo. Attempts west and east brought the same results.

It dawned on me that I was in a bog. It really wasn't a bad bog as Irish bogs go, but I was stuck there until dawn. I sat down on my little dry spot and ate a bit of chocolate, wondering all the while how the rest of the crew were faring. My head ached.

As the first light of dawn flooded the bog a half-hour later,

I discerned in the distance what I thought to be a great wall. The light grew and, just about 20 yards from me, I picked out a ribbon of road. If I could have got to that in the darkness, I might have stumbled to some sort of hiding place.

Now I hid my parachute, waded to the roadway and fairly ran along it toward the wall, for there wasn't a sign of other cover. As I got quite close to the wall, however, I saw that it was made of piled-up blocks of peat, the winter's fuel supply for hundreds of Irish families.

I hurried past and came upon a gate bearing a sign: "Keep Gate Shut." The thought came to me: "Well, we speak the same language. Maybe they'll listen to an argument if they catch me."

Deciding to head for the coast, I tore the badges and insignia from my flying dress as I walked. Around me were the tiny white cottages of the turf-cutters, each with a noisy dog. Smoke curled above the thatched roofs.

The sun started to rise and, in desperation, I looked for a hiding place. A small copse close to a cottage seemed the most likely, and furtively I climbed the low stone wall to go to it. As I did so, a child came from the house.

"O, momma," she cried. "Lookit the man!"

The family came out and I hurried away, wondering whether I was lucky enough to resemble an Irish vagrant.

The countryside was astir by now. Cattle drovers and donkey carts were on the road. Along the way I said good morning cheerfully to everyone. Dan O'Fagan said good morning from his pub door and the children sang good morning from the fence posts.

"Not bad," I thought, wondering if my red hair made me look like a native. "It can't be more than 100 miles to the border, either."

When I had walked eight or 10 miles, I sighted a railroad track and then a patch of woods overlooking it, near a coastal village. It looked like an ideal spot to wait for a freight train, and I started toward it.

"Hello," I was accosted from the roadside. "Where are ye goin' and where are ye after comin' from?"

"I'm from the south and I'm going north," I told the Irish policeman, just as if I were addressing a traffic cop back home.

"Well, them as goes north always comes into our guard barracks for a nice cup o' tay," he smiled. It was a real, nice, top-o'-the-mornin' smile, but I could feel him frisking me with his eyes for firearms. There was nothing for it but to go along.

"We heared ye wuz comin'," he said. "Five others like ye will be along in a twinkle." And then, wistfully, "Sure an' ye're all just lads, too."

In the police barracks I was fed bacon and eggs and Irish whisky, which goes down like fire and hits bottom like a sledge hammer. Keefer and the English sergeants came along soon. Bob was limping because, in landing, he had revived a knee injury which he suffered when he played with McGill University's football team.

"I had to go to a cottage," he reported. "The people said they would smuggle me into the north. So, while I was enjoying their bacon and eggs, they got the cops. Hey, look! Don't touch that Irish whisky. They gave me a shot and I nearly went through the floor."

The stories of the sergeants were similar to our own. They were in good shape.

The police and militia, arriving by the dozen, questioned us from every angle. Bob and I lied variously (and obviously) that we had brought a hundred parachutists and dropped them all over Ireland; that we had been flying alone and didn't know who the sergeants were; and that we didn't think we should be kept in a police station when our mothers and fathers came from Ireland and had been greatly interested in the Gaelic revival in America and the police strike in Boston. Keefer's name was O'Keefer and mine Fitz-Calder.

(I have learned since to swear that I am descended from the ancient Kings of Ireland and came "home" deliberately.)

When we had found out that we were at Quilty, in County Clare, we got permission to go outside and lie in the sun, for it was chilly in the barracks. We hoped, of course, to be able to get away, but the numbers of troops outside dashed those hopes quickly.

A bright sun shone on the sea, which lay calm and blue in the rock-bound inlet a mile away. All about us the land was green and in the background lay purple mountains.

While scores of Irish country folk stood gaping at us, Keefer fell asleep and I fell to thinking. I thought of the jobs we'd done and the fun we'd had together. Though I had been awake for more than 24 hours, I couldn't sleep. The letdown had been too sudden.

I remembered the tingling excitements of my first trip. It was to Rotterdam, where I released my first load of big bombs in the dock area. I was flying that night with Slapsy Maxie, a New Zealander who had been through the business in France and had flown the Atlantic twice. While he took avoiding action, he explained the various kinds of tracer shells that were being fired at us and the systems of searchlight fingers that were trying to pick us out, as if he were giving a lecture back in the crew room.

When we went to Frankfurt a couple of nights later, we were bounced around a bit by heavy anti-aircraft fire near Brussels; Maxie laughed while he worked the throttles to desynchronize the motors. On we went to find a terrific wall of fire being thrown up in one sector at the target area.

"There's something funny here," said Maxie. "I think they want us to believe the target is where they're shooting from. But do you see that bend in the river down there? That's what we're looking for."

When I dropped a flare, Maxie's opinion was confirmed. We were able to let the load go quickly and go back to England, where we were diverted to another airdrome because our own was under fog.

I did Brest in daylight with Maxie. It seems to have been the most exciting episode of my life, for our formation shot down three Messerschmitt 109's in our run-up to the target. Maxie got the Distinguished Flying Cross and the gunnery leader the Distinguished Flying Medal for that one.

Many of the jaunts with Keefer were nearly as successful. We couldn't have hit the target more squarely than we did on our first together. We just glided into Boulogne with a full moon ahead, released our stick across the docks and glided out again before Jerry knew we were there. The Air Ministry has recorded that the fires were burning the next day.

The things that stood out most prominently, though—as I lay on the green, green Irish lawn and gazed into the blue, blue Irish sky—were the things that had gone wrong and become right again, the things we had gone through and lived to tell about.

More vividly still I remember one night we headed for Berlin. An hour from the target—and after we had weathered a storm of anti-aircraft fire among the big searchlight belts—the wireless operator produced a message recalling us to base because fog was closing in all over England.

"Aw, we've gone through the worst of it now," Keefer groaned. "I feel like going on."

"But I've acknowledged the message, sir," the wireless operator said. "And my set is kicking up a fuss."

We would have to return, we agreed. Bob asked for a course for home and told me to select a target en route. We decided on an airdrome near Münster and I prepared the camera for our bomb explosions.

Sgt. Johnny Tett, the former Canadian diving champion, was with us as second pilot. One of his duties was to release the flash bomb for the photograph and he put it into the chute as we glided toward the target.

"Okay, Johnny?" I asked on the phone.

"Just about," he said; and then, "Holy smoke, no!"

There was a commotion and a flash lit up the aircraft and the sky around us. My first thought was of a night fighter or a new weapon. Johnny came on again.

"The thing fused too quickly," he panted. "It nearly went off in the aircraft. I think it exploded right beneath us."

We came around again, dropped our stuff and took a picture. We saw our fires for a good 15 minutes on the way home. Johnny didn't say a word all the way.

On one of our last raids we came home with three minutes' petrol after visiting Bremen, Wilhelmshaven and Emden in search of a suitable target. Nowhere over Germany is the anti-aircraft fire more vivid than over the northwest; that night the whole countryside spurted fountains of varicoloured shells.

The commanding officer was in a sweat when we arrived back

an hour after everyone else, and his wife made us promise at dinner the next night that we wouldn't worry him again.

The flight on which we lost Coxie from the rear turret was a nightmare. We climbed to 20,000 feet over the North Sea, always just above a field of icing cloud. After crossing the Belgian coast, the machine suddenly gasped, went out of control and spiralled dizzily downward. Keefer brought her right after losing about 3,000 feet.

Over the telephone I could hear Coxie shouting—though his voice came through like a whisper—to ask if everything was all right. I reassured him, and then the plane spiralled downward again. Bob wrestled her under control and finally the clouds divided as providentially as the Red Sea. We levelled out.

"We went into a cloud and iced up before I could do a thing," he shouted tersely. "I haven't any instruments left but my compass and altimeter. I'll have to go down below the freezing level."

We descended to 3,000 feet. It was then we found that Coxie, unable to communicate with us and apparently certain that we were spinning in, had baled out. We had lost the best rear gunner on the squadron, a boy who had three enemy aircraft to his credit and who never lost his spirit in the most nerve-racking spot in the ship. (He reports the food in a German prison camp "not so good.")

Our instruments gradually returned to normal and we bombed a coastal airdrome from so low a level that we felt our bombbursts. As we fought our way home across the North Sea in a thunderstorm, lightning struck the front guns with a flash that thoroughly scared us all and blinded the gunner momentarily. The white cliffs were never more welcome than on that night.

On our last leave we had set a record by doing Doncaster, Edinburgh, London and Southend in six days, seeing all the shows and meeting scores of friends from Canada. When we "left" our squadron, we were organizing a hockey team and we had just sold our £10 motor car for £15 because the licence and insurance were due.

Once we had tea with the King and Queen and the Princesses in Windsor Castle. We chatted about the Royal Visit and the pre-war days.

And now we lay on a lawn in Eire, away from it all, waiting for a motor convoy to take us to the quiet of an internment camp. My headache grew worse.

In midafternoon the parish priest came to see us, saying that he was "sorry." Why I chose to unloose my feelings on him, I don't know; but I stood up and engaged him in the wildest political, religious and war argument on record. They say it was pretty good. It must have been for I recall an old woman trying to collect sixpences in the crowd that looked on open-mouthed.

The convoy formed and we were driven down the coast and along the beautiful River Shannon to Limerick. That night we went behind barbed wire on the Curragh, where British troops were garrisoned in the last war. It was startling to see the streets lit up again at night, after Britain's blackout.

The Irish people? Well, they're very Irish. They've been very kind. We have been allowed considerable freedom on parole. John D. Kearney, the Canadian High Commissioner, has been like a father to us. Our parcels from Canada have been the envy of the entire British Internment Camp.

The atmosphere of horses, fishing and Irish colleens could be pretty lulling, I think. Somehow—and I believe the Irish understand too well—we aren't always thinking of those things. We can still read the papers and listen to Churchill and Roosevelt by radio.

The last escape attempt was a big one but got nowhere. Perhaps too many Irishmen know what it is to be locked up by other people. They've known all the tricks so far.

In 1942, Jack Calder and Bob Keefer escaped from their camp, but Calder was recaptured—and then released in the following year. Keefer first trained pilots in Canada, before returning to action as a photo reconnaissance pilot. After the war, Keefer ran an import-export business in Montreal and now lives in an Ottawa veterans' home.

Calder, despite losing an eye in a training crash after his return to duty, still flew bombing missions until July 20, 1944, when he drowned in the Elbe estuary after his plane was shot down over Germany.

Wing Cmdr. Mark Brown

Mark Brown, Fighter Pilot

FRANK E. CROFT
October 1, 1942

Two Hurricane fighters went streaking across the skies above Metz on the tail of a Dornier 17. It was late November, 1939. The Hurricanes attacked in turns, and after a couple of bursts from each, the Nazi went into a spiral, then fell to earth in flames.

One of the Hurricanes was piloted by the leader of No. 1 Fighter Squadron, R.A.F. The other was piloted by a Canadian member of the squadron—Flying Officer Mark "Hilly" Brown, of Glenboro, Man. The "half" plane which was credited to him at

Wing Headquarters after that brief chase above Metz was the first of a string of victories which had reached a total of 20 definite and as many probables, before Italian ground defences in Sicily brought him to his death late in 1941.

The Manitoba youth has been out of the fight for almost a year, now, and although other Canadian pilots are crowding close to his record, it remains, as this is written, the mark which all must surpass if the title "Canada's No. 1 Fighter Ace" is to appear after any name but Brown.

Mark Brown was a Flying Officer when the war began, having joined the R.A.F. in 1936. He was the first Canadian airman to draw blood in this war. When he got out of France in June, 1940, he had been promoted to the rank of Flight Lieutenant and had 17 enemy planes to his credit. In the Battle of Britain he added still more Nazi planes to his list; by the time the last of the daylight raiders had been chased out of British skies, Hilly Brown was in command of the squadron with which he had gone to France a year previously, and with this promotion to Squadron Leader came the Distinguished Flying Cross.

During the winter and early summer of 1941, he instructed a group of Czech student pilots, whom he described as "grand fellows and fine pilots." His work with the Czechs won him a military decoration from the Czecho-Slovakian government in London. At the end of summer, Wing Cmdr. Brown, as he was by then (the youngest Wing Commander in the R.A.F.), was again given operational duties—his last—when he was sent to Malta as commander of fighter operations in that zone.

Mark Henry Brown was born in Portage la Prairie, Man., on Oct. 9, 1911. His father, S. T. Brown, is a Canadian Pacific Railway man. His father's duties took the family to MacGregor, Man., when Mark was still a boy, and they remained there several years.

After graduating from Macgregor High School, Mark went to work in the Bank of Montreal. He spent seven years in the bank, in Macgregor, Deloraine, Russell, all in Manitoba, and Limerick and Saskatoon, in Saskatchewan. So quite a bit of scene shifting went on behind young Brown during his time with the bank, but he was able to work in a course with the Brandon Flying Club, where he received his private pilot's licence—his entrée to the R.A.F.

It was in Macgregor that Mark went to school, played in the town band (a faltering but loud baritone horn), worked in the butcher shop on Saturdays and played hockey in between times. He was not a hockey star, as Western standards go; but he was good enough to show the English some tricks after the game had become popular in Britain during the three years preceding the war. It was also in Macgregor that Mark displayed some real mechanical skill. He and a pal installed the first "talkie" equipment known to the town, and for three years the boys just about ran the show. The extra money which Mark earned from this enterprise was part of a thrift campaign which he had started right after leaving high school, with a flying course and training in England as the goal.

In Glenboro he received one notable bequest, however. The evening before he left for England, a neighbour's boy came running up to him with a button ripped from the tunic the boy's father had worn in the First Great War, when a member of the Royal Flying Corps.

"It may bring you luck," the boy said. Mark gratefully accepted the button thinking that the only bad luck against which he would need a charm would be not making the grade with the R.A.F. But he did make the grade; and when war broke out he replaced the top button on his uniform with the old R.F.C. button which had been thrust into his hand on the eve of his departure for Britain.

When Mark Brown showed up at the flying training school at Ansty, England, a number of students were listening to some Kentucky hill-billy songs, being sung on the radio by a certain "Hilly Brown." The newcomer was introduced, and the name Brown, coupled with the singer's name, were enough for the "Hilly" part to replace his Christian name, a replacement which remained.

Hilly Brown was just under medium height—five feet seven—chunkily built, with sandy hair, twinkling blue-grey eyes and that disarming manner with which all practical jokers are equipped. For Mark was a great joker, a prankster who usually had those around him wondering just when the next covert blow would fall, when and from what direction. After all, he was the youngest of five—and three of them girls. So it was only natural that he should have come to the conclusion early in life that the best defence was attack, with surprise the main element.

When Mark Brown left Canada, thoughts of ever levelling gun sights on an enemy plane were as remote as the possibility of hunting crocodiles on the Congo. He joined the Royal Air Force fresh from his course with the Brandon Flying Club, as one would enter a university from high school. His ambition was to become a first-class commercial pilot, operating home in Canada, and he picked the R.A.F. as being the most thorough seat of learning among the world's universities of the air.

Under the Gosport system of training, Hilly Brown began unconsciously to show what he was made of. Along with the other fledglings, his name was entered in what must be the queerest ledger in the world. It is a ledger of imponderables. The entries are made in columns under such headings as dash, courage, observation, aggressiveness, and so on. When his training days were over and his account on his ledger page was reckoned, it was found that as a fighter pilot his credits were heavy and his debits none at all. So when war was declared, Flying Officer Brown from Manitoba found himself in the cockpit of a Hurricane, roaring across the flat East Anglia countryside for France.

The battle with the Dornier over Metz was one of the few which enlivened the dullness of patrol work during those unreal days in France, from September to early the following May. In a letter to a friend in Canada, Hilly said: "What a queer war it is. The only excitement is when some officer shoots out the windows of his quarters in a near-by camp with his revolver."

About a week after he had bagged his share of the Dornier, Hilly and another member of the squadron accounted for a Heinkel 111K, and it was not long after that when No. 1 Squadron met up with its first Messerschmitt 109. It took only two such duels for the British to realize that Willie Messerschmitt hadn't produced anything which they didn't have, and that any difference between the Me's and the Hurricanes was in the British plane's favour.

Around Christmas time Hilly bagged his first Me. No clear account of the battle has been given, but later on, when an Me 109 was forced down intact, Hilly was chosen to fly it to England for examination. He was the first British pilot to fly a Messerschmitt.

Hilly entered the Battle of France with the conviction that there was not a bullet with his name on it. He was right. He took them all on, in French, British and Mediterranean skies, but it took fire from below—cannon fire—to pull Hilly Brown out of the fight for good.

It was an evening early in May, when the squadron was stationed at Neuville, that the distant rumblings of gun fire on the

Maginot and Siegfried lines presaged the flood tide of battle which in a short time was to roll on to Paris. All through the night of May 9 the airmen at Neuville could hear the guns. The roar of aircraft motors rose above the cannonading to the east, and sometimes the pounding of AA guns could be heard close at hand. It was all happening in sectors handled by the French, but at dawn the Operations Officer at Wing Headquarters had plots all over the board, and the sun was still crouching on the horizon when No. 1 Squadron was fighting it out with Dorniers and Me's at 20,000 feet.

Hilly's R.F.C. button still held its charm and he came out of that scrap with another plane to his credit. At that time the Me 110 was putting in a frequent appearance. For a while our boys were inclined to regard them with considerable awe, just as they had the 109, until they had fought it out with them. But after a few dogfights with the Me 110's, the awe was replaced by limited respect, for the Hurricanes were still on top.

The R.A.F. won the confidence of the freedom-loving world in the Battle of Britain, but it had already won confidence in itself in the Battle of France.

Hilly Brown, like every other airman in France, flew and fought from an hour before dawn to two and three hours after sunset. He slept under the wing of his plane, when he could sleep. In those days, when nerves were raw, Hilly's phlegmatic humour was a tonic for the whole squadron. The few survivors of No. 1 Squadron still tell of one occasion when they had just taken up quarters at Berry-au-Bac. Jerry came over to give the new field a pasting.

A stick of bombs burst with staccato, ear-splitting crashes. Fragments spattered against the dispersal hut and flew about the heads of the men lying face down on the turf. A stream of invective came from the men as they jumped up to rush for their planes. Hilly was heard, almost as if talking to himself, saying, "Legitimate military objective." It had been, of course, but his calm appraisal of the attack didn't prevent him from adding two more German planes to his score before sundown that day.

His fellow squadron members say that Hilly's technique was something to see, if anyone could take time out from a dogfight to watch. He seemed able to do all his manoeuvring before closing the range on his victim. Once Hilly was ready to open fire, the climbing and slipping, dodging and twisting were all over with. He would be right on the tail of the enemy plane, and could stay there until the Nazi had dropped from his sights, a flaming wreck.

He was in on the bombing of the Maastricht Bridge—a volunteer job, carried out against strong ground defences and swarms of Me 109's and 110's. It was in that fight that Hilly's plane received its first bad hits of the war—two cannon-shell hits; but he brought it back all right, and the bridge was successfully bombed by our Blenheims, under the protection of a small fighter escort, headed by Hilly Brown.

On the way home, at Rethel, the Hurricanes ran into a group of Me 110's. A savage battle was fought at a bare thousand feet. A wounded British flier, who saw most of the fight from a ditch, said later that if a movie cameraman had been on the job he would have got a picture to make *Hell's Angels* look like a Sunday-school picnic.

The Me's were escorting a large formation of Ju 87's. Six of the enemy planes were shot down—two by Hilly (an Me and a Junkers) and one each by four of the other pilots in the Hurricane flight.

The Battle of France had not been in progress many days before Hilly was promoted to Flight-Lieutenant and placed second in command of the squadron. At that time he had 13 planes definite, and 10 probables, while No. 1 Squadron had an official score of 98 enemy planes, against two pilots missing and one wounded! Toward the end of the month Hilly was averaging almost a plane each nerve-racking day.

German battle tactics were being grimly demonstrated before the eyes of the British fliers during that period. They saw the vanguard of refugees clogging the roads and presently they saw those refugees cowering in ditches while German planes strafed them from chimney-top altitudes. When the Germans had passed on, the refugees, crazed with fear, would come out of the ditches to stumble on down the road, leaving scores of their number dead and bleeding in the ditch.

Paul Ritchey, a member of No. 1 Squadron, says in his published diary of the Battle of France (*Fighter Pilot*), after having seen German airmen at work on Belgian and French refugees: "'We'll teach you Huns how to fight. We'll shoot your snooty fighters out of the sky and rip your foul great bomber to shreds; we'll make you wish to God you had never seen an airplane. We'll teach you to make war.' We knew we could, too—if we were reinforced."

At that stage of the war, Hilly was forsaking his cool, calculating battle technique. He had seen the slaughter of the refugees. Now he went into battle with less time spent on the preliminaries. He pitched into the Messerschmitts from any angle, flying like an enraged hornet, eager to open fire on any terms and from just about any position.

On May 18, Hilly was ordered to lead seven volunteers on a flight to Amiens, land and refuel, then go ahead on a special job. Over St. Quentin they ran into heavy anti-aircraft fire, although their latest intelligence hadn't placed the enemy within 50 miles of St. Quentin. The Germans were moving fast. In the first burst of AA fire, two of the Hurricanes dived down and disappeared. When the other six, who had split up and done some fancy dodging, looked around for Hilly, they found they had no leader on whom to form up. Thinking that Hilly and the other member of the flight had been shot down, the remaining six began to look around for an airdrome.

On the first one located they saw the wreckage of two Potez 63's (dive bombers), and a Hurricane was seen taxiing in toward the wrecked enemy craft. As the other six Hurricanes touched in, they were surprised to see that it was their leader; Hilly's "E" was plainly marked on the fuselage. Hilly then swung into the wind and took off in a hurry. He later told the other pilots that a Frenchman had run up to him as he was taxiing in, with the warning: "Get away quick—the Germans are just over there and will be here in five minutes."

Hilly had broken away from the flight when he had seen the two dive-bombers at work on a defenceless village near the airdrome. He had not only accounted for one of the Potez craft (the other had got in the way of the AA fire) but had encountered a German Army co-op plane, a Henschel 126, and had literally blown it out of the sky. The other pilot who had disappeared with Hilly had been hit, but he bailed out and was taken prisoner.

By this time there was not a batman in the Allied forces who did not realize that the Germans were not being held, and would not be held. On May 19 the R.A.F. and the Armée de l'Air sent every bomber they had to attack the bridges on the Aisne. And every fighter squadron was to provide protection. Hilly shot down a Heinkel on the way to the Aisne, just as an appetizer. In the actual fighting over the Aisne, there was no sure telling who had shot down what. It was a wild melee similar to some of the dogfights which were to take place in British skies before the summer was over, and no one had a chance of following a victim down to make sure he was really done for, nor of having his claims corroborated by others in the fight.

May 19 was the last day of any sizeable operations in France for No. 1 Squadron, or the R.A.F., for that matter. France was finished. The squadron was given the choice of returning to England or sticking it out in France. Hilly was one of the men who voted on staying in France and, as he expressed it, "facing the music."

The squadron hung on for another month. Finally, when it had been ordered to return to England, Hilly's score was 17 German planes shot down. He was tied with the famous New Zealander, "Cobber" Kane. The bullet with Cobber's name on it found him during the dying echoes of the Battle of France.

Hilly was not able to fly out of France. Engine trouble at the last minute saw him hurrying toward the Channel coast by any means of transportation he could find. He arrived on the coast in time, to quote him, "to catch the last boat for England."

A clearer account has been kept of the individual exploits of the squadron in France than after it was re-formed in England. Hilly rose to command No. 1 Squadron in Britain. He was by then a veteran of aerial warfare. During the fierce days in late July and August, when the Huns were coming in larger and larger numbers, Hilly added to his score. He had reached the 20 mark when on August 15—the day the Germans sent their greatest number of planes against Britain—he was shot down. He landed in the sea and was picked up by a trawler.

Thanks to his oxygen mask and helmet, the burns he suffered were minor—although he didn't think so when he discovered that his moustache had been burned off. That sandy-coloured moustache had been a source of great pride with Hilly, and losing it was a blow.

A leg injury which he also suffered on August 15 kept him on the ground for a spell; but in spite of this layoff he added more planes to his score in that late summer of 1940. With the coming of winter, Hilly was promoted to the rank of Acting Wing Commander. His value as an instructor could not be over-looked, no matter how many planes he could shoot down. So he was sent to a northern training centre to instruct a crop of Czech student pilots.

Hilly stayed with the Czech lads all winter, and his work was so satisfactory that the Czech Government in London awarded him that country's top military decoration. At about that time he was awarded the bar to his D.F.C. It was a happy Mark Brown who received orders late in the summer of 1941 to go to Malta and resume operational flying. He was in charge of all fighter opera-tions on the island of Malta, and he came on the scene just when the German and Italian airmen were beginning to step up their bombing attacks.

Mark Brown had not been at his new post very long before something happened to the charm of that old Royal Flying Corps button. During a raid on the airdrome at Kasina, on the Island of Sicily, Wing Commander Brown's plane was hit by anti-aircraft fire. He was seen to turn, then go down in a steady glide. A few days later the Italians dropped a note on Malta, saying that Mark Brown (whom they called "lieutenant-colonel") had been buried with full military honours in an unnamed cemetery.

A short time ago S. T. Brown in Glenboro was given these details of his son's death in a personal letter from Air Vice-Marshal Lloyd, Air Officer Commanding, Mediterranean Command.

The Air Vice-Marshal concluded with these words:

"There is one consolation. That is that the raid was a great success, as indeed it would be, for Wing Cmdr. Brown planned the whole operation and went over and saw to it himself."

There is no official list of fighter-pilot kills, but "Buzz" Beurling is generally considered Canada's top Second World War ace, with some 30 enemy planes shot down. Mark Brown ranks as high as fifth on unofficial lists.

Lieut.-Gen. Andrew McNaughton

General in Battle Dress

WALLACE REYBURN
February 15, 1943

Lieut.-Gen. Andrew George Latta McNaughton, 55, home town, Moosomin, Sask., is the head of the 1st Army, in the strict sense of the word, that Canada has ever had.

In this war the Canadians go into battle not as a Corps, as they did in the last war, but as an Army. This change from a Corps to an Army was made early in 1942. An Army is elastic in size and may comprise six divisions, eight, perhaps 10. But it always consists of two or more Corps, and at present has some 170,000 men.

Being in charge of such a large body of men is an assignment as complicated as that of being the head of any great corporation or business enterprise employing thousands. But in one very important regard McNaughton's position differs from that of an ordinary civilian business president. Not only is he the guiding light for the thousands of people under him—but their fate depends upon his decisions, their very lives are in his hands.

His task is to know intimately, from study or personal knowledge, the terrain into which his troops are going to move, so that the problems of transportation and manoeuvre can be understood fully and handled efficiently. He must be able to make an accurate estimate of what the casualties of any operation are likely to be and be certain that reinforcements can be sent in speedily and in large numbers. He deals with all the thousand and one problems of supply, the getting of food, fuel and equipment to the men in the field. He must ascertain the extent of Air Force and Naval co-operation and work with these other branches. He must assure himself that the weapons at the disposal of his men are suitable and sufficient for any given undertaking.

These and countless other considerations come under the supervision and guidance of a general commanding an army. To perform these duties, Gen. McNaughton arrives at his office each morning at between 9:00 and 9:15. Army Headquarters are in a large, beautifully situated country mansion. As he arrives at the front doorway, McNaughton never fails to inspect the guard. The guard consists of a sentry who walks back and forth in front of the doorway along a pathway worn smooth in the gravel of the driveway by the footprints of many a sentry before him.

The house is a typical English country seat, a big rambling grey stone affair with ivy framing its leaded windows. Its stairs and hallways are panelled, and its bathroom fixtures installed by a plumber of the old school. Theoretically it's centrally heated. It stands on a slight rise which affords an excellent view of the surrounding meadows and hedgerows. Not that the General is prone to sit at his windows admiring the scenery. The most likely position any intruder will find the General in when he invades his sanctum is with his head down over the papers on his desk. There are three tables in the room, none of them of the polished-top variety, all of them functional rather than good to look at. A large table by the big bay window is used as a conference table when he talks en masse with his chiefs. In another corner of the room is a map table, waist high, and on a swivel so that he can work at it standing up. In the centre of the room is the drafting table, which is the one he uses most.

Being a man with more regard for utility than show, McNaughton's office has little else to offer in the manner of furnishings. The other pieces in the room are mostly chairs of the campstool type, canvas and wood affairs. Before he took the room over, the walls boasted rich oak panelling, but this has long since been covered over with beaverboard on which has been pinned an array of large-scale maps. These maps, which cover the entire surface of two walls, are mostly of the area in which the Canadian troops are stationed, with coloured pins indicating the locality of every unit in the Canadian Army. There are also a map of Great Britain and a large-scale, huge map of France.

As soon as he gets into his office in the morning, McNaughton seats himself at his desk and occupies himself for an hour with correspondence, files and other routine matters. While the General is at work, should any of his office staff chance to come into the room to talk to him on some matter, it is highly unlikely that he will look up as the door opens. Possessed of tremendous powers of concentration, he becomes quite oblivious to anything that is going on around him when he "has his nose down." As any of his office staff will tell you, going into the Chief's office to see him about something entails walking into the room, standing before his desk for half a minute or so and then, when you feel that you have given him every chance of becoming aware of your presence, drawing attention to yourself by a discreet cough.

One day a clerk, thinking McNaughton was out, sailed gaily into his office, whistling a tune as he went. He stopped in his tracks when he saw the General at work at his desk and was about to mumble apologies. But apparently they were unnecessary. He departed without McNaughton giving any sign of having noticed the interruption.

Gen. McNaughton has on his desk a rubber time-stamp. Every letter or other paper that is put before him, he automatically brands with this personal stamp, so that at a moment's notice his staff can look through the files of his papers and tell him on what day and at what hour he dealt with such-and-such a document.

He smokes incessantly. The large square glass ashtray on his desk is piled high with cigarette butts long before the day is through. Though he used to smoke a pipe before the war, he smokes cigarettes exclusively now and smokes them at a rate that leaves even the most ardent smokers among his visitors a long way behind. He drinks little. His favourite drink is sherry, and his consumption of this is confined almost entirely to a glass before dinner.

After the first hour in his office dealing with routine matters, he is prepared to receive the day's D.V.'s. The expression "D.V." is army parlance for Distinguished Visitor and these may comprise officers down from Canadian Military Headquarters in London, Divisional Commanders, men from the War Office, technical specialists, what-have-you.

Any D.V. who meets McNaughton for the first time is struck by what at first glance seems to be a most unmilitary disregard for personal tidiness and neatness of attire. The General's uniform or battle dress will have been pressed to perfection by his batman, but perhaps the collar of his tunic got turned up as he put it on and he is unlikely to notice it or do anything about it until it is brought to his attention.

When he isn't on parade his peaked cap is more likely to be found sitting on the back of his head than at the approved military angle. He has not the preoccupation about "looking the part" that is evidenced by many another military man who is bent on impressing all and sundry with the importance of his position. He is interested in the job on hand and he regards the clothes he wears as necessary but not something to clutter one's mind with thoughts about. His hair is unruly and a lock of it invariably hangs down over his forehead. His friends will tell you that "he has bigger things to worry about than his personal appearance."

When you are in conversation with him he fixes you with his piercing, penetrating eyes as you speak. If you are asking him a question he weighs every word you say, his eyebrows will be puckered together in a frown of concentration and his whole attention is riveted on you and what you are saying. Then when he gives you his answer it will be the fullest and most easily understood answer it is in his power to give. As he speaks, he works on and develops each idea, each sentence, with the same precision and exactness he would bring to a laboratory experiment. But this doesn't mean that his conversation is studied and stiff. It's merely an outcome of his inborn high regard for detail and exactness. He never talks down to you and, as an officer once said, "The great thing about McNaughton is that when he's talking to you he takes it for granted he is talking to an intelligent person." There is not an ounce of sham, ostentation or pomposity in him.

He is the answer to a photographer's prayer and a joy to the Canadian war correspondents. It's impossible to take a bad photograph of him. His face contains in it so much character, depth and understanding that one can shoot him from any angle and catch him in any mood, even when he's worn out and tired from a heavy day, and the result is a superb photograph.

The correspondents wax lyrical about him because it's his expressed policy that the people of Canada have a right to know everything there is to be known about the Canadian Army Overseas, everything, that is, except certain facts that would give comfort to the enemy. He says that the men in the field must have behind them a well-informed Canada. And the way to do this is through the press.

Therefore, when a correspondent goes to McNaughton for some guidance on a story he's writing, he'll take him into his confidence. He'll tell him things that McNaughton knows and the pressman knows, too, can never be published. He'll tell him the whole story, and as he does so, point out to him what parts can be published and what parts can't. He realizes to the utmost the important link the press is between the men overseas and the people at home and wants every correspondent to have the fullest possible background on every Army topic—not just scraps of publishable information.

Best way to show how strongly McNaughton feels about furthering a sound understanding and keeping strong this bond between the Army overseas and the people back home is to mention what happened at a parade that was held in England not long ago. The King was coming down to inspect a certain unit of the troops. They were all lined up—hundreds of them—on the parade square. One of our official Army photographers started getting his equipment together and then he suddenly realized that as the parade was laid out he was going to have to shoot into the sun. His pictures wouldn't be very good. So he approached Gen. McNaughton with his problem.

McNaughton thought for a second or two and then said: "You won't be able to get good pictures, eh? H'm. There are a lot of families back in Canada who'd be thrilled to see their sons photographed with the King. All right, I'll fix it." And he called over one of his officers and had the whole parade turned round in the opposite direction.

McNaughton takes his lunch at one o'clock. His A.D.C., Lieut. Laird Bouvaird, makes an earnest endeavour to get him to eat at home on as many days as possible. Reason for this is that when he eats at Headquarters, the General sits down in A Mess, which is the one reserved for senior ranking officers, and the lunch always resolves itself into less of a meal than a conference. Lieut. Bouvaird, whose job approximates that of a private secretary in civilian life, has that particular type of regard for his Chief's health and welfare that is evidenced by every private secretary of a hard-worked boss, and he feels that the General should have a definite break at noontime, get away from work for an hour or so and come back to the job refreshed. So whenever possible he connives with Mrs. McNaughton to get the Chief to lunch at home.

Whether Gen. McNaughton lunches at home or at the mess, the eating part of the procedure is something over which he concerns himself little or nothing. He has no interest at all in food as such. He will eat anything that is put in front of him. Meals to him are merely a three-times-a-day interruption, a formality akin to cleaning one's teeth each morning. When he becomes engrossed in whatever he is doing, he often has to be reminded that he's overrunning a mealtime.

This preoccupation with what he is doing, this singleness of purpose, is something that anyone who comes in close contact with McNaughton notices as his foremost characteristic. Though an outstanding attribute and one that has meant much in the forming of his career, it had its drawbacks for one Canadian unit on an occasion last winter. McNaughton was going to inspect them. They were lined up on the barrack square at the appointed time. The General was a few minutes late. They waited. The minutes dragged on to half an hour. Still no sign of the General. An hour passed, and they still stood on the barrack square waiting. Eventually, after an hour and a half, he arrived and announced to the men his apologies. On the way to the square the Colonel had shown him a new set of intelligence tests and aptitude-gauging machines that had just reached the unit. McNaughton had looked them over. Tried one, then another, didn't leave the hut until he had tried himself out on all of them. His score was "above average, very outstanding."

Following lunch McNaughton usually spends the afternoon out of doors, inspecting field formations. These excursions may cover anything from watching an exercise to testing out some new piece of equipment. Though it is part of the function of any General commanding an army to know intimately the weapons, vehicles and equipment the men under him are furnished with, to see that they have the best possible and to help in an advisory capacity with the development of new material, there are few Generals today who devote as much attention to this phase of their work or are as qualified to take such an active part in it as is McNaughton.

His interest in science began when he was in short pants. In his birthplace of Moosomin, young Andy is remembered mostly for two things, both of them connected with explosives. On one occasion, to draw to a close an argument which was going on between his father and his cousin, he fashioned a bomb, tied it outside the window of the room they were in, set it off and finished the argument with a bang. At another time he made a cannon out of an old piece of three-inch boiler tubing and used it to shoot potatoes at gophers.

Feeling the need to give his son a wider scope for his inventiveness, young Andy's father, Robert Duncan McNaughton, who owned the town's thriving central store, sent him east to Bishop's College School, Lennoxville, Que., and later to McGill University, where he studied electrical engineering.

After an outstanding career in the Great War, during which he did such great work in the development of artillery counter-battery tactics that he was awarded the D.S.O., he returned to Canada, soon became Chief of the General Staff and was later to become head of the National Research Council. It was while in that capacity that he developed the cathode ray direction-finder, which helps airmen to find true bearings over mountainous country.

A scientist as well as a soldier, McNaughton has the scientific approach to the weapons, vehicles and equipment of his army. Photographs in the press have often displayed him looking over a tank or testing out a new field gun. But such photographs tell only half the story. McNaughton is a believer in "seeing for himself." When he comes to look over, say, a new radio-equipped truck for the Signallers, he will not be content to give it a mere cursory once-over. He'll climb in and out of that truck, seat himself at the steering wheel, crouch down under the front springs, examine the thing up and down, inside and outside, subject it and all its parts to the closest of close scrutinies. All the time he will be firing at the driver, the mechanic and the radio operators a series of questions about the truck and its parts. "This wrench in the toolbox— does it do the job it's meant to do? I notice it's made of cast iron. Don't you think it will be likely to break under stress?" And with that he will give the wrench a resounding crack on a rock. It will perhaps break and he will put forward the suggestion that it be replaced with a wrench made of wrought iron.

His study of weapons and equipment is not merely critical without being constructive. He has said often and at great length that he is not going to be satisfied until he knows that his men go into battle with the best weapons that it's possible for the cream of Canada's scientific, mechanical and industrial brains to produce. Much of the equipment of the Canadian Army Overseas is Canadian-made, and much of it is the result either of McNaughton's direct instigation or critical appraisal and suggestions.

"I am not interested in museum pieces," he has said. "I don't want 'hand-tooled' pieces that you can hold up to the light and admire. I want weapons as good or better than the enemy's and I want them fast and by the thousands, by the tens of thousands."

He was the prime mover in the setting up early in 1942 of Canada's weapon development board. He is a great believer in the development of weapons being done in the factories, in the atmosphere of mass production, as he terms it. The prototype is developed overseas, in the field as it were, and then back in Canada that prototype is developed by the people who will do the production. An interesting point is that Britain has followed this Canadian lead and has now set up a weapon development board.

None of his fellow officers can recall ever having seen McNaughton lose his temper in public. Gen. Wavell has pointed out in his now famous series of lectures delivered at

Cambridge that explosions of temper do not necessarily ruin a General's reputation of influence with his troops; it is almost expected of them—"the privileged irascibility of senior officers," it has been called. But Gen. McNaughton has never been known to avail himself of this privilege. He gets mad, certainly. He would not be human if he didn't. His office has been known to resound lustily on occasion, when something or somebody has taxed his patience. But in dealing with his men he has drawn on his understanding of the psychology of handling people and getting from them the maximum of confidence and co-operation (an essential for a successful General) and he refrains from "flying off the handle" in public.

As an example of his wisdom in this, there is the case of his visit to a certain unit in the field. He arrived in the hutments to find them dirty, untidy and showing every evidence of neglect by the officer in charge. He was shocked and annoyed at what he saw. But he did not berate the man concerned in front of the N.C.O.'s and privates. He knew that by doing that he would only make the officer the laughing-stock of the men, who would lose their regard for "the guy the General bawled out." Also the officer would be humiliated, harbour a grudge against the General for showing him up, and that also would make for bad morale. But that officer was not let off with a mere soft reprimand. He got hell from the Chief, but later in the private confines of McNaughton's own office. Thus the objective of having the hutments cleaned up and assurance that it wouldn't occur again was achieved without the relationships between men and officer, officer and commander, being impaired.

That incident is typical of McNaughton's handling of his troops. Though a General must be assured of strict discipline, he must have an understanding of humanity, the raw material of his trade. Whenever he assigns a man to perform some task he tells him specifically what he wants done and by what time he expects it to be done. Then he leaves him alone. He doesn't pester him with queries as to how the job's coming along, he doesn't flood him with advice as to how he should he doing it. He picks his men and has faith in them.

In his off-duty moments, McNaughton has nothing that can actually be called a hobby. He is an expert fisherman, but he gets no time for it. He is not a great reader—of general literature, that is. Many a reporter has been disappointed to learn that the great man does *not* spend his leisure moments reading detective novels the way so many well-known great men do. What reading McNaughton does do is confined almost exclusively to military and kindred works. But he is an avid newspaper and magazine reader and keeps more than well abreast of what is being published in the daily and periodical press of Canada.

His chief relaxation is, to quote Mrs. McNaughton, "fixing things up." He is one of the few people in England today who are glad of the fact that wartime shortages of labour have made workmen, like plumbers and electricians, scarce and hard to get hold of if something in the house breaks down. The more appliances that go wrong in his home, the happier he is, and guests are likely to arrive of an evening and find the G.O.C., Canadian Army Overseas, down on his hands and knees behind a bureau tinkering with an electric light plug.

These guests that drop into the McNaughton home are many and varied. "Feel free to drop in at any time" is no mere platitude where the McNaughtons are concerned. They mean it, whether it's said to a divisional commander or a private, and on a Sunday afternoon in the McNaughton home there is likely to be gathered there an as seemingly unhomogeneous social group as one could imagine. But no matter what station in life or rank in the Army the guests may be, the friendly atmosphere of the place breaks down any such barriers.

Many of his friends will tell you that McNaughton is the most considerate man they have ever known. Travelling in an Army staff car on his way to some manoeuvres, he is likely to turn to a very junior officer who happens to be riding in the car with him and say: "Is it too cold for you with the window open?" The young man will probably say to himself: "Good heavens, it's not important whether or not I'M cold! Who am I, a mere lieutenant, to decide whether the window should be up or down when I'm driving in the General's car?" He will be moved by this display of thoughtfulness on the part of McNaughton, just as hundreds of other officers, N.C.O.'s, privates, have been struck by similar experiences.

Such courteousness may seem relatively unimportant in judging the merits of a General. But it is part of something much bigger. Just as McNaughton would think twice about exposing a fellow traveller to the wintry winds of England, so will he think twice, many more times than twice, before he will launch his 170,000 men into an operation which is clearly hazardous.

Definite proof of this came at the time just before Dunkirk when, at personal risk to himself, he went into France to get a firsthand insight into the situation, and from what he saw made the decision that it would be foolhardy and disastrous to send men there, as had been projected by the Imperial General Staff.

But it is not to be gathered from this that he is sentimental about and perhaps soft with his troops. He displayed his ability to cast aside any feelings of sentiment or even personal friendship recently when some officers in the Canadian Army were "axed" and sent back to Canada. Because they were over age and for other reasons, these men were not suitable for their posts.

McNaughton did not allow the fact that some of them were close friends of his to influence him in the least degree. Though there were heartburnings and fervent appeals, they went. It is his firmly avowed policy to have young commanding officers in the field. Testimony of this is the fact that at present the average age of Lieutenant-Colonels in the Canadian Army is just over 32.

As a man, McNaughton may definitely be rated as great. Anybody who has been in contact with him cannot help but feel he has a mind, an outstanding mind, one of the greatest Canada has produced. One comes away from seeing him at work among his troops or from a conversation with him, saying to oneself, "That man's a genius."

But we have nothing upon which to base a statement that McNaughton is a great General. His record in the sphere of artillery in the last war was formidable. But as a General commanding a whole Army in action in today's type of warfare he is as yet untried. The test will come when he launches his army of Canadians at the enemy.

One feels that, like his performance in the army aptitude tests, he will show himself to be "above average, very outstanding."

Andrew McNaughton was replaced as Commander of the Canadian Army by Lt.-Gen. H. D. G. Crerar at the end of 1943. McNaughton then returned to Canada and a three-month political career as minister of defence in 1944–1945. After the war, MacNaughton became president of the Atomic Energy Control Board of Canada and served as chairman of the Canadian section of the International Joint Commission. He died in 1966 at 79 in Montebello, Que.

Loading bombs on a Stirling, used in Berlin raids

Bombs Away

D. K. FINDLAY
March 1, 1943

"The take-off is at eight o'clock."

The soft green of the English countryside is fading into grey. The sky is clear except for a bright band of pink clouds in the west. The aircraft are marshalled, stretched in a long line on the perimeter, fuelled and bombed and ready to go. The air crews were briefed three hours ago—they have just come over from the hangars in lorries, dressed in their flying clothes, and now they are sitting on the edge of the track with the ground crews. The bulky clothes hide the badges of rank. The lad stretched out on the ground with his hands clasped behind his head happens to be a commissioned officer, the one stuffing a thermos flask into his boot happens to be a pilot and a sergeant. To each other they are "air crew"—Jock and Don and Hap and Skipper. They are very young—about 22 would be their average age.

The Canadians are kidding their Jock gunners. The Canadians and the Scots get along very well—Jock's imperturbability over the target always tickles the Canadians. The pilot of "S for Sugar" is getting some extra attention because it is his first operational flight over Germany. He knows all the answers and drawls them out but one hand is steadily plucking up the grass. A padre comes by, but not as padre. He is in battle dress and the boys borrow gum from him.

"There's the green light, boys."

Without any word of command they go aboard their aircraft, swinging their bulky figures up through the belly hatch with a practised twist. A truck shimmers by with a gay cargo of green and red lights which are used to mark the take-off runway. At the head of the flare path stands the Air Control Pilot who directs the take-off. At five minutes to eight the motors of the leading aircraft turn over, a minute later Number Two starts up and so along the line. The ground begins to tremble, the solid roar trips and grows as another motor fires. There is something beautiful and awe-inspiring here—the ranks of whirling propellers gleaming like shields, the black wings silhouetted against the dust cloud which rises behind them, turning from yellow to pink in the sunset.

At two minutes to eight, the first Halifax four-motored bomber, with seven men and five tons of bombs, weighing 30 tons, with a wingspread of 99 feet, trundles down the track and wheels precisely on to the flare path. The A.C. holds an Aldis lamp in his hand, he sights along the barrel and a beam of green light focuses on the waiting aircraft. The motors rev up with a roaring and a billowing of dust, the Halifax hurtles down the field and, a mile away, hoists itself into the sky.

As each aircraft is airborne, another wheels on to the flare path. There is a yell from the radio truck. "Hold it! 'B for Beer' didn't get off." A red beam anchors the line of aircraft. The pilot of "B for Beer" reports that he tore off a hatch cover in his run—"and there is no blooming use freezing to death." The ground crew has a new cover in place almost as soon as the message is through and "B for Beer" comes trundling back along the perimeter looking incredibly large in the dusk—swings about and takes off.

From the other side of the field come the Wimpies—the Wellingtons, the toughest bomber in the service. It was with us at the beginning of the war and the pilots who fly it say it will be in at the finish. Heavily gunned, manoeuvrable, with a five-man crew, it is the work horse of the air. Tonight they are getting plenty of respect for they are carrying 4,000-pound bombs—one of them is enough to blow the station to bits.

From the fields nearby, Lancasters and Stirlings are being launched. The sky is dotted with aircraft stooging about, gaining height, waiting for all the bombers to get off the ground. Tonight's is a big raid and they want to strike together.

"Well, that's the lot," says the A.C.P. The field is empty and the sky is quiet. The knots of men and officers melt into the dusk. "L for London" still stands on the track. At the last moment she developed generator trouble which a sweating ground crew could not repair in time. The pilot is swearing with vexation and nervous let-down and when he comes into the mess later, everyone will say, "Tough luck, kid," and will want to buy him a drink.

An orderly calls us at two o'clock. We switch off the lights and draw the blackout curtains to look out. Good—the stars are shining and there is no ground mist. As we walk among the shapes of the station buildings, the world is quiet and black and smells of dew. We see no one about, but men are awake and moving. The maintenance crews work all night in the darkened hangars. Out on the edge of the field, in the September chill, ground crews wait at dispersal points for their aircraft.

Inside the brightly lit Watch Office, people wait, walk about restlessly. There are two girl operators with head-sets on. A blackboard tells us that two of our bombers turned back with engine trouble and landed some time ago. The Traffic Control Officer says for the 20th time, "They should be coming now," and someone puts his head through the blackout hangings in front and says he hears something. We go out on the deck to listen. There is a faint hum in the sky.

"One of ours," says the Traffic Controller cheerfully. "Come right in, boys."

Inside, the loudspeaker begins to blat. The homing aircraft identifies itself and gives the station's code name. "May I come in? May I come in? Over."

The Traffic Controller nods at one of the girls and she says softly, clearly into her mike, "You may come in. Use Number Six runway."

The Halifax comes in low, its lights on for identification, and is lost in the darkness of the field. Before it is off the runway, the sky is filling with engine throb and three more aircraft are calling down for permission to land. While Traffic Control is lining them up at different heights a fourth aircraft breaks in abruptly. "H for Harry" is in trouble—one engine not working, controls shot up. Traffic Control orders the other aircraft to stand by. "Come in, 'H for Harry.' "

From the deck we see the red and green wing lights of the damaged bomber sinking on to the field. He is down—then one light rises in a sudden arc and goes out and far away, and not very loud, there is the sound of a crash. The stillness is broken by the racket of the crash car dashing off into the darkness. A headlight goes on briefly and you see dark figures like racing shadows running on the field. Overhead more aircraft are arriving, none can be let down until the field is cleared. The Traffic Controller rushes from one mike to another, the girls repeat their messages in soft clear voices. Some aircraft are told to stooge about, others running short of gas or having engine trouble are diverted to neighbouring fields.

We stand waiting outside the operating room in the iodoform-smelling hospital. The pilot of "H for Harry" has a gash in his forehead, he is trying to smoke a cigarette that comes to shreds in his shaking fingers. His front gunner leans against the wall, still dazed.

This is their story. They had come in over the target at 14,000 feet. The flak was very heavy, the aircraft was thrown about. Something exploded under the starboard wing, blowing off the outer propeller. The control column wobbled uselessly, the aircraft went into a dive. "I told the boys to bail out if we passed 10,000," said the pilot. "She came out at 7,000. The tail gunner and the middle upper had gone—bailed out over the target—the navigator and the front gunner hadn't been able to get out." The navigator had set the homing course and gone back into the tail turret to take the gunner's place. As the aircraft landed, the throttles "froze" and the pilot was unable to cut out the motors. "H for Harry" ran off the runway and broke her back on an obstruction. The tail turret was torn off and thrown some distance.

"He didn't have to stay in the turret," the pilot kept saying, "he did it to help keep the tail down." The doctor came out of the operating room, glanced at the flight leader and shook his head.

The crews straggle back from their dispersed aircraft, get huge mugs of coffee and go to the "ops" room for interrogation. A W.A.A.F. collects the maps and code books. They sit in a group around a table and an Intelligence Officer collects their information. Some arrived over the target on schedule, spotted the dummy fires set by the enemy, found pathfinder flares, dropped their bombs and got away. Some had fought trouble from the take-off, got "coned" in searchlights and caught in flak "Gee, they threw everything in Germany at us." "The flak was like a wall, we couldn't get through. I stooged round till they 'coned up' on other kites and we got through between them." Some had been attacked by night fighters and had to take evasive action until the crew were air sick. Some had fought back—but it is a bomber's business to bomb and not to mix it with fighters. Listening to them and watching, the main impression is of tired eyes and tousled hair and voices that stumble over words.

"On the whole, a good do. Bags of fires all over the place." The target was Dusseldorf.

Released, the boys go over to the mess for a late supper. The big room is dimly lighted, the W.A.A.F. waitresses who have been on duty all day are still on duty and are as tired as the air crews. This is an informal meal. The lads wander out to the kitchens and help themselves to beer and milk. They can have bacon and eggs if they want it. Fed and warm again, with another "op" safely behind, they will talk now. This is the time to hear stories.

Every time the door opens, the boys look up. One of the flight leaders, a popular veteran of 24, has not returned. He had finished his tour of duty but he had asked for one last trip. Against the Wingco's wishes he had filled in tonight for a sick pilot. His aircraft is overdue now, it is getting near the time when "missing" must be written on the Watch Office blackboard. Through the kitchen door, with his arms full of food and bottles, comes the missing flight leader. He had come down at a neighbouring field and been sent home by car. For him, tonight will be a mixture of elation and regret—elation that he had come through his "ops" unhurt; regret that the nervous-electric time before take-off, the "wumpff" of flak and the fires in the darkness are over for him.

This scene, with variations, takes place night after night all over England.

Every morning Group Headquarters receives from its stations reports of the number of aircraft and air crew ready for operations. These reports are amended from time to time as air tests bring more aircraft to readiness or wash them out. On the basis of this information, Bomber Command selects the target and the number of aircraft to be used. Then the plan is articulated—groups notified, time for take-off and time over target determined, the kind of bombs to be carried and the proportion of incendiaries to high explosive decided upon. "Briefing" of the air crews takes place on the stations, generally in the late afternoon. In the meantime bombing-up has been going forward. The trailers trundle out their loads, the bomb bay doors drop down and the armourers climb in. The bombs are raised into position by hand winches and it is a laborious, sweaty business. Some of the bombs weigh 8,000 pounds.

On May 6, 1942, Air Marshal A. T. Harris, A.O.C., Bomber Command, said: "If I could send 20,000 bombers to Germany tonight, Germany would not be in the war tomorrow. If I could send 1,000 bombers to Germany every night, it would end the war by autumn."

On the night of May 30 he sent 1,043 aircraft to Cologne.

The Cologne raid, the first of the 1,000-plane raids, opened a new chapter in aerial warfare. It is worth a moment's review. Cologne was Germany's third largest city. It was strongly defended by 500 anti-aircraft guns, 120 searchlights and squadrons of night fighters. The night fighters were dealt with by our intruder squadrons who attacked them over their own fields. Bombers came in at the rate of one every six seconds and dropped 8,000 tons of explosives. The enemy predictor system was upset by the number of the attackers and the ground defences were overwhelmed. Photographs showed 5,000 acres of destruction, including 250 factories. The city was without water, gas or light; railway traffic was suspended for five days; a month later streets were still choked with debris.

No one knows the number of casualties. The official German figures are 411 dead and 560 seriously injured. The experience of London goes to show that the number of dead is less than would be expected from the damage. The German dead was probably not fewer than 6,000. The roads leading from the city were choked with refugees. Altogether about 240,000 people (about a third of the city) had to be evacuated.

A second thousand-plane raid took place 48 hours later on the first of June when Essen and the Ruhr were attacked. The third went to Bremen on the night of June 25/26. There was one outstanding difference between the three raids—visibility. The cities of the Ruhr will always be difficult targets because they are hidden in industrial haze, the smoke of their own chimneys, to which the defenders add more smoke. Essen and Bremen were hidden by haze and low cloud but the night of their raid on Cologne happened to be exceptionally clear with a full moon. The results were correspondingly devastating.

The boys who fly the bombers are all in favour of the big raids.

They regard them as safer because the ground defences are "saturated," i.e., the enemy predictors upset and the anti-aircraft fire dispersed. They argue like this: you can only get so many operational hours out of crews and aircraft, therefore it would be better for everyone to sit on the ground until the weather is just right, then let everybody go out together and just naturally obliterate the target for the night.

Since Bremen the R.A.F. has not used 1,000 bombers in one raid; it uses a smaller number of four-engined bombers, as it did in the mass raids on Berlin early this year. Yet there is no comparison between the blitz suffered by England in 1941 and what the R.A.F. is doing to the Reich now. Germany is being badly hurt. By her own admission she has not sufficient aircraft to retaliate in kind but she has enormously increased her defences. Her best fighter aircraft are stationed in the west. It is calculated that not less than a million and a half men are engaged with the night fighters, the anti-aircraft guns, searchlights and fire-fighting organizations. This is a substantial army to be pinned down to defensive duties alone.

As part of her defence, Germany has developed a remarkable system of decoy tactics. Their technique is characteristically thorough and ruthless. Near the city they wish to protect they find a town or village which has the same landmarks, such as a railway junction, a canal or river. They blast that town to ruins, erect dummy factories and chimneys, and at night they set out fires in it. They have even sent up their own aircraft to drop flares on it to attract our raiders to the site.

Diversionary tactics sometimes develop a reverse twist. German bombers screaming for Liverpool one night dropped incendiaries on a hill in North Wales and set the heather aflame. Next night other raiders spotted the fires and blasted the empty hillside with high explosive.

Decoy tactics have led to an improvement in our attack—the use of pathfinders. The pathfinder aircraft, equipped with the most precise instruments and manned by experienced crews, proceed to the target area and light it by flares. The navigators of the following bombers are thus made sure of the target area and are able to seek out special features in it which need a little blasting. We are so accustomed to the exploits of the Bomber Command that we forget the difficulty and strain of navigating 400 to 600 miles to find a dark spot in the darkness. The wonder is that they make such few mistakes. As the bombs go a flare explodes and a picture is taken. The pictures are plotted on target maps and Intelligence knows where the bomb has fallen.

One squadron tells a story about one of their pilots who was ticked off for getting lost and bombing off the target. He protested that it wasn't he who was lost, it was the others. When his pictures were developed, there, square in his sights, was a Diesel engine plant for which the R.A.F. had been searching.

It is said that German morale will not crack under the strain of air raids. Perhaps it won't but her transport may. That is why the Hurricanes and Spitfires of the Fighter Command shoot up every locomotive they find. The day Germany's transport cannot be maintained, that day she is defeated.

Air power is our only hope for a short war. The danger is that the Allied leaders, confused by traditional thinking, may be reluctant to rely on it. They may choose to wait, to build up larger armies to an inevitable mass slaughter and the exhausted decision of a long war.

It should be repeated. Air Power is the only weapon which can defeat Germany even within the ring of its armies.

Preparing aircraft for battle

Desert Airmen

FLT. LIEUT. JOHN CLARE
May 1, 1943

S omewhere in North Africa . . . The Arab approached the
fighter pilots clustered around a small fire outside their tent.
In his hands he carried a straw basket. On his face was the look
of an inexperienced door-to-door salesman. He shuffled silently
up, and in almost flawless Canadian greeted them, "Hiya Mac—
'oofs [*oeufs*]?"

"One of our Canadians taught him to say that," explained the
Commanding Officer of the Royal Air Force squadron which
numbered these Canadians in its roster. "Actually he taught him

many more expressions which will get him into trouble if that Arab ever tries to use them in polite Canadian society."

Wherever you go among R.A.F. squadrons in North Africa, you will find Canadian fliers. They are seeing plenty of action and loving it. One of the Canadian pilots with a Spitfire squadron was asked how he liked it. "We live in tents," he said, "and when it rains—and boy, it can rain!—everything gets damp. All our food, except the eggs we get from Arabs, comes out of a tin. We never see a movie or a girl but—" he grinned. "Boy, it's wizard!"

The Canadians in Africa complain when leaden skies drip rain— hour after hour. They complain when the mail is late or when the postman doesn't even knock once at their tent door. But there probably isn't one of them who would be anywhere else in the war if they had the chance. There is plenty of flying and plenty of fighting.

Canadians seem to fit into this kind of life remarkably well. They seem to like the informality, the almost frontier aspect of it all. They like swinging a gun at the hip. They're not so old, these boys who fly the Spitfires, that the idea of a gun in a holster isn't something to give a fellow a bit of a kick.

In his scarf, a fighter pilot has a chance to express a touch of personality. Checkered table napkins from a restaurant in Algiers made their appearance on one squadron after some of the pilots had leave. White silk from parachutes is still popular, and an added touch is a Turk's-head made from the plastic windscreen of a Messerschmitt 109 or a Focke-Wulf 190.

Life at forward fighter air field is rough. There are none of the amenities of life such as hotel-like living quarters and flocks of ground crew to swarm over every homing aircraft. The pilots and ground crewmen are comfortable and well-fed, but it's still a front-line life. The food is particularly good, though it does come out of tins, though it does include that buttress of the British fighting man's diet—bully beef. The food Canadians and their squadron mates are eating in this show is probably the best that has been supplied for any campaign in British military history.

A fighter pilot's day seems to point up toward dinner. That is the time when the whole squadron is together. The dinner hour has that intimate mood that suggests a family. Air battles are fought again. Insults—the kind you hurl only at people you know well and respect—are whipped back and forth, and the conversational gong is generally kicked around.

There is a squadron in which there are several Canadians where a simple and somehow important sentimental exercise is indulged in each evening. At nine a member of the squadron rises and proposes a toast: "To those at home. May we soon return safely to them."

You don't talk much about home in North Africa. It's one of those unwritten laws of conduct based on respect for other men's feelings and fears. When there is talk about home it is about such things as sport, or Air Force shop talk. A recent arrival at a squadron, a Canadian, was asked at dinner recently how the "Leafs" were doing. He put down his knife and fork and looked pensive for a moment. "Darned if I know if they're even in the league this year," he said. "That's Africa for you—puts you out of touch with even such fundamentals."

It's natural when someone says complimentary things about your family that you expand visibly like a barrage balloon getting ready for work. It's the same out here when someone says, "The Canadians in these squadrons are wizard blokes. I should say so."

Your boys are popular in their squadrons out here because they are never too busy to say hello, and they know their job and they do it. Their English, Scottish, Welsh, South African, Rhodesian, New Zealand and Australian fellow fliers like their "mateyness."

Canadian slang is undergoing a few changes in this campaign. No, the boys aren't getting English accents, but into their talk is creeping such examples of the R.A.F. argot as "Good show," and "actually" and "Let's face it, chaps." Actually, it's a fine and splendid thing.

There is a certain amount of reciprocity in the vocabulary trade, and Britishers are seizing on such expressions as "No percentage" as something they have been wanting to say for a long time.

There are two aspects of this campaign that parallel the war in which the fathers of many of these pilots fought—the French language and the mud. Robert W. Service wrote ballads about the mud of France in 1914–1918, but if he saw this stuff he would be moved to write a five-act play in verse. It sticks closer than a freshman pilot sticks to his squadron on his first sweep. Its consistency suggests that somewhere in its miry depths lies the answer to the search for synthetic rubber. The mud that pappy knew is sissy stuff.

Canadians in this campaign are having the same amusing adventures with French that the C.E.F. had a quarter of a century ago. And when you add the hazard of Arabic to that you have something that only the most eloquent gestures can overcome.

French-Canadian pilots are much in demand as middlemen in transactions for eggs, fruit and bread. French people are delighted to find Canadians who speak their language, and to hear about the great province of the Dominion where French is the official language.

Here in Africa, to a greater degree than ever before in the

history of aerial combat, the teamwork of the squadron is the thing. Canadian pilots are flying with young veterans of the Battle of Britain, in the world's greatest fighter aircraft.

The Canadian pilots out here are doing a great job. That's not an opinion, that's a report, a report as official as their fellow fliers can make it by their praise of their comrades from Canada, by remarks like: "The Canadians in these squadrons are wizard blokes. I should say so."

John Clare joined Maclean's *after the war and was managing editor from 1949 to 1952. He continued to write for* Maclean's *thereafter, even as editor of* Chatelaine *(1952–1956) and the* Star Weekly *(1959–1967). He died in Toronto in 1991 at 81.*

German U-Boat survivors sunk by the
Canadian corvette St. Thomas, 1945

They Kill U-Boats

ARCH WHITEHOUSE
May 1, 1943

You sit in a blister beside two machine guns. Below you is nothing but water and a few chunks of ice. Your knees are stiff and your thighs seem to have changed into stone. You grab at the plane's metal conduits, H-beam framework and hang on. You are aboard a long-range patrol bomber of the Royal Canadian Air Force, flying over the North Atlantic on the anti-submarine front.

You're dressed in the most fantastic garb man ever devised and you look and feel like a fool because you don't know how to move about in it, and you wonder if you'll ever be able to drift nonchalantly from port to starboard as the real gunner does. The patrol bomber is doing a Calgary Stampede act that makes you clutch again. You look about and find the parachute harness you are supposed to wear is stuffed in between the ammunition boxes and a spare-parts case. What does it matter? You are flying so low now that it seems a waste of money to bother about putting wings on these things. You struggle to get a folding seat down and you lower yourself to it gingerly and peer out at the depth charges that hang below the wing on your side.

Back at the base you've signed your life away and agreed to the conditions involving this little deal between you and His Britannic Majesty. He has agreed to let you ride around in his aircraft so that you can see how it is done, but in case something slips, you have no comeback.

Maybe you think you were an "intrepid airman" in the last war, but you haven't the slightest idea what this is like until you have tried it. Up here they have managed to combine the worst features of the tank, the airplane and the submarine, and call it anti-submarine warfare.

Inside the plane is a maze of mechanical equipment from which vibrates the insistent drum of power. There are seven other chaps aboard with you somewhere, but you might just as well be alone in a cement mixer installed on Baffin Land. You wonder about the others, but they have disappeared along catwalks, up ladders and through metal doors. You soon reach the point where you keep watching the other gunner across the compartment to make sure he doesn't slip off somewhere.

It's still cold and you wonder how they stand 12 or 16 hours of it. When you go hundreds of miles out to sea with a strong westerly tail wind at your back, you can't get home in a few hours, and you gamble on the hope that the weather map was right and the favourable front that was somewhere in Ontario when you left your base on the east coast will have reached the strip of runway hacked out of the muskeg and pines when you get back.

The patrol goes on for hours and hours and you become colder and colder . . .

There is a stately room in a grey stone building in Hamburg buried deep below the surface of the street. Before a massive green board a chunky man wearing the reefer jacket of a vice-admiral strides up and down, watching small lights flicker and coloured symbols move along almost invisible wires. At a group of intricate control tables, several junior officers with the stamp of the under-sea boat in their features speak with quiet deliberation into microphones strapped to their chests and respond to the vice-admiral's every gesture and command.

From tall black panels banking the sides of the room modulated voices may be heard. Their reports are taken down by alert operators and the figures and symbols on the great board are changed or moved. The vice-admiral continues his striding with automatic glances at his massive chart of operations. An oblong block of symbols is moved *en masse* and there is a decided contrast in colours. The black symbols are forming a new geometrical pattern while the red markers move ever on eastward.

It takes but a few minutes to write this, but the submarine warfare staff of the German admiralty is willing to wait weeks until these little symbols are in their proper tactical positions. A new and refreshed pack of U-boats has crept out of Saint-Nazaire and L'Orient, and their progress is watched closely by the men in the sunken room in Hamburg as they slip out of the Bay of Biscay and take up their positions in the North Atlantic.

Now we turn to another board just as big and just as elaborate with its lights, symbols and figures. The operators of the two boards are 3,000 miles apart but they are staging the grimmest and most deadly game of chess the world will ever know. Opposing the German vice-admiral we see an unnamed Canadian officer who directs operations from a combined Army–Navy–Air Force base somewhere between Cape Sable, N.S., and St. John's. The German uses submarines, radio and Nazi discipline. The Canadian does his job with anti-submarine squadrons working in co-operation with surface craft.

The Germans have the weather and cover of the ocean depths on their side. The men who attempt to beat them off are relentless, determined and cruelly cold in their calculations. They have drive and spirit, but it isn't displayed in the theatrical manner. This is important business. There's no glamour to it.

Their U-boat front starts in Ottawa. So I went to Ottawa and talked with Air Marshal L. S. Breadner, Chief of the Air Staff, and the Deputy Air Minister, S. L. deCarteret. The whole situation was explained frankly. They minimized no feature of the U-boat problem. It was a serious one.

In January, the Germans claimed 63 sinkings, totalling 408,000 tons, which is well below the rate of 630,000 tons a month they claimed for 1942—but—it is still very serious.

Canada has built more than 500 surface ships and put them into operation against the U-boat packs. Canadian air squadrons continue their patrols day after day and night after night, even when their chances of reasonable visibility and tactical operations are hopeless. Our fliers know it will be tougher when summer comes and the ice conditions change. It is known that Germany is building between 20 and 30 new submarines a month and that by the time this appears in print there will be between 500 and 700 submarines for the Germans to throw against us.

In Ottawa, I also saw Wing Cmdr. C. L. Annis of Bomber Reconnaissance. He was working on a new program of anti-submarine armament and his desk was stacked high with charts, lists, explosive data and photographs.

Annis brought out a blank chart of the North Atlantic, grabbed a red pencil and went to work. He is a tall, good-looking lad who seldom smiles. When he does it is more than worth the time you waited because you sense at once you have been accepted. Annis has been on submarine patrol and he talks the language. He explained the general setup and outlined in broad terms the defences that have been erected to beat the U-boat.

"Submarines don't just hunt in packs," he explained, putting some marks down on the chart. "They have a definite program from the time they start out from the Bay of Biscay. They work in packs in predetermined areas and they have a working schedule.

"Now, around here they keep subs which rarely cruise out of these particular areas. They are the reconnaissance groups which sit there and try to pick up the convoys a few hours or days after they sail. They trail the convoys to make sure which route they are taking. All this information is then relayed to the interceptor packs deployed out here."

The picture was taking form now, and I began to see the situation and the difficulties. Both sides were being moved by the men 3,000 miles apart who sat before the great control boards. Ships, aircraft and submarines being moved like pawns across a chess board.

"At present, we are working with this particular type of plane in this particular area. The aircraft has a range of so many miles. That means we can send them out to this point and get them back again. If they have a strong tail wind out it means they get there that much quicker but they are that much longer getting back. Simple arithmetic.

"As both we and the Germans well know, many freight convoys sail at slow speed—often less than 10 knots. If the convoy is several hundred miles from land, an aircraft may have to spend many hours, say 12 or more, going only from base to convoy and return. If the aircraft's working endurance were 15 hours that would mean it could only spend three hours with the convoy."

From Ottawa I went straight to an operations base. I served many months with an active service squadron at the front in the last war, but in two weeks with the men of the various operational squadrons on anti-submarine duty, I learned more than I ever learned in that many years on the western front.

Talk to the boys of the anti-submarine patrol and you realize you're in a war—a war that isn't too far from your back door either. Several times a week, in weather fair or foul, they go out and play their insane game of hide-and-seek for 12 or 15 or 18 hours or more. They start out before it is light and they don't get back until we "in the officers' mess" have just about finished dinner. Twelve hours of incessant vigil, skipping the whitecaps or darting madly in and out of the low-hanging cloud cover.

Two weeks up there and you wonder which is the greater menace, the weather or the U-boat. Most certainly Hitler has a very formidable and ever-attacking ally in the winds, rain, fog and snow of the North Atlantic. Here our boys meet the one member of the Axis who never surrenders.

On patrol, I have leaned over the navigation table and

watched a slim serious lad chart a course, check a position, and manipulate the most delicate instruments with fingers that should have lost all sense of feel hours before. I have crawled under the legs of an engineer who sits in a pulpit high under the wing where he keeps a lookout for submarines, with his fingers on the nerve centres of this massive winged destroyer. I have sat with the pilot and have handled the controls with 2,600 h.p. at the other end of the throttles. I have huddled amid the maze of panels, switches and gleaming cables, and studied the wireless operator's face as he listened for the signals that were the only tie with the base, miles and miles away.

Find the man who has actually fought a sub and you'll have the devil's own time getting him to talk about it. Flight.-Lieut. Bill Graham, who commands a unit of a Lockheed Hudson squadron, has had three attacks on U-boats to his credit. I found him in a hangar going over his paper work. When I asked him about his attacks, he tried to put me off.

Finally he related how he, with Pilot Officer Fred Davies, navigator, Sgt. John Dobie, wireless operator, and Flt.-Sgt. Brown, wireless air-gunner, had been posted to cover a convoy which had been heading north for some time. He sat over it, making the usual contacts with the corvettes and convoy leaders. There were long hours of sweeping back and forth, hunting and searching for the U-boats they knew were in that territory. Another hour and they would be able to turn the convoy over to the air escorts of another station farther north and another dreary patrol would be over.

Suddenly, Graham sighted a strange spattered design of oil on the water a short distance away from a corvette. It took on weird patterns as the wind brushed the wave caps. "You see the darndest things out there," Bill broke in. "I suppose it is because we have been staring so intently for so long that eventually wishful thinking takes over and produces the images. You can see any kind of submarine you want if you let it get you."

But this time it was something more substantial. The oil slick design suddenly parted and a distinct section of conning tower wearing a feathery neckpiece came to the surface. There wasn't any question now. This German was actually making an attack in broad daylight, right under the nose of the attending corvettes!

"We really can put the Hudson down fast," Bill went on. "She's a tough baby and can really take it. The bigger boys don't dare dive like that. We went in with everything cracking!"

Obviously the U-boat had missed the bomber and was concentrating on the vessels of the convoy. The conning tower was almost fully in the clear when Bill's Hudson slammed down at him. There was a mad scramble somewhere below and the sub started down again, lashing the sea in fury to get below the surface again, but the Hudson had him cold.

In the bomb bay hung depth charges fitted with fuses that would detonate the explosive below the surface. Here was the perfect setup. The selector was set to drop charges on each side of the U-boat. The others were released so that they fell at the stern and at the bow of the crash-diving U-boat. It was as simple as that.

Bill punched the release gear from not so many feet above the raging swirl of screw-churned water and there was no question as to how accurate his sighting had been. WHONG! The explosions produced gigantic cauliflowers of outraged sea. Everything went up, embossing the perfect pattern of a successful attack. In turn there was an oil slick and a whimpering series of air bubbles. Even better, as the corvettes later reported, a long length of wooden catwalk from the deck of the submarine came shooting up through the broiling seas and floated off—a scrawny length of skeleton.

To get credit for a kill you have to produce something from the inside of the submarine—or you have to bring back convincing photographs.

Bill's camera had frozen up! No pictures—no confirmation.

And that brings us to the third degree staged by the intelligence men. I was shown the 11-page submarine attack report these boys have to answer if they come back with empty bomb-racks and a report of having attacked a U-boat. The interrogation goes on for hours and the next day they do it all over again, just to make sure all the questions and answers jibe.

How they remember anything is amazing, because when the attacks take place everything happens fast. Everyone has a job to do, and here time is measured in fractions of seconds, and the results can only be positively gauged by the results impressed on a sheet of sensitized film. And yet when you get seven men, each doing a separate job, you can get seven different versions of what actually happened.

The verbal records are taken and carefully considered, but it's what they bring back inside the camera that really turns the cards face up. For sheer drama and suspense Hollywood has yet to equal the few minutes that tick off in the intelligence office when the sergeant of the photographic section comes clumping up the stairs with the first prints of those few inches of film for which the boys have risked everything.

A successful attack on an enemy submarine can only result from a perfect co-ordination of all the factors involved. The bomber must spot the target and make its attack before the submarine makes a successful crash dive to safety depth. Effective results do not necessarily produce flame, oil slick, air bubbles or floating wreckage. A successful attack will, however, produce one or several of these results in their proper sequence and within certain time-bracket limitations. An oil slick in itself is not enough. Air bubbles are not enough. A catwalk is not enough. Oil might come from a ruptured outer compartment, but that wouldn't mean the sub had been fatally damaged. Air bubbles—at the wrong time—could come from an empty tank that had been damaged. Air bubbles appearing so many seconds after other surface evidence and in a certain pattern are something else entirely.

An attack then does not always mean an official kill; but, as one of the intelligence officers told me, a lot of nasty people get a lot of headaches and they're willing to lay low a long time, or even find some excuses for cruising in less offensive waters. An attack, whether it is considered successful or not, has great morale effect on the crews of the U-boats. While Hitler may be able to build 20 submarines a month, he might find it difficult to find refreshed crews to man them.

There will be more submarine activity this summer and many sinkings will be reported, but only in very isolated cases, where the authorities believe that certain service and morale advantages are to be gained, will the successful attacks be publicized.

It's a way they have in this service. They'd sooner say it with depth charges.

We leave early.

Flt.-Lieut. Frederick C. Colborne commands one of the bomber-reconnaissance squadrons located somewhere on the East coast of Canada. Freddie is a tall pleasant chap who does more than his share of flying. He feels he has to keep up with the boys under him who are more than ambitious and have ideas of their own.

Not so long ago, Colborne's crew went off early in the morning, long before "first light," on a regular sweep. For weeks they had carried out these routine patrols, one day battling with the winds, fogs and blizzards, and the next inching their way out as far as they dared, seeking submarines that skulked well beyond the usual range of the bombers.

Colborne's crew, consisting of a co-pilot, a navigator, two wireless air-gunners, and a first and second engineer, have been together many months. Freddie has made certain of his men. He is something of a taskmaster when it comes to maintaining a strict routine of aircraft drill and regular periods of physical training, engine lectures, navigation lessons and other subjects that make a really polished outfit.

But with all this, who would believe that an ordained minister of the United Church would be found at the navigator's table? But Flying Officer Irving is just that, and this story is as much his as it is about the time they came upon a German submarine, attacked it and brought back one of the best sets of "attack" pictures RCAF Intelligence has seen.

Colborne was at the wheel that day. What happened was a tribute to the intense action drill that the young flight-commander has insisted upon since he was burdened with his second ring of braid. "I saw it," Freddie explained to me before the crackling fire of the mess, "and I couldn't believe my eyes. You must remember, I had been doing this sort of thing for more than five months, and had never even seen a submarine."

In the drill, the first pilot actually flies the bomber, but if he spots something he does not take his eyes off it. He simply taps his co-pilot on the shoulder, still keeping his eyes on the object, and holds his hand in a certain way. Flight-Sgt. Duncan, the co-pilot, knew what was wanted and placed the binoculars in Colborne's hand. Freddie put the glasses to his eyes and saw, beyond all shadow of doubt, a German submarine.

He handed the glasses back. The command was shouted over intercom microphone: "Submarine sighted! Take action posts!"

Colborne never took his eyes off the splinter of U-boat he could still see. Behind him the rest of them were taking their positions. All knew everything had to click off like clockwork. A lot of things could go wrong in the next few seconds.

Flying Officer Irving, the navigator, was pinpointing their position for the 10th time and wondering what he could take as his sermon subject when he took the chaplain's place in church the following Sunday morning. Suddenly he heard the "submarine sighted" order and all thoughts of next Sunday's possible text went overboard. He glanced at his chart, scribbled a set of position figures on a stiff card and handed them over to Warrant Officer Elden, the first wireless operator air-gunner. Elden had been hooked into his radio set, and had not heard the "submarine sighted," but he knew what had happened when Irving stuck that card in the prongs before him.

Flt.-Sgt. Blain, the second wireless operator air-gunner, helped Irving get the camera through the small doorway leading into the gun-blister compartment. It was his further duty to clamber through to the narrow aft compartment and drop sea-markers in the area so that after their attack dive, the plane could zoom away from the possible effect of the depth charges and turn and fly back over the scene of the attack. Unless markers are dropped, it is often difficult to estimate where the crash-diving submarine has disappeared.

Meanwhile, up above in his confined control compartment, the first engineer, Sgt. Thomson, had heard the warning and already was peering out of his small port window to obtain his version of what actually happened.

The submarine had heard the bomber long before the bomber

crew had spotted the U-boat. Colborne had lost not a second in preparing his crew for action. The second pilot had set the selector gear for the proper disposition of the depth charges. He had also returned to his seat with a small pistol-grip hand camera and was already shooting a set of pictures.

The sea was emerald green except where the U-boat was thrashing its screws and blasting air from its ballast tanks. Aft, Irving, better known as the Deacon to the rest of the crew, was in an argument with Blain as to who was to use the port blister. The big blister hatch, somewhat like a third of a massive transparent eggshell, was opened. The Deacon shoved the wireless air-gunner away with a thrust of the big camera and dropped to his knees on the hard catwalk that circled the port gun mounting. The big bomber was on her way down now at a million miles an hour—or so it seemed.

The big bomber leaped with the release of the depth charges. Aft, the WAG was dropping long silver torpedo-shaped objects out of the tail hatch. They all hung on, tense. If Freddie went too low, they could blow their own tail off. The pressure, as she came out of the dive, made them all bend and stand spraddle-legged. There was a broken tumult of explosion.

"Right on, Skipper!" the second WAG yelled, without knowing whether he was hooked into the intercom or not. He had seen a slice of diving rudder a few feet behind the last depth charge blossom.

The bomber screamed with the strain as she went sharply into her climbing turn. Freddie stayed with her at the wheel and then looked over. There was a distinct slab of black submarine deck as the great cauliflower blossoms of the depth charge explosions fell back, and lathered the ocean for a hundred square yards.

But Freddie wanted to see more and he banked the bomber

over steeper and held her up by sheer force with the rudder. "I could almost swear," he began, glancing over at his co-pilot. "You certain you got your shots?"

"If I haven't, the Deacon must have some beauts!"

Back in the blister compartment, the second WAG was standing behind two impressive black Browning guns, pleading to his gods for a shot at something. He turned as the big bomber came around and glanced at the Deacon in the port blister. What he saw made him twist like a salmon and dive across the compartment—just in time.

The Deacon, with his massive camera, was actually sliding clean over the edge of the gun blister. The second WAG grabbed his legs and shouted. "Judas! The Deacon nearly went out!" he yelled.

"You still got that camera?" he shouted over the Deacon's shoulder. "You didn't drop the camera?"

He grabbed Irving back, startled and breathless, but Irving lunged forward again and went after some more. Below was a telltale splotch of widening oil—then a gasp of white as if something below had suffered a great wound. There was another trickle of oil and then a series of slobbery air bubbles that seemed like great tears drooling across a strip of film.

"If you had let that go I would have tossed you over after it," the WAG said with absolutely no respect for the Deacon's rank.

"If I had let it go," Irving muttered, staring at the film counter on his camera, "I would have jumped out after it. I think I got a couple of nice shots."

A couple of nice shots!

Back at the base, the Intelligence Officers fine-combed the evidence. There was no question about Freddie Colborne's attack—thanks to the Deacon. "And," the second WAG told me on the quiet, "I must say he gave a swell sermon the next Sunday."

Someone asked him how he felt being a member of a crew believed to have just wiped out about 45 Germans aboard a submarine.

"If you only knew your Bible, you'd have the answer," replied the Deacon.

Colborne was a radio announcer for a western Canada station before he became one of Canada's U-boat aces. Today he worries more about the number of aircraft he has on his "serviceable" list than he ever did about a program being on time.

This war has done something to these boys. The responsibility they have had to shoulder and the hours they have spent in the air seem to have annealed their character years before one might expect them to throw off the lighthearted irresponsibility of youth. Perhaps it is the continued contact with the sea and the hours of battling northeasters that have put the true-tempered lights in their eyes.

We were talking about the weather—as usual.

"Sometimes we are ordered to go into alternate bases if it closes in here," Colborne explained over a pocket map the first night I arrived at his station. "We can get in at 'A' or 'B' or 'C'; but you will notice that in all cases these alternate bases are further away and while we may get good weather, we may not have the fuel to fly that far. That means a possible forced landing, and as I say, you may get down safely, but you deprive the squadron of one aircraft and one full crew, and they have to send a salvage party out to help you get into the air again. It's just not efficient. We like to get back here, if we can."

That brought up the subject of Squadron Leader Wilson who, with his Hudson crew, was rescued from an ice floe somewhere off Prince Edward Island. Wilson, pilot of a Hudson patrol-bomber flying out of a RCAF station at Dartmouth, N.S., late last February, completed his routine sweep out over the Atlantic and returned to find the weather in the Halifax area had closed in. He was advised to fly north and try to get in at another base, but on his arrival there, another front of weather had slipped in from the Newfoundland coast and Wilson found his first alternate base closed off.

With typical bomber-reconnaissance stubbornness he started back to Halifax, determined to make a final effort to get into Dartmouth. The weather there, however, was even worse than before. There was nothing to do but seek another alternate base.

Through the murk Wilson and his three comrades plunged, with zero-zero weather beating them in by minutes wherever they attempted to land. Eventually their fuel supply was exhausted and night had fallen. There was nothing to do but order the crew to bail out. One by one they jumped into the night. Wilson switched in "George," the automatic pilot, to hold the bomber on an even keel while he himself leaped to safety. With "George" at the controls, the bomber roared away into the night on the last few pints of gasoline.

Then came one of the strangest adventures in the history of the anti-submarine patrols.

Instead of dropping into an uninhabited pine-spiked waste of Nova Scotia, Wilson's crew landed on a smooth, hard area that offered not a twig of surface relief. Each member, believing he was alone and completely isolated, made the best of a bad situation and walked about in a small space to stay awake and keep from freezing to death. Not one had any idea that any of the others could be anywhere near.

Then with the cold light of early morning, each airman, blanketed with his parachute for warmth, was astonished to find three other ghostly figures moving about in the mist and gloom. By an extraordinary twist of fate, all four had landed on a floating ice cake somewhere south of Prince Edward Island.

There are several versions of this unexpected meeting of the crew, but the general story is that the navigator, the air-gunner and the wireless man discovered each other first. The pilot turned up later that morning. Wilson made several gallant efforts to get to the shore, but succeeded only in breaking through the thin edge of the flow and getting soaked. They had to burn their parachutes and harness gear to get him dry again and prevent him from freezing to death.

For four days and nights they huddled together on the raft of ice before they were eventually sighted and rescued, more dead than alive. However, a few days in hospital and all four were fit and ready for action again. When I arrived in Halifax in hopes of interviewing them, I discovered that all had been discharged from hospital and were in California. On the squadron strength-board they were listed by some wag as being in "Hollywood." Actually they were at San Diego to ferry a new plane out.

But I did learn that this amazing drama of the anti-submarine patrol had provided a bizarre anti-climax. After they had left the doomed plane with no one but "George" in charge, the Hudson went on alone, drained its tanks dry and then, with Mephistophelean mockery, landed itself in the only stretch of open space available for miles around. A small sapling standing sentry in the field attempted to enforce the landing rules and managed to damage one of the propellers.

A local resident notified the officials and a salvage party went in to take over. A new propeller was fitted, a few minor adjustments were made to the slightly damaged motor and the bomber was flown out long before her original crew had been discharged from the hospital.

But not all anti-submarine patrol accidents end with such success-story climaxes. There are many of the other kind.

Take the case of Squadron Leader "Molly" Small, perhaps one of the most beloved anti-submarine stars in the eastern air command. Small, from all accounts, was a "Hun hater" and he never relaxed his one-man war against the U-boats. As a result he had the finest record on this side of the North Atlantic. Small drove himself fiendishly and wore out crew after crew in his efforts to keep his aircraft in the danger area. He used to say, "You can't get subs sitting in the mess and talking about it. You've got to go out there to be sure of getting them!"

He fretted all one night in the mess on his inability to get out to the spot where he believed he would find submarines. His fierce intensity of purpose eventually goaded his listeners into forming a volunteer crew to attempt the almost impossible. "We can make it if we can load a few more gallons of gasoline," Small persisted. "If we can get out to ———— degrees longitude we'll get subs."

They turned off the phonograph, climbed into their greatcoats and went out to the hangars where the ground crews were preparing the big Cansos for the next day's patrols. There, Small and the rest went over their equipment. Instead of eight canisters of food they settled for three. They agreed to strip down to their lightest equipment. Spare parts were jettisoned and the mooring gear left on the hangar floor. From the gun blisters aft all the way to the nose they went, removing everything that was not absolutely essential. The jettisoned equipment was weighed and replaced with extra gasoline.

It was a brave effort to reach the ——— degrees longitude, but Squadron Leader Small's luck had run out. They lumbered down the runway, struggled into the air and crashed a few miles away. The wreck was discovered the next day.

The control officer of an operational squadron has no sinecure. A few weeks of that and you have your fingernails gnawed down to the elbows. In the first place he is responsible for every aircraft and crew on the station. He outlines their patrol to fit the convoy—and weather circumstances of the hour. If he makes a mistake a lot of swell boys don't get back. If he goes easy on his air crews several merchantmen are torpedoed out there on the North Atlantic. If the weather double-crosses him, he has to bring any number of aircraft back from heaven knows where and get them down safely.

I watched Squadron Leader Griffin one night when he had to recall several patrol-bombers. The weather had shifted suddenly and a snowstorm raged across the field for more than five hours. All this happened after nine o'clock at night and there were five aircraft and crews somewhere up there in the murk.

One by one they were first assigned to different altitude levels. Then he talked to them and found out which was entitled to come in first. His decision is based on their remaining fuel supply and the number of hours they have been in the air.

It takes courage to sit there, keep calm and talk in a modulated voice so that you don't transfer your own concern to those lads up there. You have to make hair-trigger decisions and insist on their being carried out. There are no false heroics, no faked theatrical situations. One man had the lives of nearly 40 skilled airmen in his hands and he knew it.

Griffin sat there, ashen and tired. He had to get them all in because on another desk he had already drawn up the plotted details of the next day's patrols. He was small, wiry and alert in spite of it all. He wore wings on his battle blouse and the ribbons of another war beneath them and he smiled—somehow.

The wind tore at the old barnlike building and it creaked from the basement to the lighted tower above. Outside there was nothing to be seen but a slanting design of Arctic fury. At the alternate landing grounds it was zero-zero also. Above in the storm five patrol bombers circled and waited.

"Don't worry, Griff," one of the pilots said from the 3,000-foot level. "Just give us a rocket from the tower. We know where we are now. Don't worry . . . we'll get in."

"That's courage," Griffin whispered to me, "but that's not enough tonight. This is what we call 'blitz,'" he added with a weary smile.

From the tower above, rockets were sent up and a young control operator added further advice and information. His forehead gleamed with perspiration even though the wind howled and stroked icy fingers across the small of his back.

Two motors cut a swath of flailing power through the storm at tower-window level and the old building trembled with it all.

More words, another rocket or two and hunched expectancy.

Then one by one they sifted down out of the murk and seemed to dab in lightly—like a party of stealthy stay-outs, tiptoeing in to avoid detection. Griffin reached for his packet of cigarettes, lit one and breathed deep as the WD operator chalked in the final landing-time figures.

The war birds were home again.

"How do you do it, Griff?" I asked when my own panic had subsided a little.

"I sometimes wonder," he said. "I suppose it's luck in some cases, but there's one thing they can't build into any control office. I mean, these boys have confidence in me. That's probably all I have to offer, but it works. When they lose that, all the courage and all the instruments in the world won't bring them in."

Arch Whitehouse, who fought for the Royal Air Force in the First World War, lived most of his life in New Jersey, where he died in 1979, aged 84. He wrote more than 30 books, fiction and non-fiction, but most on flying and war.

CBC broadcaster Peter Stursberg in Ortona, Italy, March, 1944

Assignment in Sicily

PETER STURSBERG
September 1, 1943

ALGIERS (BY CABLE)—The trouble with Combined Operations, I have discovered, is that it is hard on the thumb. There are some who claim that its worst hazard is the cold bath you get when scrambling ashore, but I didn't get my feet wet landing on the beaches of Sicily.

However, I used my thumb to cover this campaign more than I ever have done since I was a schoolboy. Even when we reached the heart of Sicily I had to hitchhike a ride to Enna. I rode part way into the city on a mule.

In Combined Operations vehicles have to be unloaded from ships and they cannot all be unloaded at the same time. The first ones to come splashing ashore were for the fighting forces, and we correspondents had to wait. I must have looked a forlorn figure standing there in the dust of Pachino Peninsula, watching tanks and trucks and guns go rolling past. I saw someone stop a vehicle and climb aboard and then I remembered that if you waved a thumb in the right direction you could usually get a lift, especially in this Canadian Army.

I don't think Ross Munro of The Canadian Press, who was the only other correspondent besides myself with the Canadian assault troops, ever considered possible transportation difficulties. We were too concerned with the landing itself, wondering whether it was going to be like Dieppe, to worry about that. We felt that if we got ashore without being killed we would be quite content to dig a nice slit trench and stay there all the rest of our lives. But when we did get ashore we changed our minds.

I expected to get soaked in the landing as there had been ominous reports of a sand bar in front of our beach and water between it and the shore nine feet deep. So I waterproofed my wallet and lighter and wrapped my typewriter in an anti gas cape and tied a pair of water wings to it so I could use it as a float if I had to swim.

The landing craft sheered away from the big troopship which brought us from Great Britain and moved slowly through water dark blue in the early light of morning toward the grey outline of the Sicilian shore. All around us was a host of great ships—troopships and freighters and warships—and in front of us were other landing craft. I watched these little boats disappear into the smoke screen just before they reached shore. There was the chatter of machine-gun fire and the louder noise of shell fire as a destroyer opened up in support of our infantry.

Then there was a sudden silence. Our landing craft was now close enough so we could see lines of men moving across each beach. Our boat stopped a little way from shore and I thought, "We've hit the sand bar. Now we've got to swim for it."

I could see vineyards and little white houses on shore and a town on the hills behind. The sun was shining now and the officer beside me said, "It looks like the sort of picture you get in a geographical magazine."

An amphibian vehicle, called a duck, which had gone ashore, wheeled around and splashed out to us. It came alongside and everyone piled in. A few minutes later, I jumped down on dry sand. I had landed in Sicily. It all seemed screwy. During the landing exercises on the British beaches we had waded ashore in water up to our chests and here I was in the real thing and not even my boots were wet.

I walked along a beach which was about as wide as Toronto's Balmy Beach or Sunnyside. It did not seem like war. It did not even seem like an exercise. There was not a sound of shots being fired. A column of Italian prisoners passed me. One of them threw his helmet into the sea. It was a gesture of finality—he at least was through with the war. A Canadian soldier who had just come ashore picked it up.

I sat on a sand dune and wrote my first story. Men were pouring out of landing craft and swarming ashore and larger ships were coming into the beaches. Their bows opened up like doors when they stopped and out of the hangar-like insides rolled tanks and trucks and guns.

There was the usual Combined Operations confusion in the early stages though somehow it was an organized confusion. I lugged my pack and typewriter through vineyards, sweat pouring off me from the burning noonday heat. I tramped along dusty limestone roads looking for divisional headquarters but nobody seemed to know where it was. I saw an officer standing by a peasant's hovel and asked him. He said, "It's here."

That afternoon, watching lines of dust-covered men and vehicles moving past the hut, I decided to use my thumb. The first lift I got was enough to stop hitchhiking for good. It was on a Bren carrier and the tow-headed kid who was driving it had not had his hands on the wheel for weeks and was giving it the works. We tore along the road in a cloud of white dust and skidded around a corner, just missing a grey stone wall and a cactus hedge.

I was hanging onto something that kept slipping. I said, "The next corner is where I stop. Let me off there. Thanks a lot."

The second day ashore I decided to go to Pachino. I got a ride in a truck to the town whose houses seemed to be crumbling away in the heat of the sun. There were a few decent buildings around the main square but the rest of it was a cluster of hovels. Most towns the Canadians took during the advance were as squalid as Pachino.

I found civil affairs in the charge of an American lieutenant representing the Allied Military Government for Occupied Territory, although the town had been taken by Canadian and British troops. Headquarters was in the main hotel which was about as pretentious as a cheap rooming house. The American was a tall, earnest-looking young man who had been a college librarian in New York. He was aptly fitted for the job as his parents were Sicilians and he could speak the language fluently. He had as an assistant an American paratrooper whom he had found in Pachino and he was very worried that he would lose him. The paratrooper, who looked like a Rockwell Kent drawing of an American soldier with long arms and legs, had been dropped in the wrong place and he would have to rejoin his unit when things got sorted out.

We went up to the lieutenant's bedroom. I thought, "This is like the fantastic things that happen in adventure comics—this 25-year-old lieutenant who has come out of the sea to run this town of 20,000, and his assistant who has dropped out of the sky."

The lieutenant told me his chief problem was food. He said, "People here are starving. Really starving." He was very serious, very conscientious.

We had dinner in the flyblown dining room of the hotel. We had three courses but the courses consisted of macaroni and cheese, sliced cucumbers, and fried potatoes. That was the best meal that the main hotel in Pachino could put on for the "Commandante."

I stayed in Pachino that night and decided to reach the front the next day. I got a lift in a jeep with some Air Force boys. They were driving to Ispica and they were a bit jittery about it as they were not sure it had been taken. But Ispica had been captured by the Canadians all right, although I could not understand how it had fallen to them so easily as it was on top of a cliff.

We arrived just as a Canadian officer was taking over the town. He could not speak Italian and he was having a difficult time making himself understood in sign language.

The Air Force boys were stopping in Ispica so I got a ride with a Canadian colonel who was going to divisional headquarters. I was very tired of hitchhiking, especially with a pack and typewriter. We drove along good macadam roads. It was a treat after the dusty roads of the Pachino Peninsula. We were bowling along at a good clip when I saw the lanky figure of Ross Munro standing by a stone wall. I shouted to the driver to stop.

Ross and our conducting officer, Capt. Dave MacLellan, Halifax, and two Canadian Army photographers, Capt. Frank Royal, Winnipeg, and Lieut. Alasdair Fraser, Montreal, were having lunch in an olive grove. They had just got a jeep and were also trying to reach the front. The five of us rode that jeep for 100 miles through Sicily. Al Fraser sat on the hood and Frank and I generally sat on a pile of baggage at the back.

We drove the jeep through fields and over ditches and back and forth along dusty roads to an airfield where we used to deliver our copy during the first few days, and it never broke down. It never complained.

I joined the lunch the fellows were having under the olive trees and when we finished we started up the road to the front. We were driving along when we almost ran down a civilian car containing two Italian officers and two Canadian officers. We trailed the car down a side road into an olive grove and then we saw the surrender of the commander of the 206th Italian Coastal Division, Gen. Achilles d'Havet, to Gen. Simonds.

It was a strange scene, like pictures you have seen of defeated officers handing over a sword, only Gen. d'Havet was asked to hand over his revolver. Through an interpreter, the Italian Naval commander, whom we had also captured, asked for the honour of retaining his revolver. Gen. Simonds agreed to this and just took the ammunition.

Gen. d'Havet looked more like a restaurant keeper than a soldier. He was stout and his face was stuffy. He made a point of telling the Canadian commander that he was awarded the Military Cross by the Duke of Connaught in the last war.

We never did see the front during the initial phase of the Sicilian campaign. By the time we reached the forward troops they were resting and the British were carrying the battle farther on. We drove past columns of Italian prisoners who were obviously only too glad to be out of the war. We drove through towns Canadians had captured. We saw signs of skirmishes along the road, broken pillboxes, burning trucks and dead horses. But we did not see any fighting—the offensive had travelled too fast for us.

However, we were to get our share of battle when the Canadians started the drive from Vizzini, which the British had captured, into the heart of Sicily after a two-day rest in the Modica area. We saw the battle of Enna which was the first real battle the Canadians fought, and I doubt if any correspondents ever had better grandstand seats for an engagement such as this.

The battle began in the heat of the afternoon sun with an artillery barrage on a ridge which the Germans held before Enna. We stood on a hill just a mile away and watched our shells sending up geysers of dust along the ridge. Our guns poured tons of high explosive on the German positions. Shells screamed and made noises like an express train over our heads.

The barrage lasted for half an hour and when the ridge was black and smoking, infantry began the attack. Through field glasses I watched little dots of men climbing over the dusty shoulder road close to a red house. I could hear the chatter of machine-gun fire and the heavier bangs of the mortars. There were little puffs of smoke coming from clumps of green near the top of the ridge where the Germans were evidently holed in.

It seemed an agonizing slowness with which the little dots moved across the road and up the lower slope of the ridge. They disappeared into what looked like a vineyard. The noise of machine-gun fire became more insistent and puffs of smoke seemed to be concentrating on a grey hut near the top of the ridge. Then a blue sputtering light burst in a wide arc across the sky. It was the success signal—the Canadians had taken the ridge.

Just after the battle of Enna we lost our jeep. A staff officer traded it for an Italian Fiat. It was a very dirty deal.

Ross and I were at divisional headquarters waiting for the Fiat to return from some job or other. We were very gloomy as we figured it had broken down. We knew it would not be long until it did break down.

A heavy German infantry wagon rolled into headquarters. It had been captured by the Canadians during the battle of Enna and it was driven by a private from the regiment which had taken part in the assault on the ridge. Everyone admired it and the private said sorrowfully, "The Colonel says this car is too big for me to drive around by myself. He told me to bring it here."

He pulled the car under a tree and got out and walked toward us and said, "Do you want it?" Ross almost snatched the key out of his hand. It was a massive vehicle but it looked as though it would get us places the Fiat would not. In a trice Ross had some men painting "Press" all over it.

We drove around in the German infantry wagon that day but we were a bit jittery about going too close to the front in case we got fired on by our own troops. It seemed like a good find but broke down that night and the next day we were without a vehicle again. We were determined to get to Enna that day so we decided to hitchhike. We got a lift as far as a demolition. Germans had blown a railway bridge over the road and it was impossible to pass. So we started to walk.

Enna was on top of a 3,000-foot hill and seemed miles away. We trudged up a steep dusty road in blazing heat. We sat down on the side of the road to rest and I saw some peasants and some mules coming toward us. I said to Ross, "Let's get a ride on these mules." He thought I was joking but when the mules passed us their owners offered us a lift. I scrambled on one mule and Ross on another.

The men leading the mules were a villainous-looking crew. Ross said to me, "Keep your eye on the last man." I did not see that this would do me much good as I had no weapon. The only thing I carried was a pair of field glasses and I doubted I was a good enough pitcher to hit him at 10 feet. However, I dropped back alongside him.

He was a talkative bandit. He described to me in great detail how he had killed his two neighbours.

I said, "Ah."

He licked his lips and bared his yellow fangs as he told me how he had murdered his last wife.

I said, "Si."

He went on to describe some of his other nefarious deeds. I said "ah" and "si." He was obviously delighted with my conversational abilities. Sicilians and mules turned off the road after a couple of miles so we got off and started walking again.

We hiked along a steep road until we saw a man with a gun sitting on a high crag overhanging the road. We had heard reports of armed civilians shooting our troops, and we looked at the man and we looked at the ditch at the side of the road and wished it was deeper. We shouted and he replied. He was an American outpost. He told us there was some American transport up the road.

We got a lift into Enna which was full of American troops. The central city of Sicily had been taken by United States troops although the Canadians had really won it at the battle of Enna. But the Americans who were on the left flank got there first.

A United States Army captain drove us to his headquarters for supper. The roads were clogged with guns and trucks and troops pressing through the city. Later in the evening he drove us back to the Canadian lines.

We were beginning to get vehicles now and we needed them to drive through the mountainous country in which the Canadians were fighting. We got three captured Fiats as well as a captured

Italian truck and the German infantry wagon, which was fixed and running well.

With those it looked as if it was going to be an easy war to cover from now on.

Born in 1913, Peter Stursberg has enjoyed a career that includes newspapers, broadcasting, oral history and writing 13 books. His CBC broadcasts covering the Sicily invasion were the first to bring first-hand news of Canadians in action. Stursberg now lives in Vancouver, B.C.

Canadian dispatch riders in North Africa

Victory Troops

WALLACE REYBURN and **JOHN CLARE**
September 15, 1943

ALGIERS (BY CABLE) — After going to all the trouble of getting accustomed to rain, the damp English climate, black-outs and English money, Canadians now find that they've entered a subtropical theatre of war. They've had to start all over again now and get themselves used to heat, flies, mosquitoes, dysentery, red wine and other problems.

The Canadians, whom the English refer to as "Victory Troops," find the heat here is terrific, and the locals say jokingly that they chose the wrong time of the year to visit this part of the world—"the season" here is October to January. But it is dry heat, so much so that after washing your hands it is only necessary to hold them in the sun for a few seconds and they are dry. And, although the sun beats down relentlessly from the blue sky all day long, it is blessedly cool after sundown.

The troops wear "KD smalls" khaki drill. It consists of shorts, slacks and a two-way shirt which comes almost to the knees and can be worn either inside the trousers or outside, a style known as the "maternity jacket." As for the Air Force, the boys get a wide variety of flying clothes. It's too hot for leather flying jackets in these nights but a bit too cool for just a shirt, so most of the crews compromise with a khaki battle jacket and slacks although many of them fly in the shorts they have worn around the camp all day.

It is impossible to keep clean here because dust immediately collects on perspiration. We do our own laundry. So as to save wear and tear on the shirt neckbands most troops wear a handkerchief around the neck, and although it gets dirty it is simpler to wash than the whole shirt. This may be the origin of the cowboy's neckerchief.

When evening comes it is essential to wear slacks because of the mosquitoes. All troops have been unhumorously told the problems of mosquitoes and malaria. Quinine is used for those who've contracted malaria and for fliers. The remainder take Mepachrine. Other precautions against malaria are nets and mosquito cream which is smeared on the exposed parts of the body. The troops were smearing on the cream when one man was heard to remark, "Golly, I always bawled out my wife for smearing on vanishing cream instead of coming to bed, but I never thought I would be doing it myself."

The mosquito net is erected over the sleeping bag but after frantic efforts to get it erected properly you usually find a half-dozen mosquitoes inside waiting for you. This phase of the campaign is too long a story to go into here. It needs an article to itself.

Hand in glove with the mosquitoes are flies which are the most persistent customers ever encountered. Up with the larks they set to work pestering you before you are awake and don't let up until nightfall. Taking their cue from Britain's night bombers supplemented by American day bombing, the mosquitoes and flies have worked out a round-the-clock campaign. The flies steadfastly refuse to be shooed and will park resolutely on the body and even pursue food as it goes into the mouth.

As anti-fly propaganda the Canadians paint signs on walls and the sides of buildings in big letters such as, "Flies improve with killing" and "Praise the Lord and pass the fly swatter." The danger of flies is that they are carriers of dysentery. This malady comes on you quickly and unexpectedly with no warning whatsoever.

Absolutely harmless compared with the flies but so big that their prairie cousins look like victims of malnutrition are the grasshoppers. Crickets in the evenings set up an ear-piercing noise which sounds to all intents and purposes like an entire Canadian Army using electric razors at once.

The sand varies from brown dirt mixed with twigs to fine white dust. It penetrates everywhere, and as the troops travel the roads dust wafts into the vehicles, so they tie wetted hand-kerchiefs across their noses and mouths. "It tastes like south-ern Saskatchewan and looks like a suburb of hell," commented one soldier.

Many mothers wouldn't know their own sons because many of the boys have their hair cut close and their heads shaved. They do this because it is easier to keep clean and also a doctor has quicker access if they suffer a head wound. "When they see us coming," grinned one of these shorn lads, "the Jerries must think Canada is releasing all her jailbirds to take part in the Sicilian campaign."

When one visits a Canadian bombing squadron in North Africa, the airdrome, set in the centre of a treeless waste, appears to be a seaplane base. A mirage makes the big Wellington bombers look as if they were floating on a lake. With the temperature at 102 in the shade and the wind blowing across the sand, it was like taking a peek into a blast furnace. The Canadians here took part in the strategic bombing of Sicily and Italy. They live, eat and sleep in their tents in the sand, and in the officers' mess the steward pours out iced water as if it were champagne.

It's not much like the lush fields of Yorkshire where the dew was heavy in the thick grass by the time the "Wimpeys" came back from their night's work over Germany. That was where many of these boys had done their operational flying before coming to North Africa. Many of the crews who made Italy unhappy those nights started their bomber careers in the European theatre of war. Some of them have done whole tours of duty up and down the length of the Reich. Many of them know the flak of Essen and Hamburg and have done the long haul to Berlin itself.

They find this new life strange and in many ways difficult. But the guys who have toured the Ruhr through the flak and prowling night fighters aren't going to let sand and sun and sweat get them down and they are adjusting themselves to the new kind of air war they are fighting.

At first they found it hard to get their sleep, for night bomber crews get to bed about dawn, and not long after the sun comes up the flies go to work. There aren't the same comforts they had at those big bomber stations in the north of England. For instance there is no local pub to rally around in when the squadron stays home for a night. There are no leaves to London or Edinburgh or that place in the country. There are a lot of things that are different but one thing remains the same. That is the job to be done.

Let Squadron Leader Wier Klassen, D.F.C., Lilac, Sask., who returned from a tour of operations over Germany, tell what he sees as the essential difference between bombing in this part of the world and in Europe. "There is not so much flak perhaps. At least you haven't got the intense concentration here that you have in the Ruhr. At the same time raids are not usually in the same proportion as they are in the big shows over the 'happy valley.' But they can give you personal attention here and make it pretty hot for you. Another thing is you miss the big fires that our bombers used to start in the Ruhr," Klassen said, recalling the 1,000 aircraft over Cologne.

The aircrews aren't the only ones who have to get used to new and trying conditions. In the hot sun the ground crews were bombing up and checking and rechecking the aircraft that carried the deadly freight consigned to Italy. Out on the line where the hulking Wellingtons stand, faithful old dobbins of bomber command, the sun makes wrenches and screwdrivers hot as freshly heated rivets. Sitting on the wing of an aircraft the heat scorches through khaki drill shorts and gives the boys who are working on the kites a hot seat that is no joke. It's tough working in that sun. But the serviceability has been remarkably high out here where you might expect a bit of *manana* to creep in their philosophy with the rising temperature.

Even the cooks have to do a bit of getting used to the desert life. Field kitchens have to be set up and those boy scout tricks that they had almost forgotten are coming in handy once more. Living in a country that seems to be a succession of jackrabbit pastures has its compensations. Eggs are plentiful. So is fruit. There are lemons now, and melons and even watermelon. Soon there will be oranges, and grapes are starting to make their appearance at the messes.

There is plenty of water although it may smack a bit of unfragrant chlorine. There are even showers fed by ice cold water from a spring.

When Sicily was invaded, the fliers were as keyed up as if they had been in the landing barges themselves. News of the progress of the land fighting was eagerly sought. The boys knew the fighting area well as they had taken part in the softening-up raids on the island on the eve of the invasion.

During the early stages of the invasion, the squadrons shuttled nightly across to Sicily, bombing and blasting targets in the path of their comrades-in-arms on the ground. These fliers attacked Naples and the big airfield near the City of Capodichino. They bombed Reggio and San Giovanni, mainland terminal of the ferry service that runs from Messina in Sicily to Italy. They bombed anything and everything that would make things easier for the boys sweating it out in the olive groves of Sicily.

As the boys in the United States Air Forces say, they are sweating it out here and doing a good job of it. Gen. Doolittle, chief of the heavy bombers, told them so the other day. That's the Jimmie Doolittle who led a formation of bombers to Tokyo. He knows good bombing when he sees it.

It would seem that heat and other bugbears would have Canadians grumbling, but they have been so enthusiastic over at last coming to grips with the enemy that they are taking everything in their stride. A group of Canadian nurses whose personnel was drawn from the Toronto district found themselves parked in a camp on the desert slopes of a mountainside. At mealtimes they lined up with mess tins alongside the men as bully beef was given out, and shared the daily rush to fill water bottles as the water cart made only one visit daily. Sleeping under mosquito nets in Nissen huts and looking, to misdirected dispatch riders, like an unexpected view of an eastern harem, these nurses were roughing it as well as any soldier.

As the wounded returned from Sicily, Canadians here besieged them to hear news of the fighting and they had some exciting and amusing stories to tell. Such as the story they tell of Pvt. "Coffee" Caughtry, London, Ont., who at the point of his tommy gun surprised and captured a group of Germans in a cave and marched them into captivity to find afterward that the tommy gun had jammed and was useless.

A Vancouver lieutenant told how happy the Italians in Sicily were to be taken prisoner and said the only two unhappy Italians he saw were two who had been put to work digging slit trenches. Not understanding English they thought they were going to be shot and were digging their own graves. They dug with tears streaming down their faces until the arrival of an interpreter who explained what the holes in the ground were for.

Travelling with a troop convoy to Tunis is an experience one is not likely to forget in a hurry. The thin lines on a map across the top of North Africa give no indication of the teeming traffic encountered on these main highways linking such places as Oran, Algiers, Tunis and Sousse. They are alive with assorted vehicles bringing up reinforcements and supplies and these two-lane highways are like Canadian city streets during the rush hour.

On the outskirts of Tunis the troops came upon an airdrome whose hangars were flattened to the ground and in a vacant field there was a vast array of destroyed German and Italian transport planes—a monument to the futile efforts of the Axis to reinforce Tunis. The Germans started occupying Tunis a day or two after the Allies landed in North Africa and were here for exactly six months. But there is practically no outward sign of the German occupation, which was a surprise to the Canadians visiting their first city liberated from the Germans.

The day after the Allied occupation, the provost companies had done the rounds of the city removing all German signs and notices. But talking to local people one was able to get a picture of what it was like when the Germans were here. On all sides it was said that the Germans' behaviour was absolutely correct except toward the Jews whom they treated abominably.

A Maltese bookshop proprietor said, "I am a British subject, but I am forced to admit that though the Germans bought up everything in the shops they paid for it." Then he added dryly, "Of course the money they used was absolutely worthless. It was spurious Banque de France paper money which they printed themselves right in Tunis. Nevertheless, the Germans were correct at all times in their own fashion."

The manager of Tunis' best hotel told of the Germans departing hurriedly and taking their bedroom keys with them. "But," he said, "knowing their thoroughness I am sure they are now making arrangements to have the keys returned to me through Geneva."

They're far from home these Canadians and they feel it— probably far more so than they did in Great Britain. But the mail is moving along pretty well and they're getting used to the new life. The Army is on its mettle and after the months of extensive training in Great Britain is fit to tackle any obstacle.

As for the Air Force, it is a strange experience for one who has seen some of these same boys taking off from the fields of England to watch them filing into a tent in North Africa to tell the story of their night's work. There seemed to be a break in time and space somewhere and then the scene lost its strangeness for there was something familiar and recognizable in their faces. Something that would always be there no matter how much they got around this man's war. They were grinning under the sweat and the airdrome dust. They were grinning the same big cocky grins that were at once a cry of joy on being home and a challenge to the next time they went out into the night.

They may be sent to a lot of funny places but these lads don't change.

Canadian troops landing at Kiska, 1943

Kiska Canucks

JAMES A. MACLEAN
October 1, 1943

MAIN STREET, KISKA VILLAGE, ALEUTIAN ISLANDS—I witnessed the Kiska landing from a grandstand seat in one of the first Canadian landing barges to hit the beach. And together with thousands of tanned surf-soaked Canadians I climbed across the rocky back of this treeless muddy island and down into this bedraggled unpainted Japanese village.

I was amazed at the extent and depth of the Japanese defences and at the amount of equipment left behind. I was more amazed at the fact that we met no Japanese gunfire. But I can't answer the question as to how or why they left. Instead, the thousands of Canadian troops here are more interested in the answer to two other questions: "Where do we go from here? And when is the next mail due from home?"

The first flush of landing was over. And so was the momentary disappointment at finding no target for our guns. The rain was pouring down again and the fog had closed in. The 6,000 Canadians in the assault force have had time to think. And here is the way they reason things out:

"We," they say, "wanted Kiska badly enough to prepare to take it by force. We were prepared to help the Americans take this forsaken rock at a price. We got it without paying that price. So why kick?"

That's how the average rawboned, muddy, cheerful Canadian soldier who helped take Kiska has things figured out. Today he sits huddled in his poncho in a drizzling rain, beneath the tattered wing of a wrecked Japanese Zero seaplane, warming his hands over a gasoline fire—Japanese gasoline. And he's thinking of home.

For months he had been trained and hardened for the fight he expected at Kiska. For months he had drilled into him the latest methods of fighting and for months he had been waiting to put that training into practice.

Then he found that the Japs had fled without waiting to fight—for the first time in this war.

The story really starts in April, 1943, in Vancouver, at a conference between Maj.-Gen. G. R. Pearkes and American Gen. John DeWitt. The Japanese then held Kiska, the best submarine harbour in the entire north Pacific, a base the United Nations wanted for operations against the Japanese naval units based on Paramuchiro 700 miles to the west. The Americans were preparing to go ahead with plans for an attack of the type successfully launched against Attu.

Gen. Pearkes plied the American with questions. He found they both agreed that a two-pronged attack against Japan, from the north as well as from the south, was the best and fastest means of crippling the Nipponese.

The Canadian Pacific Coast Commander explained it to me as follows:

"If Canada is to be regarded as a power in the Pacific, she must take part in operations against Japan. The correct and only way to defend Canada's west coast is to carry the fight to the Japanese across the international dateline. The Japanese have concentrated most of their power in the south Pacific—the area they covet most. If we hit them there and only there we are like a boxer using one arm. But if we can rock Japan from north and south, the Japanese will be forced to split their naval force to guard their own home shores. No matter how they dispose their forces, under a two-pronged attack they will be weakened."

Canadian participation in the move on Kiska was agreed upon and on several occasions Prime Minister W. L. Mackenzie King hinted at the coming operation in the House of Commons.

The London Fusiliers, the Winnipeg Grenadiers, the Rocky Mountain Rangers, and the Regiment de Hull were picked to form the nucleus of the three combat teams sent into action by Canada. This plan of battle affected the average soldier in several ways. Naturally he wasn't let in on the ultimate objective this early in the game, but there was no doubt in his mind that something big was in the wind. Battle training and combined operations got into full swing at a number of training centres on the Canadian west coast. Day after day the Canadians now on Kiska went through gruelling workouts—iron rations, three-day manoeuvres, barge landings, practice scaling and climbing down mock landing nets.

Day after day it went on. And the scuttlebutt, or rumours, flew thick and fast. Gossip had it that the various units were being trained to take part in operations anywhere from Siam to the Italian Alps. Many of these rumours were started deliberately to help keep the real objective dark.

Meanwhile, transports were being collected at various Pacific coast ports, and Canadian and American naval and air stations began gearing themselves to handle the job of convoying. Many who took part in the groundwork were completely unaware of the significance of their job.

Sailing day came and with it the issue of clothing and equipment such as were being worn by the Canadian machine gunner, resting in the mud in the lee of a hill to my left. He'd thrown his rain cape over a packing box and he'd got his head and shoulders inside, writing a letter to his wife.

Clad in American-type helmets and carrying American ski-troop-type rucksacks, rubber muckluks, rain suits, web belt and attachments, spare jackets and pants, arctic parkas, face camouflage paint, and some types of American small arms, these Canadian lads boarded their transports—the same ships that carried the American troops into Attu. Crammed in the holds of these transports, or lashed to their spray-swept decks, were hundreds of tons of explosives, tractors, bulldozers, artillery, and motor transport.

The convoy stood out from a western Canadian port and steamed west before dawn. The force's objective was still unknown to most of the troops aboard. Overhead, out of sight in the fog, planes of the Royal Canadian Air Force wheeled and circled. Around the host of grey 10,000-ton transports charged units of the Royal Canadian Navy. Later, the naval escort was taken over by the American North Pacific Fleet.

Below decks the tension grew. Army censors found themselves facing a growing volume of troop mail—those last letters written by soldiers before going into battle. Card games flourished on the hatches on deck. Carbines, antitank guns, and Bren guns were taken apart and cleaned and put together again for the 100th time. Magazines and books became treasures. And rumours rolled off the production line with clocklike precision. News from the outside world was cut off to prevent the enemy from picking up coded newscasts.

Gradually in the minds of the officers was etched an unforgettable image of Kiska: "Twenty-five miles long, five miles wide. Shaped something like a bat. Four-thousand-foot semi-active volcano at the north end. Japanese work parties sighted inside the crater. Main resistance probably expected in the central part of the island. Heavy anti-aircraft defences on the plateau north of the main harbour on the east coast. Similar ack-ack dispositions south of the harbour and more around Gertrude Cove. Machine guns, caves, tunnels, operations posts, radio station and equipment in the harbour area. Damage already done to submarine sheds and seaplane hangars on the main harbour beach. Warn the men again about booby traps."

The convoy steamed on—due west. It dropped anchor at Adak Island, the advance task force base for the operation. These Canadian troops streamed ashore and wound uphill, waving greetings to American sailors and soldiers. Ribald wisecracks were fired back and forth. The Canadians wound their way uphill back of the harbour to await the signal for the final re-embarkation on the last leg of the trip.

The rain came down that night, and with it the Canadians got their first real taste of Aleutian weather. There are some, of course, who claim that it never snows or rains in the Aleutians— it snows or rains in Siberia and just blows past the Aleutians. An even more select group claims that the weather comes in so horizontally that roofs are really unnecessary—a stout set of walls will suffice.

The Canadian pennants fluttered soggily along the picket lines that night, and on almost every other night until sailing time. The deep-churned mud around the tents became stickier and seemingly bottomless.

Sailing time came—on Friday 13th. Down from the hill came the Canadians, headed for the docks. They were loaded with equipment, fresh from final manoeuvres, armed with last-minute information and toughened and ready for battle.

As the troops streamed past me, an endless line of marching men, trucks, and guns, I found their faces hard to read. Many were bothered, I know, by the letters they'd left unwritten. I was in that spot myself. There never seemed to be time. Generally the faces of the troops were impassive. Not happy, but certainly not sad. This was their biggest adventure and they knew it. And each beginner at the game of war was anxious to acquit himself well. I was in that spot too.

One by one the transports pulled away from the dock and slid into position within the destroyer screen offshore. My transport was the last to leave. Aboard were the Winnipeg Grenadiers, lineal successors of the battalion wiped out by the Japs at Hong Kong. In from the bay drifted the strains of "Alouette," deep-throated from the men of the Regiment de Hull in a transport ahead of ours.

I slept late the following morning and perhaps it was just as well. News correspondents got no sleep for the remainder of the trip.

On deck the Grenadiers were playing cards or reading, their life jackets around their waists or within reach. Or they were talking to the Filipino mess boys or to the battle-wise crew of the transport. The transport had gone through the bombing of Dutch Harbour unscathed, although she lay there loaded with high explosives and without a pound of steam pressure in her boilers. She'd been to Attu, too, and the Canadians aboard her were missing no bets on picking up anti-Jap tips from her veteran crewmen.

The Filipino mess boys were the Grenadiers' favourites, and it was an esteem that worked both ways. All of the mess boys had families in the Philippines—and an implacable hate for the Japs. It wasn't a demonstrative hate. It couldn't be gauged by anything the Filipinos said themselves. But it was shaped for me to see.

One night when I was on my way to the galley for a cup of coffee, a lithe little mess boy with a thick shock of black hair touched me on the elbow. The passageway was dark but I heard him murmur, "This way, sir, please." He guided me into the kitchen and asked me for my sheath knife. The knife, like most of those issued, was not really any too sharp. Five minutes later I walked out of the kitchen with an edge on that knife capable of splitting a piece of paper in half edgewise. I found out later the Filipinos had stayed up half the night sharpening Canadian knives.

We had our first attack alarm that night. It was my first, as it was for hundreds of Canadian troops aboard—many of them had never been to sea before. Somewhere off to starboard an American destroyer shrilled the alarm. The transport's alarm bell cut through the silence like a knife. There was no panic. But the alarm came as a definite shock, like a dentist running his drill over a nerve.

The next few minutes seemed like hours. No one knew whether to expect air or submarine attack. The muzzles of the transport's guns in the armoured "buckets" topside moved limberly in ready arcs. The seconds dragged. I thought of the tons of explosives in the hold and crossed my fingers.

Out of the fog came a steady drone. A plane. The 17-year-old American machine gunner next to me listened intently and then relaxed. "It's one of ours."

The all-clear sounded two minutes later. I looked at my watch. What had seemed like hours had lasted just nine minutes. The young gunner rewrapped the breeches of his twin weapons in canvas and scuffed his toes on the deck. "I wish my folks would write me occasionally," he said.

Our convoy was chosen to create a diversion off the south coast of Kiska in order to facilitate the landing of American troops on the other side of the island. Also, there was some hope by the Navy that Japanese naval units could be lured into action with the outside fringes of our naval cover. We were circling in the fog, not knowing whether to expect enemy fire from the land or sea side.

Shortly after the alarm and the diversionary circling we got good news. The captain pinned up a brief bulletin on the door of the officers' mess. It said, "American troops have landed on the south beach head and have taken their first objectives without resistance." Things were going well.

We steamed on through the night toward the northern end of the island where we were to open the northern beach head. The fog was endless and solidly black. The only light was the greenish-white glow of phosphorescence in the water. The transports nudged their way through the fog to within 1,000 yards of the island. Kiska looked black and deathly silent. The anchors went down with a rattling crash and I was sure then that the noise would waken every Jap for miles.

Through night glasses I stared hard at the ink-black shore. No sign of life. No noise. To the left the huge base of the Kiska volcano could be seen jutting out of the sea. Two-thirds of it was hidden by the low-lying fog. Then, at dawn, the fog and darkness lifted.

From all over Bamboo Bay came the roar of winches and the faint shouts of men. The Canadians and Americans were pouring ashore in force. Scores and scores of blue-grey landing barges of all types sped in an endless conveyer belt to the beach, pounding through the icy surf and kelp to the sand bars just off shore. The Canadians, their faces daubed with greenish-white camouflage paint, swarmed over the sides of the transports, down the thick rope landing nets and into the barges bobbing in the Bering swells beneath.

There were 250 Canadians in the first barge from our ship. And half way to the beach we thought the fireworks had started. Blue smoke and explosions rolled out across the bay from the hills above the beach head. We thought it was Japanese artillery or mortar fire. It turned out to be advance engineers destroying the thickly sown booby traps and land mines, devices that claimed Canadian casualties in the next few days.

Our barge hit the sandy beach and down the twin ramps the Canadians streamed ashore—waist deep in the freezing water. Loud-speakers ashore were blaring warnings to "Keep out of the grass—it's filled with mines." Two captured Japanese machine guns stood silent on the sand next to rows of mines already located and dug up. The gunner next to me cursed as the surf poured over him, wetting him to the skin, and helped me nurse my portable typewriter through the waves to the shore.

From then on the occupation of the island went on at a pace that was breathless. Canadians, heavily laden with guns and equipment, swept across that mountainous terrain like a prairie fire. I had to abandon all my equipment to keep up and even then I never did catch up with the advance patrols.

The weather was perfect for the first two days. After that the rains set in and the island turned into a morass of mud and icy water. Even souvenir hunting became boresome. The tons of enemy equipment abandoned when the garrison pulled out lost its attraction. The Japanese clothing stank with an animal odour, and the bullet-riddled ramshackle buildings on the Kiska harbour water front seemed to settle down further in the mud.

Kiska is no place to spend a vacation. So when the rains came again on the third day, the thoughts of the Canadian assault force turned back once more to home—to a country that has trees, real milk, dry quarters, and sunshine.

Your Canadian soldiers went ashore on this forsaken island with a particular job to do. A relatively small job in the vast mosaic of global war. Within a few days, unexpectedly, that job was done—Kiska was taken.

And now, as I said before, there are two questions that the Canadians on Kiska are asking themselves, and they are waiting for the answers.

"Where do we go from here? And when's the next mail due from home?"

The Kiska Canadians never did find any Japanese on the island—they had all escaped a few days earlier. But there were casualties in the invasion: one Canadian wounded and more than 20 Americans killed, mostly through friendly fire during thick fog. Afterwards, the Canadian units all ended up in Europe. One group, part of the Canadian-American First Special Service, or "Black Devils," was the first to enter Rome.

Flt.-Lieut. Coleman Perkins

I Was the Wireless Operator . . .

FLT.-LIEUT. COLEMAN PERKINS
as told to GORDON SINCLAIR

January 15, 1944

It was moonlight as we crossed the North Sea to Juist in the Frisian Islands that lie north of Holland. Our task was to mine the sea lanes off the Dutch coast around the Islands. We carried two mines of a ton each and two 250-pound bombs.

Our Wellington was one of Number 9 Squadron, RAF, one of the oldest and finest, and one of the first squadrons to attack Germany in this war. I was the wireless operator.

When all goes well the wireless operator on a Wellington has about the easiest of the five jobs aboard. Usually, after the flight is under way, the wireless operator takes up observation position in the astro dome, the greenhouse-like half sphere amidships, and just before and during the attack he stands facing the rear of the aircraft, in the dome, to watch what's developing and report to all hands, especially the pilot.

As we neared the "gardening area"—that's what we call the area to be mined—I went on the intercom to report, "There seems to be a strange aircraft above . . . Let you know if it gets any closer."

Sgt. Vic (Trusty) Trustrum, Toronto, our pilot, left further observation of that shadowing plane to me and to our tail gunner, Bill Hall, Newcastle, Eng., while he and Kerry Kermode, the navigator, who came from the Isle of Man, studied the charts. But as the minutes passed there was no further sign of the strange aircraft. We kept stooging on around 800 feet. I could hear Trusty and Kerry talking about the various peculiarities of the island's shape. No sight or sound came from below.

Then, as we flew over the tip of Juist, like a flash of lightning we were trapped by 10 searchlights. Trusty immediately threw the stick forward and the nose dropped down and we were, into a steep dive.

Flak thumped around us. It was green and yellow and red—all sorts of colours. The searchlights that held us were a kind of purplish white.

The violent dive threw me against the steel of the astro tower. My intercom plug came out of the socket and I lost contact with the rest of the fellows. There were so many explosions right outside the aircraft I couldn't count them. I was thrown against the side of the ship. I knew we were too low to bail out.

It was an all-out dive, the steepest I'd ever been in. We were diving so fast the Nazi gunners couldn't keep us in their sights. I was still pressed against the side of the aircraft, not able to do anything. I wasn't particularly frightened. Everything was happening too quickly. But I remember mumbling to myself, "Well, this is it. I guess it's all over . . ."

All of a sudden there was a terrific wrench. Trusty had pulled her out of the dive and we started to climb. I picked myself up and plugged into the intercom. The first thing I heard was the excited voice of Joe Miesen, Arkansas, our front gunner, saying, "Hey, I've got a fire here in my front turret!"

I picked up the fire extinguisher that was near my wireless set and started forward. The thought of a big fire in the front of the aircraft made me a little shaky. We had to lay our mines and we had to get away from there, but the most important thing to be done was to get the fire under control. I plugged into one of the intercom sockets near Joe's door and said, "Okay, Joe, I've an extinguisher here." But his voice came back over the intercom, "I think it's all right. I think I can handle the fire myself." Just at the minute he said it, Hall, the rear gunner, started to shout, "Weave, for heaven's sake, weave! They're firing at us. And closer. Let's get out of here."

I rushed back beside the pilot and then realized his intercom had been shot away. He was staring ahead, concentrating on getting us out of that mess. His hands actually looked as if they were stuck to the stick with glue. I nudged him and made a weavy motion with my hand to indicate an evasive course. Trusty threw the ship about. I reached over and plugged his intercom plug into another socket. The flak kept going by in big red bursts.

I started back to the astro dome. By the time I got there Trusty had thrown the searchlights off. Over the intercom I could hear him muttering to himself in amazement over how our wings could pull out from such a steep dive just a few feet from the sea with a full load of explosives. We were so low the waves had ripped off my trailing aerial.

Then I heard Trusty say, "There seems to be something wrong with the starboard engine." But he decided to proceed with the mine laying. He brought her down to 500 feet so we could lay the mines.

We got the mines safely into the sea roads, then Kerry gave us a course and we set off for home. Back at base as we started to come in to land the weather was a bit tricky, with a ground mist making things difficult, and Trusty found we were coming in too high. He pranged the throttles forward to go round again and just then there was a terrific shudder from the starboard engine. We had to stick the nose down and make a forced landing.

When we got out we found just a stub of a blade on the starboard prop. A shell had gone straight through her. We had suffered 19 other hits, yet our Wellington was back in the skies two or three nights later, good as ever, out on a bombing raid.

Military bombing is never haphazard. It's as scientifically accurate as skill and experience can make it. We know before going out what we're supposed to hit and we take pictures, immediately after the bombs are gone, to see what we do hit. Next day a chart in the briefing room shows the score: what we went after and what we got. No secrets are held back and each crew knows how the other crew scored. Although it doesn't happen very often, the crew consistently off aiming point gets a ticking off from the CO.

Dropping the photoflash flares to take those pictures is one of the less pleasant jobs of the wireless operator. Bombs go down heavy and fast and true. The flares go down more slowly and explode at a predetermined height set by a fuse cap. The flares are, roughly, four feet long and about six inches in diameter. They're black with little fins on them.

It's the wireless operator's job to extend the flare chute out the side of the aircraft and, when the words "Bombs gone" come through the intercom, to see that the flares get away properly. They burst at the proper height above the ground to light things up below so the camera can get the picture.

Flare dropping is no fun. The flares are worthless if released before the bombs, and after the bombs have gone the pilot generally has to take violent weaving or evasive action, twisting and turning at 300 miles an hour. So the flare dropper gets tossed and upset and spilled about.

One night in our Wellington we were carrying four big flares and many bombs to Essen, home of the Krupp works. It was a clear night. Over the intercom came word from the navigator, "Okay, we're coming up to the target now."

The pilot brought us over the target on the first run; the bombardier reported "Bombs gone" and I dropped a flare. Then another and another. The fourth and last flare stuck.

I guess it was because the flare didn't get into the chute properly and also that we were weaving so violently. Maybe that combination did it. Anyhow, while we were trying to duck the multicoloured flak at 200 miles an hour, I tried with all my strength to push that flare through the chute. It wouldn't go.

I picked up the stick used to extend the chute and pushed at the flare. That didn't work. And any minute now the flare might explode. The explosion would have been equal to that of being hit by a 75 mm. shell.

Everybody was intent on his own job when I reported, "Skipper, I've got a flare stuck here in the flare chute. I can't get rid of it."

Flak was bursting around us so it didn't surprise me to hear Trusty say, "We've got troubles enough of our own. Keep heaving."

Between trying to keep my balance in the twisting ship and keep from getting my head bashed in as we pitched about and trying to push that flare through the chute, I was in a lather. Already the flare's period of usefulness was gone but we probably had good pictures from the other three flares.

Then Miesen, the front gunner, came up from behind his two guns to help. We both pushed at the flare, but it still refused to budge. Trusty and Kerry, from the front, kept asking how we were doing. We were doing badly.

To this day I don't know how the flare failed to explode. But I do know that after what seemed an hour—actually it was only about 20 minutes—the photoflash flare finally got away. I stood there for a minute after it had gone, not doing anything or thinking of anything.

That was a pretty close call. I still feel a bit funny sometimes when I think of it now. However, the only time that Wellington of ours got us into real trouble was because of her stout heart, and it was during a raid over Bremen when she brought us to target too soon.

That night everything seemed to be going so well we were all surprised when Kerry, the navigator, went on the intercom to say, "We're going to be on target in six minutes, Trusty . . . That's going to be far too early."

"I can't go any slower."

"Well, I'm afraid we're going to be there too early."

We really didn't know then what it was going to be like to be first on the target. At the moment everything seemed quite peaceful so we kept on. We were in by ourselves, well ahead of the others.

As we ran up on the target, lights seemed to spring up from everywhere. I suddenly knew we were going to have a tough time and that we'd be lucky to get out of it alive. I braced myself against the sides of the aircraft. The flak seemed to be all around us. There were ugly red flashes, which left trailing black plumes of smoke. They seemed to be so close you could reach out and touch them.

The front gunner, who was new with us on that trip in our Wellington, suddenly got out of his turret thinking we were out of control. He stood near the pilot, putting his parachute pack on. Trusty said to him, "Everything is okay. They haven't got us yet." But the gunner just stood there. He didn't get back into his turret or do anything.

We might have been in the missing category but just then the other aircraft began to wheel in and the Nazis weren't able to give us their undivided attention. We dropped our bombs and set course for home.

Shortly after that trip to Bremen I was transferred to a Lancaster, D for Donald. I was sorry to say goodbye to that old Wellington. When I first crewed up on her she was already a veteran of the war in the skies. She was just the sort of ship I looked forward to being on when I left my home in Fonthill, Ont., to enlist in the RCAF on Aug. 14, 1940. I trained at Brandon, Man., and Calgary and went overseas in July of the following year, and was posted to Number 9 Bombing Squadron a few months later.

At first I took a dim view of my new skipper on the Lancaster, D for Donald. He was Gordon Fry, Londoner, five years in the RAF but never on ops. I thought he'd be game but inadequate and probably too proud to ask the rest of us for advice. I was wrong. He turned out to be one of the finest and coolest pilots I've ever met.

Our first briefing with the Lancaster was for Bremen and I had a feeling that this time we'd catch it. I'd had a rough time over Bremen before and here we were going in with a green chief.

I was glad the wireless operator on the big Lancaster had one of the busiest spots in the ship. I had to check all gear before the takeoff, making certain the demolition equipment was in order because it is imperative that secret apparatus should not fall into enemy hands in case we are downed. I see to the photoflash flares, and, of course, the wireless

On this assault on Bremen our Lancaster was in the last wave over the target, and looking ahead at the flak we had to fly through it seemed to all of us an impossibility. They were throwing everything up. Nothing, you'd think, could move through that and live.

The flak was coming up from many miles outside Bremen and concentrating over the aiming point, which was the harbour. We stood there in the plane and looked at it with more detachment than we felt.

"Is it always this bad?" the skipper asked.

"No, sir, this looks worse than usual." Coming into flak is like approaching a big hill. As you come near the hill in a motor car it looks steep, almost insurmountable. Then as you get close it seems to flatten out. That's how it is approaching a flak-protected target. You stand there and swear no aircraft ever built can fly through in safety. Then you drone onward, weaving this way and that and after what seems an endless length of time you emerge at the other end of the target and defences thin out. That's how it was this first night with Gordon Fry as our pilot.

As we started into the heavier part of the flak, I thought this was a real test for a new skipper. Everywhere I looked there were searchlights—there seemed to be hundreds and hundreds of them, and in some places there were 20 or 30 concentrating on one aircraft.

The flak was thick. The red flak, that burst in big clusters, seemed the most frightening. Below them were streams of yellow and red tracer that were coming up to discourage anyone coming in below 10,000 feet. It was like a nightmare and it was all colours and you stiffened and got ready for the worst to happen. You didn't think of anything or say much; you just waited there, clinging to the sides of the aircraft as it twisted. All around were the searchlights and all the colours of the flak. We came through it all right—how we managed to, I suppose I'll never know.

Our second Lancaster assault was over Essen and we saw the "flaming onion." This is a phosphorescent projective, which looks as big as a large bomber as it twists at you. Momentarily it seems to float along beside you. It's a big shell in its own right, but, in addition, from it shoot tails of flame. It looks like a whirling onion of white fire or, perhaps, like a vast flying octopus, with grasping arms of fire probing into the night.

On one hand I suppose its purpose is explosive, like other shells, but it is also an incendiary. But they are so big and spectacular to watch that no one can miss them.

A few nights after the encounter with the flaming onion our squadron was briefed to bomb the Heinkel works at Wismar on the Baltic. I didn't fly. The chaps came back with good reports, but intelligence was dissatisfied and after two nights we were ordered to return and hit harder.

This time D for Donald was briefed to attack at 5,000 feet. We carried a 4,000-pounder and hundreds of incendiaries. With a block-buster it's dangerous to fly lower than one mile; otherwise you might get crippled by your own explosive.

Because of the earlier dissatisfaction we were determined this night to reduce the place to a shambles. All hands were tense and silent as we neared the target. Then the bombardier reported, "Sorry, skipper, all I can see is fields. Better do another run."

"Okay, we're down to 4,000, a bit low, anyway."

"Upper gunner here, sir . . . Fighters to starboard."

"Bombardier here. We'll bomb this time. I can see the target."

Our four motors roared, flak burst around and below us yet the silence in our aircraft seemed intense when the bombardier again reported, "Okay, skipper. Right . . . Right a bit . . . Steady . . . Steady . . . Bombs gone."

I was standing amidships by the flare chute and observed that the photoflash flare dropped properly as the words "Bombs gone" came over the intercom. I stooped down and shone my flashlight into the bomb bays to check that the bombs were gone. The first can of incendiaries I saw was full. Then I noticed the other cans seemed to be full as well. I reported at once.

Flak kept on bursting beneath us as the pilot's voice came over very coolly, "Has the 4,000-pounder gone?"

As I hurried up to the inspection panel over the block-buster the intercom buzzed with a warning, "Tail gunner, here . . . We're into the balloon barrage . . . Wires on both sides."

I got to the inspection panel. I had a quick sinking feeling. There was the huge bomb still aboard.

"The 4,000- pounder is still here!" I reported.

"Well, we will have to do another run," Fry said. "But let's check everything."

There was a pause.

"Okay, bomb doors open."

But as the pilot said this I noticed that the bomb doors were not opening. I reported:

"Bomb doors still shut, sir."

"Better get on the hand pump," the skipper said. "See if you can pump them open."

I went to the pump beside my wireless seat and began pumping. But the pump refused to take hold. I reported:

"This pump's not working. I see hydraulic oil on the floor."

By now all the planes should have left. We were still in the target area. We'd been there about 14 minutes. Nobody spoke for a minute after I reported the pump wouldn't work. Then the bombardier broke into the intercom, "The bomb weighs two tons. Two tons will force the doors open. I'd say let her go."

We all seemed to be waiting for something to happen. Nobody said anything. The gunners were at post. The skipper was stooging around near the target. Then, after what seemed a long time, one of the gunners said, "Well, have you fellows made up your minds yet or do we stay here all night?"

Just then, cool as ever, the skipper spoke over the intercom: "We will just have to take it back."

For a minute I was half sick as I thought of all the defences we'd have to fly back through along the Baltic coast. Nobody else said anything. We turned and headed for home.

We were all pretty quiet on the way back. But luck was with us. The defences were quiet and we got through without trouble. A few miles from home the pilot reported to our base, "D Donald here . . . We have all bombs aboard . . . What are your instructions?"

"Hello, D Donald . . . This is Jetty. Stand by."

We proceeded to circle base. It was forbidden to land an aircraft containing a block-buster, not so much because that plane and its crew would vanish if the bomb detonated, but because the entire drome would be seriously damaged. In our case we couldn't get rid of the bomb so we rather expected they'd order us to head for sea and bail out.

Soon, however, came the impersonal command, "Hello, D Donald . . . Jetty here . . . Pancake . . . Pancake."

This is an order for a routine landing. "Going in for a landing, chaps."

We had been circling our own base for about 10 minutes. Now we started down. All of us seemed to be gripping our seats or our chute harness. I think I whispered a prayer under my breath. I heard the skipper say, "If I'm not careful I'm going to make a mess of this."

Now we were almost down. Everything seemed to be taking longer to happen than it should. There was a heavy bump. I braced myself, putting my feet against the floor. Then the gunner said, "Gently did it, skipper. Nice work."

Shortly after that I completed my 200 operational hours with Number 9 Squadron. I was posted to Number 16 Operational Training Unit in England and applied for remuster to pilot—I hope as a fighter pilot because they are the lads who have the fun and get a chance to show initiative.

Journalist and broadcaster Gordon Sinclair achieved national exposure as a long-standing panellist on the popular CBC-TV program Front Page Challenge, *from its debut in 1957 until his death, at age 83, in 1984. Earlier, Sinclair was a popular reporter for the* Toronto Star, *which sent him all over the globe to file his idiosyncratic stories.*

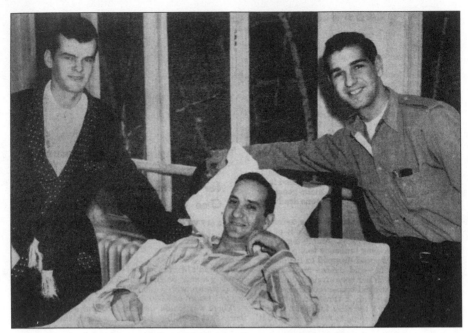

*Flying Officer Ted Greenaway, Capt.
Robert Coffman and Wireless Officer Ron Snow,
in a Montreal hospital, 1944*

Three against Death

ROBERT E. COFFMAN
March 1, 1944

*This is a tale of Ferry Command, of the great circle route
where men fly over the roof of the world—and sometimes have
to come down. Ron, Ted and I came down in the trough and
for 10 grim days clung to the ice-dripping eaves. But let me
begin at the beginning . . .*

We belonged to Ferry Command of the RAF and had flown
together for several months taking bombers from America
to Britain, to Morocco and Algiers, and by the southern route

across Africa and down the Nile valley—and once to India. Flying Officer Norman E. (Ted) Greenaway of the RCAF was the navigator, a slender good-looking boy of 23 from Camrose, Alta. Ronald Snow was the wireless operator, a tall dark boy of 22 with a handsome smile, a Bluenose of Digby, N.S., who had come to Ferry Command from the Canadian Merchant Navy. And I was the pilot, long and lean and 32. My home is in Baton Rouge, and Ted and Ron used to kid me about my Louisiana drawl. I had been a professional flier for seven years and had come to Ferry Command from the T.W.A. We were oddly assorted, as you see, but we liked and had absolute confidence in each other from the start. When you have that you stick together as a team.

In October, 1943, we were asked to fly an old Hampden bomber from Scotland to Canada—our second job of that kind. We started on Oct. 10 and made the hop to Iceland all right. We were held three days at Rejkjavik by weather, but on the morning of the 14th we hopped off for Montreal. It was a fine day and after three hours we sighted the white peaks of Greenland, 150 miles away. Then, without warning, our port engine died for keeps. You can't keep a Hampden up very long on one motor, so I told Ron over the intercom to send out an SOS. We were losing altitude about 100 feet a minute and were about an hour's ordinary flying time from the Greenland coast. Ted worked out our position and Ron had to send it on the emergency battery because the main generator operated from the port engine and had gone dead with it. That SOS was never received.

We lightened ship, pushing machine guns, ammunition drums, bombsight, personal baggage out of the hatches. But we kept losing height. And flying on one engine the kite had a growing tendency to flip over on its back. Finally our air speed dropped to the danger point and over she went—and again—and again—

falling in a tight spin with her nose straight down. If you've ever watched a winged maple seed spinning to the ground you get the idea. I throttled down the starboard motor and gave the ship full right rudder and a lot of forward stick, hoping to force her out of it before we hit the drink. We dropped 3,000 feet in less than a minute, diving straight at the sea, and I thought, "This is *It*." But she came out of it at 1,000 feet and I eased back the stick and pointed her nose for Greenland. About 15 miles from the coast we were down to 500 feet and I decided to bring her down on the water. We hadn't enough height to clear the cliffs and I didn't like the look of Greenland anyway. That country stands on end, a high plateau covered by the great icecap, with a jumble of alps sticking out of the ice to a height of 5,000 to 8,000 feet.

There was ice on the sea, too, and a vast pack of bergs and floes, but I spotted a clear lane in it and told the boys I was going down. I called Ted back out of the nose, because his plexiglass was sure to cave in when we hit the water. With luck we'd get down unhurt and have a few seconds to scramble out before she sank. Our low port wing bothered me, so I cut the motor and turned away from it as I dived, to bring her to an even keel. I levelled out at about 40 feet and left the wheels and landing flaps up—the kite would stop quick enough when we hit the drink. I lifted the nose once or twice to slow her up and when we were a few feet from the water I lifted her again, just enough to stall her. The tail slapped down on the sea and the drag of it pulled the ship down on her belly with a whack that ripped off the bomb bays and stove in the plexiglass at the nose. We were going about 76 knots, at a guess, and water flew everywhere, inside and outside the ship. The racket was terrific. Solid spouts of water shot in through the nose and the bomb hatch. Ted was thrown hard against a fitting and got a nasty gash in his shin.

I yanked my phone cord clear and so did Ted, but Ron forgot his and the cord pulled his helmet off when he scrambled through the rear upper gun hatch. In that first rush of water I thought we'd gone right under. Then I saw blue sky through the upper hatch. We had to move fast. She was sinking like a stone. Ted grabbed the emergency kit and we climbed on top of the ship and looked for the dinghy. It was a raft, really, a small thing of thin water-proofed fabric, shaped like a six-foot rubber tire with a fabric door in the central space, and stowed deflated in the rear of the port engine nacelle. A carbon-dioxide cartridge inflated it automatically when the ship struck water. And there it was, bobbing at the end of its mooring. We went out on the port wing, already three inches awash, got in with the emergency kit and paddled clear. The ship gave a quarter roll to the right and went down, a little more than a minute after she hit the sea. That was about 11:00 a.m. Greenland time on Oct. 14. We were a good 15 miles from the coast with a big field of pack ice between us and the shore. There was no sign of the ship but a patch of oil and four slim pieces of board. We salvaged the boards and Ted and Ron lit cigarettes—I don't smoke—while we considered the situation.

Our chief emotion was relief. It had been touch and go. Now we were safely down, and in the dinghy, and over there was the shore. We started for it, using the little metal and canvas paddles, as cheerful as could be. It took us some time to get the hang of paddling the dinghy. The thing was circular and if you paddled too much or too little on one side it simply spun. Also it was tipsy, and we had to sit or lie just so, and be careful how we moved.

Before long we entered the ice. There were leads among the floes and we followed those that opened toward the shore. Often we had to fend off with our hands against the ice—one slit in the dinghy's fabric might have been fatal. Progress was terribly slow.

By dark we were well into the pack and the air turned bitterly cold. Our boots and gloves were soaked and began to freeze. Ron and I were opposite each other so we opened the leg zippers of our flying suits, laid our legs together, and then zipped up the suits as far as they would go. And Ron took Ted's feet inside his jacket against his breast.

The moon was nearly full and there were millions of stars, so we had something to steer by and plenty of light for seeking leads in the ice. But it was an eerie experience. Some of the bergs towered 200 feet in the moonlight and—this is the weird part—were bobbing up and down with a slow and ponderous motion *in a perfectly calm sea*. Later we knew why, but it was very mysterious and disturbing there in the night.

Soon we noticed by the stars that we and the pack were drifting southwest. This general movement and the strange slow dance of the bergs produced a series of tremendous collisions all through the pack. The floes ground together with shrill squeals; the little bergs groaned and growled, and the big ones boomed like thunder. The big bergs were unsteady, too, and now and then one rolled over and set up a surge amongst the floes; and again one would split apart with sounds like gunfire and a splash you could hear for miles.

We learned to give the big ones a wide berth. All this clash and movement filled the night with an uproar like nothing on earth, but there were moments of stillness like the calm of a crowded room when all the voices happen to stop together. In these moments there was a peculiar rustle and tinkle all over the place. The skin of the sea was freezing lightly and the ice crystals whispered together like fragments of thin glass.

For 20 hours on end—14 of them in darkness—we paddled and pushed and pulled that frail thing through the ice. It was strange enough to the two Canadians. It was weird to a man from Louisiana. I felt like Sam McGee in the Yukon ballad. But when dawn broke we were close in to the coast and in fairly open water. We had a good look at the Greenland shore for the first time, and what we saw was discomforting. We had been steering for a shallow bay with a wide fringe of dark cliffs. Now we saw that the "cliffs" were in fact the blue face of an enormous glacier extending up and down the coast for miles; and that glacier was launching masses of ice into the sea at frequent intervals—hence the great concussions we heard from the coast in the night, and hence the bobbing of the bergs, and their tipsiness and the deep fractures which caused them to fall apart in the milling of the pack.

And we were now in the edge of the coastal current, where a peculiar overfall of the water bounced the dinghy like a cork. So we steered for a huge rock standing out of the sea on the southwest side of the bay. It was of grey stone, speckled with patches of ice and snow, and rising to a height somewhere between 1,000 and 2,500 feet. Long afterwards we learned its name—Umanarsuk, the Eskimo for "shaped like a great heart."

We reached it at seven on the morning of Oct. 15, weary and stiff with cold. Ron landed first but his hands were numb and he lost his hold and nearly fell back into the sea. When he got a firm grip we tossed him the line and he drew us in through the surge. Ted and I scrambled out. Then the line parted and we nearly lost the dinghy and everything in it. Ted and I jumped into the water and grabbed it just in time. The sea was something less than 30 degrees Fahrenheit and it nipped our legs and thighs painfully. We knew we must find a ledge where we could rest together and where the dinghy would be safe from wind and sea, so we started up the rocky slope, dragging the thing, clawing for a hold in the crannies.

About 100 feet up was a ledge, a poor thing, just big enough for the boat. We left it there temporarily and went on to a better ledge about 50 feet higher. There we shed our wet flying suits, wrung them out and spread them in the sun to "dry." What a hope! In that latitude in October the sun describes a low arc in the southern sky. For two hours before and after noon there is an illusion of warmth, no more; enough to melt the snow a little in the sheltered places. We discarded our shoes, frozen hard as wood, and wore only our flying boots.

We took stock. I had woollen underwear and socks, flying boots, a shirt, a suit of RAF battle dress and a U.S. infantry winter hat with a cloth crown and fur side pieces. The other boys wore pretty much the same, except that Ted had a flying helmet and Ron had no headgear at all. Besides these we had shoes, leather gloves, and flying suits, all soaked with sea water and impossible to dry.

We threw the gloves and shoes aside and used the flying suits (and the salvaged boards) to make a couch between us and the rock. Ron tore a fur collar from a flying suit to make a covering for his head. The emergency kit contained a Very light pistol and a couple of dozen flares, a small flag on a telescoping aluminum shaft, a helio mirror, 135 malted-milk tablets about three-quarters of an inch square, 12 small squares of barley sugar, 12 sticks of chewing gum, 12 pint tins of water, a pack of benzedrine "energy pills," and a first-aid kit. And we had a few soaked chocolate bars in our pockets.

We went down and dragged the dinghy up to the second ledge, and just got there when we heard aircraft engines. I grabbed the Very pistol and Ron took the flag. They passed right overhead, a Fortress and a Liberator, headed for Iceland at 10,000 feet. I fired six flares and Ron waved the flag, all useless.

From that height we were invisible. The sober truth about our situation now dawned on us. Aircraft coming over Greenland fly very high to keep clear of the peaks—and those mountain ranges extend almost to the sea. And planes flying the other way start to pick up height for the icecap crossing when they are still far out to sea. On our rock at the foot of the coastal shelf we had no more chance of discovery by passing aircraft than three dolls on a sidewalk in lower Manhattan. This was confirmed later in the afternoon when another Lib went over, about 10 miles from us and very high. We shot flares and waved the flag, but it did no good.

I didn't know much about the east coast of Greenland, and all I knew was bad. The great ice stream from the polar basin pours down the coast to Cape Farewell, blocking navigation except for a few whalers and sealers in summer, and giving the whole east face of the continent a permanent Arctic climate. The Danish settlements are about Cape Farewell and up the west coast; the nearest was well over 100 miles straight overland from us, and God knows how far over those skyscraping mountains. And a voyage down the coast to Cape Farewell on the flimsy raft was impossible on account of the ice; it had taken us 28 hours to make 15 miles and we had well-nigh perished.

Other fliers had come down on Greenland and lived to tell the tale; but they had landed in the snow inland, with dry clothes and the plane cabins for shelter, and the wrecked plane itself as a mark for searching aircraft. They had been supplied from the air with snowshoes, Arctic clothing, sleeping bags, food, stimulants, ropes, and so on. And they'd had a mighty tough time at that. We had nothing but the damp clothes we stood in and the contents of the emergency kit. We were marooned on that windy rock between the glacier and the sea. As for rescue by

344 Second World War

sea, it was October, the beginning of the Greenland winter, when ships had no business on that coast at all.

All this was pretty grim. It was better not to think about it. Ted climbed 500 feet up the rock and planted our flag in a cranny. We hunted for a cave but found none. Our four bits of board were too wet to burn. We thought of birds' nests for fuel; there were none. The rock had no vegetation but lichens and a small plant shaped like a shrivelled Brussels sprout, bitter and inedible. But we found a water supply; on fine days the noon sun melted the snow a little and the water lay in fissures of the rock.

We decided on a daily ration—three bits of chocolate and three malted-milk tablets (or three pieces of barley sugar) per man. Ted and Ron had 20 cigarettes and they allowed themselves three a day, lighting one and passing it back and forth.

At dark we deflated the raft and spread its limp fabric over the flying suits to make a bed. We lay on it, huddling for warmth, unable to sleep. The sky was overcast and toward midnight a wind sprang up, whipping snow and sleet. We crawled under the dinghy fabric, tucking its edges under our heads and feet and lying on the sides to hold it down. The storm tore at us and beat upon us all that night, all the next day, and all the following night.

The true nature of our problem in survival was clear in the first few hours, and we saw that the only key to it was that thin waterproof fabric of the dinghy. We must lie close together and cover ourselves with it, tucking it tightly at the sides and ends, not merely to keep out the weather but to hold in the warmth of our breath and our bodies; and we must stay that way, wrapped in that yellow shroud, breathing the foul air over and over, day and night, conserving our heat and our energy, until rescue came—or death.

There was nothing romantic about it—our fight with the

North. The posture was unheroic and the weapon miserable. Fight is the wrong word anyhow. In a fight you can feel magnificent. There was nothing magnificent about Umanarsuk except the setting. That was grand enough.

I saw its full grandeur in our third day on the rock. The sun shone in an empty sky and we tried to scrape the snow from our ledge, for it melted enough to keep our bed continually wet. We could never decide whether the sun was a blessing or a curse to us, for that reason.

We determined to plant our flag on the peak of Umanarsuk. It would take a great effort. Ted's feet were badly swollen so Ron and I swallowed benzedrine tablets and set out. The pills aroused our energies, for we were still pretty strong. The sensation for six hours was marvellous. (Days later when the strength had gone out of us we tried them again but the effect was nil—like flogging a dead horse.) It took three hours of hard climbing—desperate in places—but we planted the eight-foot flagstaff firmly on the summit.

The view was wonderful. Eastward lay the sea, covered with ice floes. West of our rock, and only 50 yards across the channel, rose a sheer cliff of grey rock, and above and beyond it the wild peaks of the mountains. Immediately north of this cliff the land receded in a wide half-moon, the glacier face, miles in extent. The whole thing was like a huge stage, with our tusk of rock near the right footlights and the sheer blue-green walls of the glacier for a backdrop. We came down very tired, but we could see our small red flag with its yellow square snapping bravely—far too bravely—on the summit. Within 24 hours it blew to shreds and vanished.

That night was cold and we lay close with our arms about each other, shivering continually. During the first two days we had suffered the traditional pangs of hunger, and dreamed of food whenever we dozed. Ron and I fancied thick juicy steaks. Ted could see only a cup of scalding coffee and a pile of buttered toast. After that our stomachs ceased to trouble us. So it was with our frozen feet—the feeling simply withdrew. We tried to bring it back; each rubbed the other's feet and took them inside his jacket for hours, without result. The toes had turned a queer grey-white and felt like old rubber. Our clothes were never dry. Apart from the snow-sodden things under us, our breath condensed on the inner surface of the dinghy and dripped down the sides upon us. There was nothing we could do about it and we put up with it.

We drank plenty of water from the rock fissures, and toward the end ate snow, which we could claw under the sides of the fabric without going outside. Our kidneys functioned normally, but for lack of food not one of us experienced the slightest bowel movement in the whole time we were on Umanarsuk.

We talked, but not very much. Old companions don't, as a rule. Ron mentioned his people in Nova Scotia; Ted his wife and baby in Montreal; and I talked of my wife and youngsters down in Baton Rouge. We doubted that our SOS had been picked up, but we figured there would be a five-day search for us when we failed to contact the Greenland wireless stations. That gave us two more days to hope—providing the flying weather held.

On the fourth morning we turned out before dawn to stretch our stiffness after the night's cold. The northern lights were giving a wonderful display, shooting up from each mountain peak like sheafs of spears. The day broke clear—good flying weather; but about noon a scud came up, with a rising wind, and we huddled under the fabric. By dark it was blowing great guns and there was a tremendous sea. The breaking waves on Umanarsuk threw sheets of spray clean up to our ledge, 150 feet above sea level. We

stuck it for a while but soon we lay in a pool of salt water and had
to get out.

The day before, Ron and I had noticed a good ledge another
150 feet up. We decided to make for it. That was a nightmare. As
soon as we stood up the screaming gale caught at the dinghy fabric and nearly dragged us off the ledge bodily. Somehow we hung
on to it, and to the rock, and slowly, painfully, crept up the steep
face of Umanarsuk with it. The fabric flogged in our numb grip. It
seemed to conspire with the wind to catch us in awkward places.
In the pitch dark we had to fumble for hand and foothold. But we
reached the ledge at last and crept exhausted under the fabric,
tucking the edges under our bodies to hold it down. We lay there
on the bare rock through the night—and through the next day
and night. During the day we crept out one by one to eat snow,
and we found a four-inch crack in the rock full of water. I looked
up and saw that the flag was gone.

It was the fifth day on the rock, the sky black, the gale still at
full force. There would be no search for us after this. There was no
blinking the hard fact, so we faced it. As fliers we had known
loneliness—you are always lonely in the sky. But that is an exhilarating kind. This was a sombre loneliness that turned our
thoughts to the one Being present with ourselves. My wife had
given me a little Saint Christopher, which I kept pinned to my
undershirt. A man's religion is like that, something personal to
him, not for the eyes of others. We had been close to death
before; but danger in the air is immediate and all-absorbing and a
flier's thought is fixed upon his instruments.

Now here was death again, not leaping any more but creeping
slowly, and there was time to think at last. It was Ron who suggested prayer. He comes of a seafaring people whose lives have kept
them close to the Almighty. We discussed a prayer in common.

Ron and Ted were Protestants—the United Church of Canada. I am a Roman Catholic. We found that our different religious teachings contained many a thing in common. One was the Lord's Prayer. It was simple, yet it said everything. It was humble without whining. It was what we wanted. So we repeated it aloud together, then, and every day and night that remained to us.

On the sixth day the gale blew out and the sun shone. We crawled out to get from it what comfort we could. We sunned our feet; a mistake, for the thin warmth aroused a gnawing pain in them and we suffered agony through that night. And through that night a snowstorm beat upon us, and all the next day. By morning our feet had lost feeling again. It was actually a relief. We were feeble now. The slightest movement was a struggle. Our bones ached and our hips were chafed raw. We lay in silence except for the daily and nightly prayers. When the sun was high we looked at each other in the queer yellow twilight under the fabric. Our faces were gaunt and bearded, our lips dry and cracked. Only our eyes seemed truly alive. We had smeared our cut hands with an antiseptic jelly from the kit, and they looked inhuman, all gentian-violet patches with the pale and bloodless fingers sticking up. The nails had ceased to grow with the first freezing of our fingertips on the voyage through the ice, as if our bodies had begun to die even then.

On the eighth day the snowfall ceased, but the clouds hung dark and now and then there was a faint haze over the sea. We got out and tried to dig the snow away from our resting place, but we were too weak even for that. We sat in a kind of lethargy with our backs to the rock face, looking seaward.

Suddenly Ted cried, "There's a ship!" We got to our feet and stared. Far to sea, 10 miles perhaps, we made out a small dark shape in the haze. We were doubtful. We had been fooled many times by the ice. Some bergs from the glacier had dark patches of moraine on their flanks and at a distance you could make out fun-nels, deckhouses, anything you chose. Yet this thing *did* look like a ship. You could make out two masts. Then we noticed it was moving north, against the coastal drift. There was no sun for the helio. I took the pistol and fired half a dozen flares at five-minute intervals. A flare is a poor thing in daylight, a dull red spark falling swiftly into the sea, a thin trail of blue smoke, nothing more. The ship or illusion, whatever it was, disappeared. Ron had some bitter things to say of the watch—if ship it was; for the rest there was only a miserable silence.

As if our misfortunes were not enough we discovered now that snow water had leaked into our last small tin of barley sugar and dissolved it. We drank the liquid and sucked the paper. Now we were down to a straight ration of milk tablets—one at daylight, one at noon, one at sunset—plus a fragment of chocolate the size of a postage stamp. On really bad nights, when there was storm or intense cold, we dipped into our reserve and swallowed two extra tablets apiece between dark and dawn. Otherwise we stuck to it.

The ninth day was cloudy and cold. We stayed under the fab-ric, clawing a handful of snow at intervals to stay our thirst. We repeated our prayer, though some phrases had no meaning for us now. "Give us this day our daily bread"—our hunger had left us long ago. "Deliver us from evil"—death seemed no longer evil; we wished devoutly that the Hampden had never come out of its spin, all those days ago. But "Thy will be done"—that meant something, everything. All that night we shivered under the fab-ric, hearing the familiar thunder and plunge from the glacier, the groaning squealing chorus of the pack. The stiff current eddied about Umanarsuk and brought opposing masses of ice together in the narrow channel behind it, and all that sound went echoing along the cliffs. It always seemed louder at night. It seemed to fill the world.

On the 10th morning—Oct. 24—the sky cleared and toward noon we crawled out feebly and sat against the rock. Our ledge would have made a fine sermon on the vanity of worldly goods. We had thrown our wallets aside long ago—they got in the way, lying down. Loose coins had fallen from our pockets and lay strewn over the sodden flying suits—English, Canadian, Icelandic, Indian—the small change of our travels. My identification pin lay rusting in a crack of the rock, my pocketknife in another.

Suddenly a sound of aircraft engines. We stared into the sky and saw a plane five miles to the west, like all the others flying at about 10,000 feet, too far, too high to see three human specks on Umanarsuk or the faint red sparks we shot into the air or the glint of the little mirror in Ron's hand. It dwindled and vanished.

That seemed the last straw. The sun had no comfort for us now. There was only the cold wind, which pierced our damp clothing like despair itself. We crept under the fabric for the last time. Something—a desire to cover our emotions probably—set our tongues wagging. We talked in our cracked and rustling voices about anything and everything—Ron mentioned that our middle names all began with E, and we discussed that gravely, as if it were a matter of the first importance. We talked in that empty way for three hours while the sun dipped into the afternoon. Ron crawled out, muttering, "Got to get snow." And then, in that afternoon of lost hope, when I think we had all resigned ourselves to death and were wondering who would be the first to go, Ron's voice came to us, cracked and excited. One word—"Ship!" We scrambled out, from instinct more than anything else. We had been tricked so many times for anything like real hope. Far out to sea we saw it again, that illusion of two days ago, the two masts, the low stubby hull.

We propped ourselves against the rock and took up the helio mirror and pistol. Our hands were too numb to hold either very long. Ron fired flares at five-minute intervals, then I fired flares. Soon we were down to our last three, and I had no faith in them. It was the helio or nothing. The sun was bright and in the right quarter. The steel mirror was four inches square with a hole pierced through the centre, and there was a separate sighting disc, also pierced. You held the reverse side of the mirror to your eye with one hand, and with the other held the sighting disc six inches beyond, and you squinted through both holes at your objective. You caught the sun on the mirror and waggled the thing slightly to make it flash—needless in our case because our bare hands shook like leaves. It was an effort just to hold them up.

We took turns, one working the helio while the others tucked their hands under their armpits, trying to coax some life into the fingers. Every half minute we passed the mirror from one to another; and steadily, soberly, we repeated our prayer aloud. We didn't go down on our knees. For one thing it seemed better to work the helio from our full height. But apart from that I think we all knew this was the end, one way or the other. If this last hope was denied we wanted to take the blow standing up, as a man should, and looking out over the sea, I think we all felt that.

We worked the mirror a long time. It seemed impossible that the glint of that small thing could be seen at 10 or 15 miles. We were asking for a miracle. Once Ted thought he saw a flash from the ship but we were not sure. A small dark shape detached itself from the ship and came slowly toward us. We sighted the mirror on that lesser thing and kept flashing it, passing it quickly from hand to hand, and flashing again. The object drew nearer. It became a boat, with the gleam of oars rising and falling, it pulled straight for the rock. But we kept working the little mirror; long after we made out the figures of the men, long after we saw the face of the steersman looking straight up at us we kept flashing and flashing and flashing.

At last they drew in to the foot of Umanarsuk. We were dazed, thanking God in our hearts and minds and it seems to me aloud. We began to clamber down with our clumsy and senseless hands and feet. Then, slowly, we realized that we were going back to the world, where certificates and identification papers and suchlike were things a man must have. I went back and picked up my wallet. Ted's was in his pocket. Ron's had vanished under the snow and could not be found. He took the Very pistol for a memento, and Ted the helio. I had the boat knife. The rest we left, the piled flying suits bearing the impress of our bodies, the scatter of coins—everything. Those Indian annas and rupees will puzzle some explorer in time to come.

The ship was the whaler Polar Bear, under charter to the U.S. Army, up there to establish a post in one of the east Greenland fords before winter closed in. The crew had not noticed our faint signals at all. But—mark how the Almighty works a miracle—the ship was the last one to make the trip down the coast. And her engines had broken down—which was why she had stopped. On deck at the time was a U.S. Army Officer, Maj. John T. Crowell of Isle au Haut, Me., a man with sharp eyes and the strength of his convictions. He happened to see a gleam on Umanarsuk. It might have been ice glittering in the sunshine—anything. He notified the crew. They were doubtful. He insisted. When finally they detected the far flash on the rock another consideration arose. The Germans had set up one or two meteorological posts on this coast during the war. Was this another? Was the flashing a trick? Crowell decided to find out, and came off with a boatful of men armed with rifles and tommy-guns. Yes, that was how they came to us, armed and hostile, ready for anything. When they recognized our uniforms the steersman cried, "How long have you been there?" I tried to tell him but my voice was little more than a whisper. Instead I held up my hands and let him count my stiff white fingers and thumbs.

We had the best possible treatment on the Polar Bear and at the U.S. Army Post in Greenland where we were taken. From there we were flown to Montreal where, in the Ross Memorial Pavilion, some of the ablest doctors in Canada fought to save our feet. Ron got off lightest. There is something indestructible in a Bluenose. I lay in hospital until Christmas while the life came slowly back to my fingers and toes. It was Ted, the most steadfast of us all, who suffered worst. After six weeks the doctors and nurses managed to save his feet, but they had to amputate practically all of his toes. He took it with his quiet smile, and Ron and I—and surely you—take off our hats to him. That boy from Alberta had a courage as steady as our Greenland rock itself. Remember the name—Norman Edward Greenaway. You don't meet his kind every day.

There is one thing more to say. We three intend to fly again.

All three men returned to Ferry Command, survived the war and had numerous reunions thereafter. Robert Coffman married a Canadian nurse he met while recuperating in hospital in Montreal. After the war, he moved to New York City and began a brief career as a commercial pilot. In 1949, he moved to the family plantation outside Natchez, Miss., where he raised cattle and crops and occasionally flew small planes for oil companies. He died in 1991 at 80.

After the war, Ron Snow went to Buenos Aires to train radio operators. After a few years, he returned and worked for

*Canadair in Toronto, before moving to Ancaster, Ont.,
where he owned a successful flooring business. He retired in
1991 and still lives in Ancaster.*

*The baby that Ted Greenaway talked about was the first
of six daughters and one son born to Greenaway and his first
wife, who died in 1985. After the war, Greenaway completed
his education at the University of British Columbia in Vancouver and ended up co-owning a successful paving company
in Saskatoon.*

*After his ordeal, Greenaway always had difficulty walking
and had to wear special shoes to compensate for his lost toes.
He remained a heavy smoker until shortly before his death following a stroke, at the age of 80, in 2000. A few years before
his death, he opened up an old trunk that had been stored and
forgotten. Inside was a single object — the mirror they had used
to signal the ship.*

A Sherman from the Ontario Regiment in Italy, 1944

Tank Battle

L. S. B. SHAPIRO
September 15, 1944

S OMEWHERE IN FRANCE (BY CABLE)—It was growing toward dusk. A squadron of 15 tanks growled slowly into a shallow valley near the wood of Langannerie, in the heart of the German belt of fortifications guarding Falaise. The tanks were Canadian—Shermans—and they were moving gingerly as a flank patrol for General Simond's brilliant knifelike attack of Aug. 8 on the Caen "hinge" around which revolved the lifeline of all Field Marshal von Kluge's divisions in Normandy and Brittany. Not many hundred yards to their left the clamour of a close infantry battle rent the evening atmosphere; but here on the flank the countryside lay ominously placid on the bosom of nature.

In the hollow of the valley 12 of the tanks stopped, then shunted individually to places of uneasy concealment—behind hedges or under foliage of overhanging trees. The three remaining tanks moved at a dead slow pace in a triangular pattern up the far slope of the valley.

Close to the summit, two of the tanks stopped. Out of the turret of the third the troop leader emerged and stood on tiptoe, his microphone pressed to his mouth and binoculars to his eyes. This single tank inched closer to the summit. Then it halted. Standing on top of his tank the troop leader could peer over the hill. His binoculars swept the vista; then he slithered back into the tank.

"Reference six Panthers 800 yards in front. Also six plus Panthers left, 350 yards. Over." The troop leader was reporting to his formation.

The reply came quickly. "Wait. Over."

The formation commander's tank came forward to join the troop on the reverse slope of the hill. Together the two officers— a major and a lieutenant—proceeded on foot to a point of vantage on the crest of the hill. Their practised eyes pierced the camouflage and quickly identified the turrets of the enemy tanks. There were 18 Panthers deployed in a small orchard; some lay above ground, concealed by shrubbery and nets; about 10 were dug into the ground, and only their long-barrelled cannon with its distinctive muzzlebrake protruded. They were being used, as the Germans have been forced to use their tanks, as part of a defence line rather than as a mobile striking force.

The major and the lieutenant marked the Panthers' location carefully on their large-scale maps. They noted, too, that several hundred yards southeast of the Panther nest a ridge of high ground led to a high stone wall stretching beneath a row of trees. The stone wall offered a direct observation of the Panthers at 700 yards' range. They studied the terrain painstakingly then crawled back to their tanks. In the hollow of the valley a quick huddle of war was called.

"We've got a good 40 minutes till darkness," the major said. "This is the plot. We'll move nine tanks to the reverse side of this slope where Jerry can't see us. Now you, Joe"—indicating his second in command, a captain—"you'll take the other six tanks and get along the high ground to the southeast. It won't be easy, but we'll lay down smoke for you and you should be able to get through to that high wall under the clump of trees. When you get there you can get a shot or two at them over open sights by coming out from behind that wall. And you'll also have a good observation post there to let us know back here how our fire is hitting. If we go at 'em from two angles we might do plenty. All right. All set?"

Ten minutes later the evening calm was shattered by whistling fire from nine Shermans each mounting 7.5 cm cannon. Some of the shells were raining down on the approximate Panther positions; these were high explosives intended to distract the Germans. The majority of our shells were smoke, ranging on the ridge of high ground to the southeast, and through the rolling billows the captain's six tanks slithered toward the stone wall flanking the Germans.

Within one minute the Germans had recovered from their confusion and opened fire on the Shermans they could faintly see—the six moving through the smoke along the ridge. One Sherman was holed by a well-aimed shot; its driver was killed, the survivors scrambled back through the smoke. Five tanks reached their objective behind the stone wall—and the battle was on.

Harassing fire came from the nine Shermans which remained behind on the reverse slope. These gunners had no direct vision of their targets. Their shots were wide for a few moments—until correction came over from the captain now observing from over the stone wall. At the same time the five tanks which had run the gauntlet of smoke shells made their thrusts. Each in its turn darted about 15 yards into the open, took two or three shots, then reversed gear and swung back to the concealment of the stone wall. The German 7.5 is considered more powerful than our gun (both have the same calibre) but the Sherman has a power traverse which allows it to take quick aim and often to get three shots away before the Panther's heavy-handed traverse can swing to fire its first shot.

The battle was now fully engaged. Indirect fire from the nine unseen Shermans was causing the Panthers to move constantly in a narrow area. And as each Panther moved from under the camouflage, one of the five Shermans on the flank darted from behind the stone wall to take a quick shot over open sights, then reverse to shelter. It was as ludicrous as it was deadly—this game of peekaboo played by 32-ton monsters. Sometimes the Shermans darted out in two's, seldom in three's, poking their shells at 700-yard range.

None of the tanks—enemy or ours—attempted to engage its adversaries at closer range. There was no "cavalry charge" here. The iron giants poked out of their hiding places, fired and scurried back. The Sherman is loath to move over open or exposed ground in the face of the superior muzzle velocity of the Panther's gun; and the Panther is too wise to seek out a Sherman which can emerge from its concealment and fire so much more quickly.

The Panther is—ineptly titled!—the lumbering giant of the

tank battle; the Sherman is the lithe stinging warrior. Each has respect for the other's distinctive qualities.

For 30 minutes this immobile battle flared—like an artillery duel at close range. In the deepening dusk the Canadians could see three flamers and two smokers among the German tanks. Their own losses were now two tanks holed and helpless.

As darkness fell the firing tapered off, then ceased. Tankmen don't like to fight at night—and that's mutual. The darkness, fog and fixed antitank weapons are the tankman's most implacable enemies.

Throughout the night the rival monsters remained in their general positions. The men inside them listened, their ears sensitive to the merest noise. They started when they heard the roar of an engine and the clank of tanks, then relaxed when these noises ceased after a few moments. This was just the restless movement of tanks, changing their positions by a few yards every now and again—in case the enemy might be ranging his guns for a quick salvo at the first streak of dawn.

They waited, like nervous giants, all night. The exhausted men inside took turns trying to sleep. They could not. A tree rustled in the breeze. An owl hooted. Every brief noise was transformed by their tense minds into the visitation of an infantryman crawling through the darkness to plant a "sticky" bomb on their armour. Throughout the night the men talked by radio. Something like this:

"Message from Charlie. For Abel. I hear something moving 40 feet at your nine o'clock. Can you see anything? Over."

"Message from Abel. For Charlie. Nothing here except a couple of daisies cooing on the grass. Daisies aren't equipped with AP (armor-piercing shells). Go back to sleep. Out."

"Message from Charlie. For Abel. Better look again. I think I see a shadow moving about your 12 o'clock. Repeat, about your 12 o'clock. Shall I try my pistol? Over."

"Message from Abel. For Charlie. For Pete's sake don't try pistol. Shadow is only Hank who's gone out there for a minute. No explanations necessary. He'll be back. Take it easy. Out."

So it went all night. These hard men encased in thick steel were "sweating it out," straining their eyes for the first evidence of dawn, plotting how to get a bead on a Panther—and knowing all the time that a Panther, just 700 yards distant, was plotting to get a bead on a Sherman. Wondering which of them will pop out and shoot first. That first is so important. Wondering and plotting and waiting and trying to get rest . . .

As a soft light suffused the dark of the eastern sky the men were on their toes. Exhaustion was no more. Motors were sputtering, then roaring. Warming up. For a full half hour before moving into battle a motor must be raced and thoroughly warmed. The first AP shell was in the breech. The loader was standing by with two more shells. They waited. The light was broadening and deepening over the eastern sky. The crew commanders stood out of their turrets and strained their eyes. A single Sherman inched forward from behind the wall. It was almost time.

"Traverse right . . . Seventy-five . . . Steady . . . Seven hundred . . . Fire!"

A burst shattered the dawn. Then another and another. The Sherman reversed 20 yards into concealment. The Panthers replied. From over the hill our nine tanks were firing now, too. The battle was on again.

For 10 minutes the firing was sporadic. The Shermans had to conserve ammunition; they were at the end of their supply line and they were outnumbered. The Panthers may have had a supply of ammunition dug in. The commanders were fighting carefully.

No swirling, fluid tank battle was this. Rather it was reminiscent of a couple of dogs in separate cages, snarling and straining to paw each other through wire netting.

Suddenly a cloud of dust enveloped the Panthers—and a thin streak of dust rolled toward the northeast of the battle area. The Panthers were breaking off and getting out. The captain relayed the news to his formation leader over the hill. In a few minutes the main body of nine Shermans was on the crest and firing over open sights at the retreating enemy—but before any pursuit by Shermans could be organized, the whine and crack of an 88 shell shook the area of the stone wall. Apparently a battery of these deadly German guns had found the range.

The nine tanks reversed to their original positions on the far slope. The formation leader radioed to his second in command: "Get back here along the same ridge. We'll lay smoke for you." The four remaining Shermans along the stone wall moved back under a smoke screen.

The second in command rejoined his formation leader in the hollow of the valley. Together they walked over the hill and examined the burned-out wreckage of six Panthers. They counted their own losses—two tanks holed but recoverable; two men killed, two wounded.

"A tidy little show," the formation leader said. And the tank battle was over.

This was typical of the way the tanks fought in Normandy. It is a far cry from the great tank battles on the plain of Champagne in 1940 or the Russian steppes in 1942. The function of tanks as cavalry is feasible only when the enemy line has been smashed open and there is a clear field for exploitation. In a close campaign, when opposing lines are firmly based, the tank is a support weapon for the infantry; it is not by itself an independent attacking force.

This radical change in tank tactics was due to a very simple technical reason: during the last two years the development of the antitank weapon has far outstripped the development of the tank. German 88's and the British 17-pounder have become too powerful and accurate for any tanks now in being. Our Sherman has cause to fear the German "bazooka" wielded by infantrymen no less than the vaunted German Tiger tank fears the shoulder-fired Piat. In short, the science of armour piercing has outraced the science of armour plating.

The ideal solution, of course, is to combine the protective and mobile qualities of the tank with the fire power of armour-piercing weapons. This has been done to a limited extent. The Allies have equipped a percentage of Shermans with 17-pounders, while the Germans have mounted 88's on Tigers. But at present we have a great many more 17-pounder Shermans in action than the Germans have Tigers.

But there are limits to the elaboration of artillery equipment on tanks. The more powerful the gun the less manoeuvrable is the traverse and the slower the tank. It boils down then to the question: does the tankman prefer mobility and quickness of aim and fire against range and weight of fire power?

The answer so far as Canadian tank warriors are concerned is: mobility and quickness of aim and fire. They prefer their lithe Sherman with its 7.5 mounted on a power-driven traverse to the ponderous Panther, even though the latter's 7.5 outranges the gun mounted on our tanks. Thus it is very fatal for a Sherman to approach a Panther over open country at 2,000 yards because the Panther's gun will smash our tank before it can get into effective range. On the other hand, in the peekaboo battle amid the hedges and woods and farmhouses of the Normandy countryside, the Sherman is so much quicker on the draw.

Some day—if the war lasts long enough—when tanks have developed armament capable of meeting fixed antitank weapons on even terms or better, we may see them sweeping like cavalry into enemy positions. Today they are being used in close support of the infantry along the lines developed largely by Maj.-Gen. Hoffmeister, DSO and two bars, of the Canadian Army; sometimes they are used in place of infantry for defensive flank protection. They are distributed in small packets among battalions and companies. But the men who command tanks long for the day when they can be employed as popular imagination would have— in open battles of magnificent scope and decisive result.

Until then, men like Capt. Joseph Fuger, Pointe Claire, Que.; Lieut. G. K. Henry, Montreal; and Cpl. Henry Beverley, Winnipeg —expert tank warriors of the Normandy battle—will continue to fight their Shermans within careful rules dictated by bitter experience.

Theirs is a job like an airman's, with something added. It requires nerves of steel, quick decision, technical skill of the most exacting kind. And something more—an ability to maintain the mind at trigger edge for many hours under the mental torture of imminent death. The airman's moment of battle climax is come and gone in a moment; the violence of a tank battle is slow and excruciating.

He lacks the soaring freedom of the fighter pilot, or the comforting sense of catlike mobility which comes to a rifleman when he is advancing over a battlefield. The tankman sits with four others in a Sherman, surrounded by high explosive shells, with every moment bringing a new possibility that he will be holed and shattered. The tank commander shares the confined space with his driver and co-driver, who doubles as a loader, gunner and wireless operator. He has a very keen sense of claustrophobia;

occasionally he leaves his turret open though it would be safer to shut it.

He rolls into the shadow of a hedge, keeping his eyes on the skyline. Suddenly the silhouette of a tank rises over the distant ridge. Its dappled camouflage tells him it is German. His mind must be faster and sharper than he ever thought it could be. Is the enemy a Panther? Or a Tiger? Has it an 88 or a 7.5? Should he take a shot at it? Is it 1,200 or 1,800 yards off? Why has it suddenly and boldly silhouetted itself? Are there other enemy on the reverse slope, planning to ambush him? Has he been seen? Is the terrain right for a winning battle by a Sherman? Can he get around to the Panther's soft side or are their 88's within range?

The answers to these and a dozen other questions must fall into his mind immediately—before the plan of battle can be formulated. Sometimes he has less than five seconds to weigh the answers and put the conclusions into lethal operation.

Day in and day out the tankman undergoes this ordeal. He is the toughest warrior of them all.

Lionel Shapiro, one of Canada's top war correspondents, was Maclean's chief foreign correspondent for nearly two decades. After the war, Shapiro had great success as a writer of plays, short stories, screenplays and novels. His The Sixth of June *won the Governor General's Award for Fiction in 1955. He died of cancer in New York City in 1958, aged 50.*

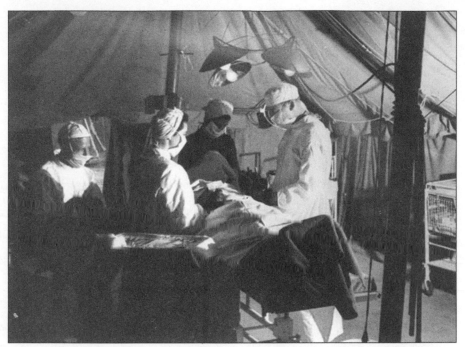

Operating in a Canadian hospital behind the lines in France, 1944

Surgery Under Fire

L. S. B. SHAPIRO
April 1, 1945

WESTERN FRONT (BY CABLE)—One day, while driving just behind the front, I visited a Canadian general hospital, a tented community sprawled over several fields beside a road which had come to be known as "Harley Street." I enquired at the orderly room for the medical officer commanding and was informed he was busy at the moment in the resuscitation ward. I then asked for the lieutenant-colonel in charge of medicine; he, too, was occupied in the resuscitation ward. Well, was the chief surgeon available, I asked. The orderly sergeant shook his head. The chief surgeon was also in the resuscitation ward.

My journalistic curiosity was thoroughly aroused and I strode across a dust-dry field to see what might be happening in the resuscitation ward to command the undivided attention of the hospital's most skilful talent. In the dim light struggling through flaps of the big tent I could see about 20 stretcher cases being prepared for surgery. Bottles of blood plasma hung lavishly from pulleys. Nurses moved among the men, wiping the sweat from the stubbly faces of the wounded and injecting morphia into the arms of the most restive.

Huddled over one stretcher case was the officer commanding, the chief medical and surgery officers, another doctor and a nursing sister. I edged toward this bedside consultation to catch a glimpse of so distinguished a patient.

The wounded man was a German private. His left arm had been almost shot away at the shoulder and the consultation was being held to devise the best ways and means of saving the man's life.

Here was a prime example of the curious irony of war. Perhaps an hour before, the whole of Canada's wealth, energy and scientific knowledge had been concentrated upon the destruction of this German; and now a part of that wealth, energy and scientific knowledge was frantically concerned with trying to preserve the same German. It is only a short drive from the front line to the most forward hospital and the drive encompasses a strange commentary on human behaviour. War is a field day for the sciences—the science of destruction plays in counterpoint to the science of preservation.

But if wars have to be, it is reassuring to know that the science of preservation is making strides at least as great as its rival.

Of 10 men who died of wounds in the last war, seven would have been saved by methods developed in the intervening years. To the front-line hospital of today there is infrequently such a thing as a hopelessly wounded man. If he retains the spark of life when he is brought in, the chances are that modern medical science will not only save his life but also return him to his home a useful human being.

Advances made in the chemistry of antiseptics and the technique of surgery are not wholly responsible for the new standards of lifesaving in war. An alert and courageous system of fully equipped yet highly mobile surgical units following close behind the assault troops has resulted in an immense saving of time between the battlefield and the operating table. In surgery time-saving is akin to lifesaving.

A classic example of how speed and skill combined to save a Canadian soldier's life came in Normandy when a private from a western regiment suffered a normally fatal wound in the battle for Caen. A thin piece of shrapnel, three quarters of an inch in length, had penetrated his heart. Within two hours he was on an operating table in a tent within our gun lines, and Maj. John Hillsman, Winnipeg, was cutting an opening, six inches by four, in his chest. While the tent quivered under the blast of our heavy guns, Maj. Hillsman closed the wound in the soldier's heart with three silk stitches. Now fully recovered, the man will carry a bit of shrapnel in his heart the rest of his life. Only a fully equipped surgical unit manned by expert technicians and located close to the battle area could have saved this life.

Canada—long noted for the excellence of her medical schools and the talent of her doctors—has endowed her fighting Army with a hospital system second to none in a world at war. The Royal Canadian Army Medical Corps is composed of men and women who combine technical ability of an exacting standard with the courage of front-line troops. They not only solve problems which would tax the ingenuity of a hospital staff in any quiet city in Canada but they work their miracles often in primitive conditions and frequently in momentary danger of losing their own lives. When you read of the Canadians launching an attack in Germany you may take it for granted that RCAMC officers and other ranks are braving enemy small-arms fire with the forward troops and that a hospital unit of varying size is close behind, well within deadly mortar range from German batteries.

When the Canadian 3rd Division stormed ashore between Bernières-sur-mer and Courseulles on June 6, three field ambulance units, completely equipped to perform major operations, arrived with the troops and were functioning before the beaches were cleared of the enemy.

One of the toughest ordeals of the campaign was sustained by the 6th Parachute Division, which held the left flank of our beachhead across the Orne River. For a full month the men of this division clung to their position under almost constant mortar-shell and machine-gun fire from an enemy entrenched 300 yards away. It was vital to Montgomery's battle plan that this position be held. Communication with this division was precarious because the Germans could fire on our pontoon bridges over open sights. A Canadian parachute battalion was with the 6th Division. As did the whole division, the Canadians lived in slit trenches during the whole of this terrifying month. And with them were the medical officers of a field surgical unit, their sensitive scalpels and fingers saving lives within easy range of German rifles.

The RCAMC is so intricately organized and so highly mobile that it functions equally effectively when the front is static and

when the line surges forward at the rate of 20 miles a day, as it did
when the breakout and pursuit developed out of Falaise. In order
to understand how the system works, let us examine the succession of medical units, from the stretcher-bearer, who goes in with
the forward platoon, to the huge general hospital, which operates
in the rear areas with a capacity of from 600 to 1,200 beds. All
units have varying degrees of mobility, from the legs of the
stretcher-bearer to the great motor truck convoys which move a
general hospital overnight.

The stretcher-bearer, who slithers forward with the platoon,
reaches a wounded man within a few moments of the shellburst.
He applies first aid—usually morphia and a spray of sulpha pow-
der—and carries the man to a jeep especially equipped to accommodate four stretcher cases. The first stop for the patient is the
regimental aid post, where the unit's regular medical officer goes a
step farther in applying emergency treatment. Thence the patient
is transported by jeep or ambulance to a field dressing station,
which usually includes a surgical unit for critical operations.

If the patient's condition allows further movement, he is
driven a mile or two to the rear to a field ambulance unit, which
is a slightly more ambitious establishment than a field dressing
station. He may be given further treatment here, depending on
his condition, or be moved directly to a casualty clearing station
[CCS], a miniature version of a general hospital where every type
of treatment is available. But the system is geared for fastest possible evacuation of patients able to be moved, in order that
accommodation in forward units may be held open for new cases
streaming from the battlefield. The final step is the general hospital, where a patient may remain indefinitely if necessary.

As a rule the regimental aid post [RAP] is on the edge of the
actual battlefield, the field dressing station and the field ambulance

unit about two miles back; the casualty clearing station is between five and eight miles from the battle area—just beyond normal effective shell range—and the general hospital anywhere from 15 to 40 miles to the rear.

Attached to no permanent unit but moving freely to where they are most needed are field surgical units. These mobile teams often function at regimental aid posts when a very heavy battle is raging, or they may bolster the surgical staff at a casualty clearing station when it is particularly crowded.

The system is elastic enough to ensure that every soldier wounded in battle in the area of the 1st Canadian Army will not lack for immediate and expert medical treatment within the shortest possible time. When British, American and Canadian forces are fighting close together there is complete interchange of medical services. The wounded, no matter of what nationality, are brought to the nearest medical unit for treatment. The urge for healing knows no national lines; it ignores even no man's land.

On friend and enemy alike the front-line surgeons perform operations with endurance and ingenuity no less than technical skill. During a recent battle, I watched a Canadian surgeon work in a tent pitched on a muddy field. An hour before, the place was as wild as a swamp in northern Quebec; now the location was endowed with electricity, from a portable power plant, pure water, sterilized linen and all the paraphernalia necessary for major operations. The surgeon worked for 10 hours—from nine at night until seven in the morning—and averaged better than one operation per hour. His only respite was a smoke outside the tent while his assistant was applying anaesthetic.

As dawn was breaking, the last patient was wheeled away and the surgeon removed his rubber apron. He was too exhausted to go immediately to his quarters. He sat on a ration box outside the tent and smoked and watched the dawn come up. Then an orderly appeared. "I wonder, sir," said the orderly, "if you could look at one more patient. The RAP is puzzled about the case."

The surgeon nodded wearily. A few moments later the new patient was wheeled in. He looked in good shape; his eyes were bright and he was smiling.

"Nothing much wrong with me, doc," he said, "just picked up a bit of shrapnel."

For 15 minutes the surgeon examined the soldier. There was a small wound on the man's right side, between his hips and his ribs, where a single flake of shrapnel had penetrated cleanly

"Well, mister," said the surgeon, "I'm going to put you to sleep for a while just to find out where that shrapnel has gone."

While an anaesthetic was being administered, the surgeon smoked outside the tent.

"The man looks pretty good," I said. "Why operate on him here when you're so tired? Why not send him back to a CCS?"

The surgeon shook his head.

"It's a trick case," he replied, "and I can't take any chances with the boy's life. If the shrapnel has penetrated his intestines he may be in a bad way at any moment. On the other hand I may find after I open him up that his intestines are intact, in that case I'll just sew him up and he'll be no worse off, except for a scar on his stomach. But I'll have to operate to find out for sure. He deserves every care we can give him. After all, he and a lot like him are the best we have in Canada."

He smiled wearily, tossed away his cigarette and returned to the operating tent.

It is this urge for healing, this frantic anxiety of medical officers to thwart the free run of tragedy on the battlefield, that has kept them at work devising new techniques. In the strange laboratory of a front-line operating tent they have continued their research and have presented medical science with new developments of permanent value.

Maj. William Mustard, Toronto, a casualty clearing station surgeon, has provided partial alleviation of the greatest fear that comes to a wounded man that he may lose an arm or leg. After long research, Maj. Mustard has achieved notable success with a method called venous transplants, which was developed under easy gun range of the enemy. Maj. Mustard's problem was this: when the main artery of a leg or arm was severed on the battle-field, blood circulation ceased in that part of the leg or arm below the severed artery and it was almost always necessary to amputate in order to save the patient's life.

Maj. Mustard developed a method of re-establishing circulation by a system of glass tubes to connect the severed artery and by the use of a solution called heparin which prevents blood clotting. Prompt use of venous transplants has already saved hundreds of men from a cripple's fate. Maj. Mustard's method has not yet been perfected; it does not work in every case, but his work is being studied by research laboratories all over the world. Thanks to Maj. Mustard, amputation will someday be a rare occurrence.

Maj. Lawrence Rabson, Winnipeg, another CCS surgeon, has done distinguished research work toward saving the lives of men suffering from multiple wounds. Maj. Rabson's method is known as interval surgery and it has resulted in a sharp drop in the number of soldiers who die on the operating table. Maj. Rabson observed that seriously wounded men can withstand only a limited amount of anaesthetic and operation trauma before the breath of life begins to falter. In the precious little leisure time left to a front-line doctor, he developed a schedule of "staggering" the stages of surgery necessary to treat the patient's wounds, thus giving the soldier's natural urge for self-preservation an opportunity to rally. Maj. Rabson's research has aroused interest among doctors everywhere.

Thus Canada's front-line surgeons, oblivious of danger and discomfort, carry on in the spirit of the oath they took as graduate students. Some have been killed in action, many have been decorated for bravery. All of them have conducted themselves with courage and unselfish industry in the noble and exacting task for which they voluntarily gave up the comfort and profit of their Canadian practice. For those of us who must see humanity squirm and twist through the shadow of Armageddon toward the ideal of a better world, it is comforting to watch the healers at work. They provide a glittering demonstration that all is not insanity, that the instinct of mankind for compassion and nobility runs strong within us and may yet become a flood tide.

Filming street action in a Dutch town, 1945

Camera Commandos

L. S. B. SHAPIRO
April 15, 1945

WESTERN FRONT (BY CABLE)—When Col. Ernest Dupuy, U.S. Army, opened the control switch of a microphone in London on the morning of June 6, 1944, and spoke the words, "This is D-Day," he broke the biggest news story of the war. The Second Front—long dreamed, doubted and decried—was at last a reality.

Dupuy scooped the world by official consent. While he was uttering the fateful words, Canadian Army cameramen were scooping the world by their own resourcefulness and courage. On

Thursday morning, June 8, newspapers in Britain and America printed the first still pictures of the Normandy beach assault. A few hours later movie theatres, from Edinburgh to Cornwall and from Flin Flon to Florida, showed the first motion pictures of the great battle. These still and motion pictures were the Canadian Army's gift to an impatient world; they were 12 to 36 hours ahead of battle pictures from any other source, military or commercial.

Scoops on D-Day required the ardent co-operation of Lady Luck — of course! No exact arrangements were possible for the dispatch of film and stories to England, newspapermen and photographers simply piled their material into a press bag, rushed down to the beach, and handed it to the skipper of any landing craft pulling out for the cross-Channel trip. Some press bags fell into the proper hands on arrival in England; others were misplaced for days in the frantic ports of southern England; a few were lost by enemy action.

But there was one way of giving Lady Luck a nudge and a flying start, and that was to get the material early and get it away as quickly as possible. Canadian Army cameramen nudged Lady Luck to the extreme limit of that beautiful girl's capacity to take punishment.

H-hour struck at 7:30 a.m. Twelve minutes later Sgt. Bud Roos, Toronto, moved inshore with "Don" company of the Regina Rifles. As it was making for the beach at top speed, the assault landing craft struck a mine. Roos was hurled into the sea. He bobbed up with his movie camera still firm under his right arm and he splashed ashore amidst a hail of German fire power. Roos didn't know whether his film had been ruined by water but he realized it would serve no purpose to examine the rolls. He dug a slit trench and began shooting film.

Lieut. Don Grant, Windsor, Ont., a still photographer, came

in with the Winnipeg Rifles three minutes after Roos and had an even more exciting landing. As his assault craft, ramp down, raced inshore, it hit a sand bar and Grant toppled into the water. This turned out to be lucky for Grant because the moment he hit water, machine-gun fire raked the craft and most of the men behind him were mowed down. Grant got ashore, discarded his ruined camera, and began shooting pictures with a candid camera he had wrapped in oil silk inside his battle-dress blouse.

At 8:20 a.m., while the battle on the beach was still in its earliest stage, Capt. Frank Duberville, Ottawa, and Sgt. Bill Grant, Vancouver, managed to come ashore dry by riding on top of a self-propelled gun. Duberville had a still camera and Grant a cine outfit. They scrambled behind dunes, made their pictures, and kept a watchful eye for any beached craft that might be pulling out for England.

Three more photographers came ashore on D-Day—Capt. Colin McDougall, Ottawa, Capt. Ken Bell, Toronto, and Sgt. Alan Grayston, Montreal. They took pictures and raced their negatives to the skippers of small craft making ready to depart the hellish beach.

All these men, landing with different units at distant points along the beach and sending back their film by a variety of ships, played their part in implementing Lady Luck. It turned out that the pictures shot by Sgt. Roos were useless because his film was drenched. But those shot by Capt. Duberville and Sgt. Grant proved the outstanding pictures of the invasion and scored a clean 12-hour beat on the world. This was a sensational piece of Canadian publicity. The majority of English-speaking newspapers and every newsreel advertised the Canadian contribution to the D-Day achievement.

This scoop launched No. 2 Canadian Film and Photo Unit on

the most exacting assignment ever given to noncombatant personnel on active service—the picture record of the western European campaign. Thereafter CFPU men were in the thick of every
battle, often moving with the most forward units, and on a few
occasions positioning themselves at a vantage point in no man's
land in anticipation of a clash.

Unlike a writing war correspondent, who can get a more
rounded story and more pertinent detail by viewing the battle
from a comparatively safe distance, and interviewing the troops
when the peak of fighting has passed, photographers must be on
the spot to get action pictures—on the spot both in the literal
and colloquial meanings of the term. Realizing this well in
advance of active operations, the Canadian Army decided that
the pictorial record of our fighting troops should be made by soldiers, not by civilians. Professional newspaper photographers were
recruited into the Army and trained like any other combat troops.
Soldiers already in the Army who showed an aptitude for photography were given special courses in Britain's famed Army school
of photography at Pinewood Studios and transferred to the Film
and Photo Unit.

Thus a highly skilled unit of soldier photographers was ready
to accompany Dominion troops into battle. These men carry arms
as well as cameras; they can shoot with a lens or a Piat; they can
lead a section of infantry in battle—if the need should arise.

The need has arisen on many occasions. A classic example is
that of Sgt. David Reynolds, Toronto, who dropped into Normandy with the 1st Canadian Parachute Regiment the night
before D-Day. In preparation for his assignment, Reynolds went
through a full course as a paratrooper, including the requisite
number of parachute jumps. When he floated to earth, east of the
Orne River, he had strapped to his body still and movie cameras

as well as a full complement of combat weapons. He was the first cameraman to land on French soil.

Reynolds dropped wide of his rendezvous area and came down in a deserted stretch of land, losing his movie camera during the descent. After wandering in the dark for more than an hour he joined a small unit of British paratroops making for a cluster of houses. The British officer in charge, having lost his own sergeant, assigned Reynolds to lead a section into the first house. As he pushed open the door Reynolds spotted a German officer in the hall. The Nazi went down under a burst from the photographer's Sten gun. Other paratroops whom Reynolds had assigned to approach the house from the rear killed two more Germans. Having fulfilled his fighting mission, Reynolds was released to apply himself to taking still pictures. After a few shots he made his way through enemy-held territory to the beach and sent his film to London.

During the month-long battle for Caen, our Army photographers lived with forward units. When that city was finally cleared as far as the Orne River, CFPU men began work on a documentary feature, the script of which had been prepared in advance. Maj. John McDougall, Montreal, the officer commanding the unit, wrote the script and directed the shooting. He recorded in his diary:

"To the best of my knowledge *City* is the first film to be shot from a prepared script on an active battlefield. For the past two days I've had my little crew working in Caen and it's rather unpleasant. Jerry is on the other side of the river, a few hundred yards away, and he's dropping plenty of mortar stuff into the town. This naturally doesn't make for pleasant picturemaking."

The product of this dangerous task was *You Can't Kill a City*, which was shown in theatres all over America and Britain. Film critics, highly impressed with the film, can scarcely believe it was photographed under enemy fire. Capt. Michael Spencer, Ottawa, was co-director and Sgt. Al Grayston did most of the cinematography.

A CFPU photographer was one of the first Allied soldiers to enter Falaise. A few days later, when the battle of the gap was at its most furious, five Army photographers, under Lieut. Don Grant, went forward in a Bren gun carrier to take action pictures of a machine-gun exchange at close quarters. Four of the men were wounded —all except Lieut. Grant. Though pinned down for five hours by enemy fire, Grant managed to arrange the evacuation of his wounded. This was one of the exploits which won for him the Military Cross.

The job of taking pictures has cost No. 2 Canadian Film and Photo Unit three killed and eight wounded. Pte. Lou Currie, Springhill, N.S., a driver, was killed by mortar fire during the bloody battle for Carpiquet airfield. Sgt. Jimmy Campbell, Hollywood, Ont., was killed by mortar fire at Fleury-sur-Orne, on July 20, as his movie camera was turning. Lieut. George Cooper, standing a few feet from him, removed Campbell's film, sent it to England, then returned to bury the sergeant.

During the assault on Walcheren Island, most furiously defended point on the Scheldt estuary, Sgt. Lloyd Millen, Winnipeg, set up his cameras on an assault craft carrying the first wave of infantry. The craft suffered a direct hit as it approached the Island. There were no survivors.

Other photographers have had hair-raising escapes. Lieut. Cooper, Ottawa, raced his jeep into Fleury-sur-Orne one day last July seeking the headquarters of a Canadian infantry battalion. He found, to his intense discomfort, that the town was occupied by Nazis. Apparently, the scheduled Canadian attack had not yet been mounted. Before Cooper and his assistant, Sgt. Len

Thompson, Regina, could turn their jeep around, eight Germans rushed out of a house, waving their arms in surrender. Half puzzled, half delighted, Cooper took them into custody. As he was marching them out of Fleury, all hell broke loose. Canadian artillery opened a barrage preparatory to assaulting the town. Cooper, Thompson and two of their prisoners flung themselves into the cellar of a farmhouse; the other six scrambled away in the confusion. The owner of the house, a French farmer, was also in the cellar and produced several bottles of beer which were shared by Canadians and prisoners alike. They emerged when a Canadian battalion stormed into the town—but Cooper, who is now in Canada, will not soon forget the artillery fire. "It was a dickens of a pasting," he said on his return to our camp, "worse than any Jerry barrage I've ever been under."

Probably the most important work of the unit is its contribution to the permanent record of this war. Every foot of original negative shot by the men at the front is deposited in government vaults in Ottawa where it will be available for war historians and film editors charged with patching together the picture story of Canada's fighting effort.

When the war ends, most of the Canadian Army's still photographers will probably drift back to their original newspaper offices. Also returning to Canada will be about 30 young men who have proved themselves among the world's top movie cameramen—men who started the war as combat troops, drivers and clerks. They will not be satisfied to go back to their humdrum jobs; they are married to a movie camera. In this circumstance lies promise for a movie industry in Canada.

Meanwhile, the war pushes into Germany, and Canadian Army cameramen go forward with the troops. This afternoon I saw an infantry battalion edging through a wood in Germany preparatory to storming a fortified town. A movie cameraman moved with the troops. Suddenly a series of eerie whistles sounded through the trees and German mortar fire spattered the area. Like the trained troops they are, the Canadians became invisible within 30 seconds. Every ditch, mound and cluster of trees hid its complement of troops. Mortar shells kept falling with sickening persistence. The area which had hummed with activity now appeared lifeless as a South American jungle—except for the glint of sun upon a lens. The cameraman had his head above ground and was filming the explosions.

On arrival at the main press camp late this evening I mentioned the incident to Maj. McDougall. "Must your men," I asked, "go forward at the head of the leading infantry?"

"Sure," he replied, "we can't take any chances. The Russians willing, a Canadian cameraman has got to be first into Berlin. He won't make it hanging around the back areas."

A glider preparing to land in enemy territory, 1945

I Crossed the Rhine with the Glider Troops

STANLEY MAXTED

May 15, 1945

Londdon (by cable)—I could hear the whispering whistle of the air that operated the glider's flaps. It was a mild replica of what you hear from the brakes of a transcontinental train or a streetcar coming to a stop. A Spandau machine gun, which sounded just outside the glider like an explosive typewriter, was tearing wicked holes through the fuselage. It was mixed with the slower slam of 20-millimetre incendiaries, for a fraction of a second before something exploded inside my head. The sour smell of burnt cordite was suddenly everywhere. I went down on one knee in the shelter of wicker baskets full of gasoline cans. Something hot and sickly was dripping over my right eye and off my chin.

Just then some giant kicked the glider in the stomach. There was a great rending and horrifying bounce. There was another bounce and some more rending, and then everything seemed to be hurtling through space, and daylight filled with dust was suddenly all around us. I watched, fascinated, as the Bren carrier that was chained to ringbolts in the floor went inexorably out of the nose of the glider, carrying the whole works ahead of it. I don't know why, but I noticed the steel caterpillars going round with its traction, as two signallers who had been lying on top of the carrier were wiped off like bread crumbs. Some battering ram had hit me in the small of the back—it was a jeep trailer that was chained to the floor just behind me. It had punched forward about six inches and then, mercifully, the chains and eye-bolts held.

My pal, public relations officer of the parachute regiment, Peter Cattle, was lying on one elbow, with blood making a spider web over his face. One of the men was on the floor, staring fixedly at nothing, as a bird might look at a snake. One of his legs, rigid in front of him, was quivering in a convulsion. Halfway up the side of the fuselage another man was pinned across the chest by wreckage. I couldn't see his face, but, through the sudden, awful quiet that lasted for a few seconds, I could hear his breathy groans as he tried to cry out and couldn't. Just over my head his legs were thrashing around like a small child's when you tickle him.

That was how we hit Germany, east of the Rhine.

Some days before, I had had a signal to return from the 9th U.S. Army, north of Cologne, and report in London—that was all. On reaching London, I learned there was a job to be done with the 6th British Airborne Division—colleagues of those wonderful men I had known at Arnhem. Where they were going, what they were to do—or when, was not discussed. That suited me all right. If I didn't know, the chances were that very few other people did either. When too many people know about operations of this sort, you can be pretty sure there's trouble waiting for you at the other end.

Maj. Roy Oliver, who led our little party out of the shambles at Arnhem, arrived with his colleague, Capt. Peter Cattle, who dropped with these men of the 6th in Normandy on D-Day. We drove out into the English countryside for several hours, and toward evening were convincing a sentry at the gate of what looked like a concentration camp that we really had a right to come in and be locked up with the rest of the lads. The camp was an orderly collection of Army huts, neat as a new pin and bleaker than charity. The whole was surrounded by barbed wire. If you wanted to go for a walk you could—through the alleyways between the huts. Here we would be kept incommunicado until the take-off.

We each drew three blankets for our stay there, as well as the usual shell dressings, entrenching tools and such items of equipment as were needed. It's always a nice moment when the sergeant hands you, for instance, a little morphia kit, with a hearty "Better 'ave it, y'know, sir—you never know, do you?" The officers' mess consisted of long trestle tables and benches in a hut, at one end of which was a row of kettles full of plain but appetizing food. The anteroom had as its main item of furniture a bar, around which the officers gathered each evening, drinking draught ale in mild quantities until the finish of the nine o'clock news, which was the signal for bed.

The second day, Roy Oliver ambled into the hut with a roll of maps under his arm. He gave two to each of us, together with a very much enlarged aerial photograph of some fields, two railway lines and a lot of trees. As Peter unrolled his two maps and scanned their contents, he grunted, "Oh—Oh, so that's it." The maps were of the territory beyond the Rhine and just north of Wesel. That told us something, anyway. Roy said the general would tell us the rest after lunch.

"Well," says Peter, "now we know where to have the flowers sent, anyway."

After lunch we went up to the briefing room. One end of it was plastered with large maps and a model of the ground we were dropping on, and the objectives the air-borne men had to capture. We had barely seated ourselves on a semicircle of benches when brisk steps sounded outside the door and intuitively we stood up. I can't imagine why, because no one told us it was the general—but there was suddenly something compelling in the air and—well— we just stood up.

You meet men like Gen. Bole once in a while, and usually in distant places. When you do it's an event—the very entry of a man like this into a room has an impact that needs no announcement. Your attention is drawn and held, like filings to a magnet. He is lean and hard-bodied and quick, and has a trick of flinging a fact at you that's as bald and gruesome as a skull. Then his frosty blue eyes soften and crinkle up as he tacks on some *non sequitur* phrase that takes half the sting away. He looks younger than he is, and heaven knows that's not very old. Someone told me he was 38 but, be that as it may, it was strange at first to see a major-general's insignia on those driving young shoulders. His quick, clipped phrases deftly sketched out the picture. Then he would stop for a second with a "clear?" Then, knowing quite well that anyone with half a brain had grasped what he meant, he'd go on to the next point.

"Well, gentlemen, you'll be glad to know that this time we're not going to be dropped down as a carrot held out for the ground forces. This time the Army and the Navy are going to storm across the Rhine, and just when they've gained Jerry's attention in front—bingo! we drop down behind him. The trouble is that the only dropping zones in the vicinity are fairly well-packed with 20-millimetre ack-ack guns and machine-gun posts. That means we'll have to fight for our landing and dropping zones. As a matter of fact, we'll have a helluva fight when we first get down. If things go according to plan with the 2nd Army, we'll be fighting like stink for the first day. However, things never go according to plan, so we'll be ready to fight it out for 48 hours.

"This operation will be real teamwork. Under my command will be the 1st Canadian Paratroop Battalion, which will drop on this high, wooded feature here. The American air-borne division to the south of us and ourselves make up a corps under the command of the American general, Ridgeway, for whom I have a great regard and affection. He's a helluva fine soldier. We operate under the command of Field Marshal Montgomery, and over us all is Ike Eisenhower. That, gentlemen, is a real Allied team, and should make the sparks fly. Unless I miss my guess, the initial tough fighting should break the crust of the remaining good troops the enemy has against us, and then I think we'll swarm out all over Germany.

"The Ox-and-Bucks will land here, and will immediately go for these three bridges here across the Issel. The Ulsters will land here, and will first clear this area to the east, and then hare into Hamminkeln and clear and hold the town. The parachute regiments are landing here, here and here. With their objectives taken they will establish contact with each other and fight their way with their support elements back to my headquarters, which will be here. It's a German headquarters now, but that's all right—there'll probably be some good brandy in the cellar.

"That's the plan, gentlemen—but it probably won't go that way at all, so we must be ready for anything. All I hope is that when the 2nd Army comes up we may have orders to climb aboard the tanks and swarm out beyond our objectives—then we can knock 'em for six. That's all, gentlemen. Any questions? Clear? Right—and good hunting."

I don't know who put the words into our mouths, but we all stood up and chorused, "Good luck, sir."

We straggled back to the hut without saying anything much, and everybody got their maps out, spread them on their bunks and studied them, comparing the notes we had taken with the corresponding features on the map. It was going to be important to know parts of that map from memory. On the next bunk to mine was a kid of 21, who from time to time came out with some of the most naïve questions imaginable. He represented a London daily paper, and this was his first assignment. His enthusiasm was terrific, but it was plain to see that he hadn't the foggiest idea of what he was in for. He was an engaging kid, and quite new to the business. He had been in the merchant marine, but should never have been sent on a thing like this for his first job. Just now he was fairly bubbling at the thought of how upset the Huns were going to be when they saw all those gliders and parachutes coming down on them. That night when I was half asleep, he reached his arm across and tapped the blankets over my shoulder. He enquired, very softly, "I say—can a war correspondent win the VC?" I mumbled something about no, a war correspondent couldn't win the VC—and anyway, all he was supposed to do was to make darned sure that everybody heard about the guys who did win them.

Thursday night—the last night we spent at this camp—Peter

and I went down to the men's canteen to find out what they were talking about. Upstairs was a big room with a piano in it. It was wreathed in smoke, and packed with glider pilots, paratroopers, men of the various air-borne infantry regiments—all bunched round on chairs and drinking strong tea out of large brown enamel mugs. One of them was sitting at a tinny old upright piano with several of the notes missing. When we came into the room they were bellowing something to the tune of "John Brown's Body." The verse went, "Should like to meet the sergeant who forgot to hook me up." Then came the chorus, "Glory, glory, what a helluva way to die, And I ain't gonna jump no more."

On the way back to the hut, I heard a knot of them chanting the song of the paratrooper whose chute hadn't been packed properly, "They scraped him off the tarmac like a daub of strawberry jam," and then pretty soon the whole place became dark and silent. Crawling into my blankets a few minutes later I was still thinking of these men and the way they look death square in the eye, and snap their fingers in his face. I wondered what their private thoughts were—or maybe they didn't dare to think.

Next day—Friday—we moved for the night to a jumping-off camp near our airstrip. The building used to be a golf club. Here we met Jock Roberts, the tall, rawboned and redhaired young Scot who would be stickleader in our glider. Jock doesn't talk much, but he knows his job. After dinner I listened to the nine o'clock news with him and heard that the Germans were expecting an air-borne attack north of Wesel. Jock turned to me, with a slow twinkle in his eye, and put out his hand. "It's been pleasant knowing you," he said. I managed a sickly grin, and said, "Yes, wasn't it?"

Up in the room where our bunks were made up, people were scribbling mysterious notes and doing things to their equipment.

Reveille was 3:30 a.m. Getting ready for bed, the atmosphere was as taut as a violin string, but the morning would end the intolerable period of inaction—of being shut up with nothing to do but think. Tomorrow, no matter what the next sundown might bring, the thunder of the beginning of the end would be heard along the Rhine. We turned the lights out and went to sleep. Young Bill, the merchant marine kid, was restless for a few minutes, and then slept like a baby.

I seemed to have just closed my eyes when somebody shook me and said, "Breakfast is in an hour." Awareness seeped through sleep, and a lead weight descended on my stomach. Breakfast was a rugged affair—sweetened porridge without milk, and a big steak with mashed potatoes and parsnips.

At 4:30 in the morning trucks took us out to the airfield. It was beginning to be daylight. On an oversized runway hundreds of gliders stood, faced by hundreds of four-engined bombers to tow them.

We loaded up, and with a terrific din the first tugs moved down the runway   regular as clockwork, one every 30 seconds. Then it was our turn, and I felt the sluggish movement along the tarmac, the picking up of speed, the old feeling that this thing would never get off the ground with all this weight in it—then a smooth rise and fall as we became air-borne. We were on our way.

England's green loveliness eased by under us to terminate where white cliffs held in the English Channel with its lace edges of lazy white foam. Sunny sparkling sea—then the sand dunes of the Belgian coast, the pock-marked scenes of months-old battles —Holland—then western Germany. Squinting ahead, through the tiny round porthole beside me, I could see the smoky windings of the Rhine. My stomach tightened up into a knot.

We did our last recording as we crossed the Rhine, and in the middle of talking, I saw, through the little porthole, the unbelievable sight of the glider, which had been flying alongside, now a couple of hundred yards away bursting into flames. I looked away, to the one ahead, and it burst into flames, too. Little sparkles were showing like pinpricks in the sky around. Next, a glider out beyond the others just broke in half without burning and emptied two vehicles and a lot of little pinmen, sprawling and whirling, without any parachutes. It was difficult to think of what I was saying.

There was a bump while I was trying to finish—and we were on our own. That well-remembered soaring feeling was with us. The big Hamilcar was coming in, with the rush of the wind in her wings, to touchdown. I just had time to see a thick white German-made mist on the ground, then that slamming through the sides of the glider started. That was when the explosive typewriter spat its message through our plywood skin. We had hit a railway embankment that took away the undercarriage, careened into an orchard that took the wings, and then just piled up.

The two glider pilots had the floor taken out from under them by the Bren carrier, but were unhurt—as were the two signallers that were brushed off when it plowed through the nose. Bullets kept crashing through the wreckage, but, heading for the daylight, I found myself lying face down in a ditch beside a hedge. Peter was lying ahead of me. We were both trying to burrow down into the ground with our noses, when a mild-voiced doctor, who seemed to bear a charmed life, bound us up and directed us to his aid post in a German farmhouse. From here we could see down the railway track to a station marked Hamminkeln. We had come down about three miles away from our dropping zone, and now the crashed glider was under fire and we couldn't get to it. In that jeep trailer was a sending set, with which I was going to make history by broadcasting direct from an air-borne fighting zone, and my portable recorder. London was listening in for me—and just over there, so near and so far, was all that lovely equipment. For an awful moment I wanted to sit down and bawl, then I remembered that the next best thing was to find the others, get the whole story, and somehow get it back to England.

Even with the landing they had, the 6th Airborne men had all their objectives by 1:30 that afternoon, and so Peter and I gradually made our way back to where the Devons were clearing out Hamminkeln, and then back across the fields to divisional headquarters. There, the young general, sparkplug of the air-borne men, told us that he expected to make contact with the 2nd Army before dark, and firm contact before morning.

Back where the lads were digging slit trenches for the night, we learned that the kid, Bill, hadn't been heard from and neither had his glider. I thought of those flaming in the air, and how he had wanted to win the VC. I looked around at smoking patches here and there that marked burned-up gliders. Wherever he was, the kid was in pretty grand company that night.

I'm looking at a letter from Jock Roberts that has just been delivered in London. Among other things he says, "We made an effort to get back to the glider next day. It was still under fire, and one of my fellows caught a packet. I went again later, only to find it a burned-out wreck and everything destroyed. I'm sorry. I was captured that night after delivering some ammunition, but we managed to turn the tables and bring quite a crowd back with us."

See what I mean about these air-borne fellows?

Stanley Maxted fought with the Canadian and British armies during the First World War and was wounded three times. Afterwards, he became a popular tenor on radio and in 1935 became Toronto regional director of the precursor of the CBC. When the Second World War begin in 1939, Maxted was in London helping the BBC produce variety programs. He became a BBC war correspondent, and in one famous broadcast from Arnhem, he began an interview with a paratrooper with the words, "Hello, son." It really was his son.

After the war, he became an actor, working in the West End and in several movies including I Am a Camera. *He died at the age of 68 in 1963.*

A North Atlantic Allied convoy

The Nightmare Convoy of the Atlantic

JACK McNAUGHT

May 15, 1952

At noon on Dec. 28, 1942, the captain of the Canadian destroyer St. Laurent, then nine days out from Britain and bound for North America, looked thoughtfully at the grey Atlantic, the pale sky and the long plodding columns of merchant ships in convoy a mile or so astern. Then he left the bridge, went down to the crowded mess deck and made a speech to his men.

"You joined the Navy for a reason," he said, "and that reason has arrived. The subs are gathering around us now and tonight there will be 10 to 15 of them. The going will be rough, but I know you are up to it. After all, we don't all expect to be old men."

In these words, stocky, spade-bearded Lieut.-Comdr. Guy Windeyer, RCN, broke the news that, bad as the run had been so far, it was about to become tragically worse. And five days later, when Slow Convoy No. ONS 154 at last won through to the other side, 14 of its 46 ships had been sunk, more than 100 merchant seamen had died, and it had made bitter history as the hardest-hit convoy ever escorted by the Canadian Navy in the Battle of the Atlantic.

The story of ONS 154, a closely guarded wartime secret, begins on Dec. 19, 1942. At nine that morning, the destroyer St. Laurent and two corvettes, Chilliwack and Battleford, sailed seaward down the narrow twisting River Foyle from the naval base at Londonderry, Northern Ireland. The three other corvettes of the all-Canadian escort group, Napanee, Kenogami and Shediac, had been in England having a new type of radar installed, and they joined at the mouth of the river. HMS Burwell, a destroyer of the Royal Navy which was also to have joined, broke down at the last minute and had to stay behind.

Even with two destroyers the escort would have been barely up to strength, and Burwell's failure was disastrous. But when he learned of it, Windeyer, who as senior officer of the group was chiefly responsible for the safety of the convoy, simply said, "That isn't too good," and went on trying to light his rain-wet cigarette. And ONS 154 put to sea—44 merchantmen, one rescue ship, one special service ship and the six fighting escorts.

Toward dawn on Dec. 20, a signal from Admiralty came in saying that 90 to 100 U-boats were estimated to be at sea in the Atlantic. And for the next two days the wind rose slowly and steadily, blowing from dead ahead and holding the convoy down to the pace of a man walking (it wasn't much more than that at its scheduled best, a scant eight land miles an hour). At midnight on Dec. 22, the wind had become a gale and it went on rising until sunset on Christmas Eve.

Nothing bad happened that night and Christmas Day dawned on a sullen but submarine-free sea. The wind had now died to a soft, curiously greasy breeze; yet its violence had left a strong ground swell running which was to play a sinister part in the hard time ahead. Because four days of struggling through the storm had used a great deal of the escort's limited fuel, more oil would have to be taken on at once.

There were two tankers in ONS 154—the American E. G. Seuber and the British Scottish Heather. At that stage of the war Canadian escorts had not had much practice in fuelling at sea (later the operation was standardized and became relatively simple) and transferring oil from tanker to warship by pumping it through a heaving jerking six-inch hose was a formidable task.

The destroyer, as the only ship of the group fast enough to overtake a U-boat running on the surface and therefore tactically the most important, ordered Scottish Heather to drop behind clear of the convoy and made the first try. All day long lines were heaved from St. Laurent's bow to the tanker so wire cables could be passed to hold the ships at a steady distance from each other during the actual fuelling. And all day long the lines snapped, one by one in maddening sequence, as tanker and destroyer slid down the steep ground swells and pulled convulsively apart.

Toward dusk, just when the sweating seamen had managed for the first time to make cables fast and oiling could have begun, a steeper swell than ever rolled by. Whereupon St. Laurent's officer of the watch made a brief entry in the deck log: "Attempts at oiling failed. Towing wires and hose parted." And her medical officer wrote in his diary, "It was a hell of a way to spend Christmas," adding a heartfelt two-word comment on the destroyer's Christmas dinner—"Shepherd's pie!"

Besides the frustration of not getting fuel, and the dismal substitute for turkey and fixings, the day brought a further unfestive note. An afternoon wireless message from Admiralty warned the convoy that a number of U-boats were within 100 miles of its position.

That made it more urgently necessary than ever to refuel and next morning, the 26th, St. Laurent ordered Scottish Heather to drop astern once more and tried again. Just before the second attempt, a large sewer-pipe-shaped aircraft flew up and circled the convoy, safely out of gunshot range. Although nobody was able to identify it positively, it seemed pretty certain to be a Nazi and a signal was made to the convoy to keep alert. However, as the strange plane merely flew round and round awhile and went away, oiling proceeded as if it hadn't been there at all. And this time St. Laurent took on 100 tons before the hose broke—enough to let her stay with the convoy the rest of the way across to Newfoundland with any luck.

But the luck of ONS 154, such as it was, had already begun to run out.

At 2:30 that afternoon, a Coastal Command aircraft unsuccessfully attacked a U-boat 22 miles astern of the convoy. It was fully surfaced and overhauling the convoy at twice the speed of the slow merchant ships. And soon before dark another signal from Admiralty warned that even more U-boats were now closing in on the lumbering freighters.

This confirmed what the senior officer of the escort already knew. St. Laurent and the rescue ship Toward, a small shabby-looking vessel whose duty was to pick up survivors after a torpedoing, were fitted with a special radar device for tracing enemy submarines. In the destroyer, this apparatus was housed in a sort of steel hut abaft the torpedo tubes, connected with the bridge by a telephone which, instead of ringing a bell, gave a sudden ghastly howl like a mad dog being strangled. Throughout the day of the 26th, the bridge phone howled almost incessantly as the operators in the hut reported U-boat after U-boat, many of them apparently within 50 miles and none farther than 150 miles away. These reports, and a stream of similar ones passed from the rescue ship by signal lamp, told their own story of trouble ahead. It wasn't long coming.

About nine o'clock that night the corvette Shediac, commanded by Lieut. John E. Clayton, RCNR, and stationed on the left and a little ahead of the convoy, got a suspicious blip on her radar and went off to investigate. Five minutes later, she sighted a U-boat on the surface about a mile and a half from the convoy, fired star shells (projectiles designed to burst in the air and drop a bright flare attached to a little parachute, thus lighting up the target) and followed with rounds of high explosive from her single four-inch gun.

The U-boat wasn't hit and at once crash-dived, so Shediac moved in to make a depth-charge attack after finding the enemy by means of asdic—a detection apparatus that bounced echoes (they sounded like ping-pong balls being batted) from the hull of a submarine which would otherwise have been safely hidden in deep water. The attack failed and contact was lost soon before 10 o'clock. Meanwhile, the ships of the convoy had begun to fire snowflake rockets, which gave much the same illumination as star shells and were used for the same purpose. And up and down the lines of merchantmen, alarm gongs clanged and the crews of the one or two naval guns each ship carried went to their action stations, ready to shoot if the U-boat surfaced again inside the lumbering columns, now bathed in a light nearly as bright as day.

On the far side of ONS 154, the corvette Napanee, under the command of Lieut. Stuart Henderson, RCNR, fired star shells and quartered back and forth to see if the submarine had passed clear across the convoy underwater and was going to risk coming up to periscope depth for an attack. And at about 10:30, St. Laurent, whose radar had spotted a U-boat on the surface seven miles ahead of the convoy, increased her speed to 20 knots and dashed off to the hunt.

Napanee quartered in vain, the first U-boat commander having wisely decided to stay submerged and make himself scarce for a while. But the destroyer, overtaking the second U-boat about half an hour later and just after the Nazi had dived, made asdic contact and started to run in to drop depth charges.

Before St. Laurent could get directly above the submarine to do this, the attacker suddenly and dramatically became the attacked. From a point beneath the surface half a mile off St. Laurent's port bow, the hissing white track of a torpedo streaked straight at her across the black waves. The destroyer's wheel was put hard over and the torpedo raced along her flank, maybe a hundred feet away, and disappeared harmlessly into the night astern. And after that, although St. Laurent did her best to pick the enemy up again on asdic and hunted for another half hour, this U-boat disappeared too and the destroyer raced back to join the convoy.

By then it was close to midnight and ONS 154 was momentarily safe; darkness and quiet descended once more. St. Laurent's medical officer took advantage of this unexpected lull to enter in his diary his impression of the earlier alarm.

"The escorts scurried around according to a prearranged plan," he wrote, "while the convoy slowly plodded on. It reminded me of going for a walk with my dog. As I walk down the street he is all over the place, investigating this and that, and here and there leaving a 'calling card,' just as we left depth charges."

The lull ended abruptly a couple of hours later, at 2:05 in the morning of the 27th. One after another the thumping crash of torpedo hits sounded in the convoy and flames broke out on four stricken merchant ships—the British Melrose Abbey, Empire Union and King Edward, and the Dutch Soekaboemi. All were hit within an hour and a half of the start of the attack and all sank quickly. The King Edward went down in less than two minutes.

While King Edward and the other torpedoed ships were sinking, the escorts were attacking the half-dozen or so submarines which had been lying in wait ahead of ONS 154 and now converged to strike. At about three o'clock, St. Laurent sighted a U-boat on the surface (the sea was day-bright again with star shells, rockets and the flames of burning ships) moving in fast on the convoy.

The destroyer opened fire, first with her Oerlikons—20-millimetre automatic cannons—and then with her main armament of 4.7-inch guns. The U-boat, a thousand yards away, dived to periscope depth and kept on toward the convoy. But the destroyer closed in to drop depth charges and, although it is doubtful whether the submarine was actually sunk, that particular enemy gave no more trouble that night.

The other U-boats had lost their earlier advantage of surprise and were beaten off by the escort in a series of attacks
which, like the destroyer's three o'clock fight, failed to sink a
single submarine for sure. But they at least staved off any further
torpedoings and allowed the rescue ship Toward to pick up 160
survivors and the corvette Napanee to save 20 more, so that the
loss of life was kept down to about one man in five from the four
sunken ships.

By dawn the Nazi wolf pack had gone off to gather on the surface, safely out of range, and wait for the other U-boats of the
mid-Atlantic patrol which had been ordered by radio from Germany to join them.

Trouble was piling up like a thundercloud on the belea-
guered convoy. Only St. Laurent and Chilliwack had so far been
able to refuel. The tanker Scottish Heather had been torpedoed,
but not sunk, soon after Chilliwack finished refuelling, and had
been forced to turn back to Britain. Napanee, Battleford and
Shediac were running critically short of oil. Kenogami, whose
radar had broken down the night before, had consequently gone
on fewer fuel-consuming U-boat chases than her sister corvettes
and still had a fair amount left in her tanks. The oil-starved
escorts had to try to fuel as quickly as possible from the remaining tanker, E. G. Seuber.

Besides the threatening disaster by which three corvettes
might soon find themselves drifting, their boiler fires dead and
their engines stopped, what could well prove another tragedy
was in the making. At six in the evening Napanee, which had
stayed behind the convoy to protect the rescue ship and was 18
miles astern, relayed a message from the master of that valiant
little vessel to Lieut.-Comdr. Windeyer: "Have insufficient food
and water for survivors now on board. Request another rescue

ship be detailed." And in the whole of ONS 154 no suitable ship could be spared.

The piercing howls of St. Laurent's bridge phone started coming at shorter and shorter intervals as the operators reported the U-boats closing in again. This time there seemed to be twice as many as there had been the night before. A signal from Admiralty bore out this gloomy estimate and a further signal ordered the convoy's course altered sharply southward when dark came.

Windeyer answered the alter-course order, which under the circumstances was wonderfully welcome to him, with one of the most remarkable signals of the war at sea: "To Commander-in-Chief, Western Approaches, from St. Laurent: Psalm 119, Verses 97 and 98." And when the astonished and faintly outraged admiral opened his Bible to decode this cry from the deep he read, "O how love I Thy law! It is my meditation all the day. Thou through Thy commandments hast made me wiser than mine enemies: for they are ever with me."

Although the convoy was now in mid-Atlantic, too far out for protection by land-based aircraft from either Britain or Newfoundland, there was one last faint chance of help from the air. Among ONS 154's ships was the Fidelity, a special service vessel of the Royal Navy on her way to a secret mission in the south Atlantic. And Fidelity had aboard a small seaplane. If it could be flown that afternoon it might be able to find some of the U-boats which were following unseen below the edge of the horizon and force them to dive. This would slow them from their surface speed, potentially more than twice the convoy's seven knots, to a submerged crawl. ONS 154 could thus gain a little distance on its deadly pursuers, make a surprise turn under cover of darkness, and perhaps escape altogether for a few hours or the whole menacing night.

Windeyer accordingly signalled this plan to Fidelity, whose captain was at first unwilling to carry it out. Fidelity, a converted tramp steamer, had no flight deck; the only way of getting the seaplane into the air was to lower it over the ship's side by means of a derrick and leave it to take off from the sea. That would have been risky enough in mid-ocean even in a flat calm; but a rough wind was beginning to blow and the gale-made swells were still running high. Under those conditions, the captain of Fidelity felt, asking anyone to try was pretty much the same as asking them to commit suicide.

However, he eventually did ask and two officers at once volunteered. Both were Frenchmen serving in the Fleet Air Arm, one a black-haired young college student and the other a greying middle-aged dentist who had escaped from Nazi-occupied France by stealing an aircraft and flying it to England.

Just before sunset the plane was lowered and it taxied slowly across the choppy waves to a strip of sea made somewhat smoother by St. Laurent's having raced ahead and flattened it with her foaming passage.

Gathering speed the seaplane, with the dentist at the controls, roared along the destroyer's wake, skittering over the first few swells very neatly. Then came a swell higher and steeper than the rest—a hissing hillside already beginning to curl and break.

The little aircraft hit it with a splashing crash, nosed down, and drove straight on in. The landing lights were jarred on by the shock and for an instant the plane could be seen through the green water, with the Frenchmen still sitting in the cockpit, like a child's toy in a bright glass showcase. The lights went out, dusk cloaked the sea again, and there was no sound but the wind.

St. Laurent's wheel was put hard over and she nosed back to the place where the plane had crashed. It was now nearly eight o'clock, the sea was dark, and it took some time to spot the two heads bobbing in the water. Wind and current had swept the men half a mile apart. The destroyer was brought close alongside one man and he was pulled out of the water; a sea-boat was sent away to get the other.

The two Frenchmen, alive and little the worse for their crash, were no sooner aboard St. Laurent than Fidelity reported by radio-phone that her asdic had caught the sound of a submarine nearby. And two minutes later she reported her main engines were broken down.

St. Laurent had only time to make a hurried and fortunately successful effort to drive the U-boat off by dropping depth charges when an ominous signal came from Battleford. A little earlier this corvette, stationed ahead and to starboard of the convoy, had sighted something black and sinister outlined against a break in the clouds on the western horizon. She had instantly given chase and now identified the menace as the first of four surfaced U-boats, running in on ONS 154 in line-ahead formation, perfectly spaced one behind the other as if they had been on a peacetime exercise at high noon.

What happened then was told afterward in the terse report of Battleford's captain, Lieut. Fred Beck, RCNVR. "The nearest U-boat was trimmed down and soon dived. The second was difficult to see, being below the horizon and therefore not silhouetted. This was followed by radar only after the initial sighting. Fire was opened on the third and fourth U-boats . . . while the range was closed on a zigzag course. One U-boat was believed hit . . . but this claim was later withdrawn because of the lack of further evidence. U-boats three and four flashed Morse to each other and turned."

St. Laurent had overtaken the convoy, which was now being attacked from all directions at once. The time was 8:20, barely half an hour from the start of the attack, and already three merchant ships had been sunk. One of them went down with such shattering swiftness that the master of another merchant ship, passing the spot a minute later, reported that "only a few white star sparks were noticed on the edge of a large cloud of whitish smoke." He saw no wreckage.

It soon became clear that instead of 15 U-boats, which had been forecast in the gloomiest estimate, there were certainly 20, quite possibly 25. One-quarter of all Nazi submarines then in the Atlantic had gathered to attack a single convoy. To beat them off there were at first only St. Laurent and four corvettes. ONS 154 had made an emergency turn at dark and Battleford, then miles away and busy with her own fight, had not got the signal which ordered the turn. Consequently she had had to hunt blindly—her radar had failed—until she caught up again and so was missing from much of the main battle.

The rest of the vastly outnumbered escort raced in and out among the plodding columns, attacking where they could and turning from one enemy to engage another whenever the second seemed a greater threat. U-boats were everywhere. "At one stage," the captain of Shediac reported later, "torpedoes were so numerous in the convoy that the officer of the watch remarked, 'Here comes ours now, sir,' as if next week's groceries were being delivered."

Every merchant ship was firing snowflake rockets, and these and the star shells fired by the escort lit the ocean all around.

Most of the swarming U-boats had dived, but others took advantage of the light, stayed on the surface and closed in on the ships they had chosen for targets. As they came, white streams of tracer bullets poured from the machine guns in their grey-green conning towers, crossing red-and-white answering streams of tracer from escorts and the convoy, the slamming orange flashes of heavier guns and the immense livid blasts of torpedo hits. Pinpointing this gaudy nightmare were the little red lights on the lifejackets of men floating in the sea and the waving flashlights of men clinging to rafts or crowded into lifeboats.

The escort, fighting desperately, could do nothing for them. "Fortunately the water was warm, about 60 degrees," St. Laurent's medical officer wrote in his diary, "but I must say it is a terrible thing to have to pass survivors in the water and be unable to pick them up." He added, sadly, "This was about the most demoralizing experience of all."

The rescue ship could do no more than the hard-pressed escort. So those who lived through these new sinkings (by 10 o'clock four more merchant ships had gone down, bringing the night's total until then to seven) would have to be left to drown or die of thirst unless the rear ships of the columns could drop astern and pick them up, in the face of great difficulty and danger, as the convoy went slowly on into the dark.

When the attack ended a little before midnight, as suddenly as it began, another three ships had been torpedoed. In the four hours it had taken to drive them off, the U-boats had sunk 10 ships. This, the heaviest shipping loss in a single attack during the whole Battle of the Atlantic, might also have meant the heaviest loss of life. Instead, at least 500 of the 600 or more men of their crews were saved. The salt-stained and cockroach-ridden old tramps that brought up the rear of ONS 154 had done their work in spite of all.

In the first light of morning on Dec. 29, Lieut.-Comdr. Windeyer on the bridge of St. Laurent took stock of the position. None of the escorts, every one of which had been repeatedly fired upon by surfaced U-boats and attacked with torpedoes from those underwater, had been even slightly damaged and none of their men had been wounded. But there were only 31 merchant ships remaining in the convoy out of the 46 that had sailed. None of the U-boats had been sunk for sure, although in the excitement of the fight there were times when captains had thought differently. The commander of one corvette signaled to St. Laurent, "Praise the Lord and pass the fuel oil: I got one of the bastards." Thus it was fair to suppose the Nazis had only hauled off to surface out of sight below the horizon astern for a day of fresh air and battery recharging and were following ONS 154 at their leisure to strike again when night came.

Three of the five corvettes had enough fuel to get the rest of the way across. But unless Battleford and Shediac got more oil they would have to leave the convoy almost at once.

However, the prospect, bleak though it was, was still not hopeless. The Commander-in-Chief, Western Approaches, had signalled during the night that two destroyers of the Royal Navy, Milne and Meteor, had been detached from a mid-ocean hunting group and would reinforce the Canadian ships at five o'clock that afternoon.

The two destroyers were right on time. Just as they approached the convoy, Milne had four torpedoes fired at her in quick succession by a lurking U-boat—they all missed. At the same time the escort's radar began to pick up numbers of other U-boats on the surface nearby. The newly arrived destroyers capped the bad news with a signal that their fuel was so low they would have to fall out again the following day.

All night the escorts crisscrossed through and around ONS 154, ready to head off the expected attack before it could develop. But no serious attack was made, although here and there a pattern of depth charges was dropped over a U-boat creeping under the convoy. Once again no submarines were sunk, or at any rate none whose destruction could then or ever be proved. Yet no merchant ships were sunk and no escort hit; so the night's work could be reckoned a success.

Next day, Dec. 30, ONS 154's situation became desperate. Milne and Meteor left the convoy at 10:00 a.m. Soon after that Shediac ran so short of oil she had to detach and head for Ponta Delgada in the Azores. And Battleford, almost but not quite as fuel-starved as her consort, left with her in case Shediac should run out of fuel altogether and have to be towed. This in fact happened next morning when the two corvettes were still five hours away from port.

Lieut.-Comdr. Windeyer signalled the convoy to make an emergency turn at dark. Then, he wrote in his official report, "I told Calgary (15 knots), carrying women and children, and Advastus, to escape if in their judgment they had an opportunity. It should be borne in mind that at this stage I considered we were done for, that the departure of Milne, Meteor, Shediac and Battleford had been observed and that tonight would see our final carving with only four escorts (St. Laurent, Chilliwack, Kenogami and Napanee) left to take the bowling."

At 7:30 p.m., St. Laurent's searching radar found a surfaced

U-boat less than two miles ahead of the convoy. The destroyer raced at the enemy, who dived in time to avoid depth charges and was not seen or heard again. And this, which was thought merely the first U-boat of a great pack, turned out to be the only one. There were no more attacks.

At dusk on Dec. 31, after a quiet day of fair weather, HMS Fame joined ONS 154 from Newfoundland. Later HMS Mansfield, USS Cole and two ships of the Third Destroyer Flotilla also arrived, and on New Year's Day Commander Windeyer (he had been promoted that morning) handed over to the captain of Cole, who was senior officer of the new escort.

St. Laurent, Chilliwack, Kenogami and Napanee, their duty done, turned away and sailed for the Canadian Navy's Newfoundland base at St. John's.

Fourteen ships of the convoy under their charge had been sunk. More than 100 merchant seamen had died. That was a disaster and a defeat. But 31 ships were brought safely into their North American port with 2,000 people aboard them alive and well.

And that was victory.

Lieut. Comdr. Guy Windeyer, who had spent three sleepless nights on the St. Laurent's bridge during the attack, was relieved of his convoy command during the fighting by the ship's medical officer. The executive officer replaced Windeyer for the remainder of the battle. After the convoy reached Halifax, Windeyer was transferred to Vancouver Island where he spent the rest of the war training landing craft crew. After the war, he farmed on Vancouver Island where he died in 1984.

Jack McNaught, who wrote under several pseudonyms, was best known as James Bannerman. As Bannerman, he contributed numerous pieces to Maclean's for more than two decades, until 1967. But few were as realistic as "The Nightmare Convoy of the Atlantic." That's because McNaught, as a member of naval intelligence, was an officer aboard the St. Laurent during this memorable battle. He died in 1970, aged 68.

Photo Credits